DATE DUE

PUNCHLINES

PUNCHLINES

PUNCHLINES

THE VIOLENCE OF AMERICAN HUMOR

WILLIAM KEOUGH

PARAGON HOUSE, NEW YORK

First Edition, 1990
Published in the United States by
Paragon House
90 Fifth Avenue
New York, NY 10011

Copyright © 1990 by William Keough

Designed by Deirdre C. Amthor

Library of Congress Cataloging-in-Publication Data

Keough, William.
   Punchlines: the violence of American humor/William
Keough.—1st ed.
      p.   cm.
   Includes bibliographical references (p.).
   ISBN 1-55778-084-6
   1. American wit and humor—History and
criticism.   2. Violence in literature.   I. Title.
PS430.K46   1990
817.009—dc20   89-27569
                                                              CIP

Manufactured in the United States of America

10 9 8 7 6 5 4 3 2

To Sean, Leyla, and Goldie who make me smile.

CONTENTS

ACKNOWLEDGMENTS

Any book of this sort, of course, is a collaboration, and I point the reader toward the notes and sources where I attempt to pay ample tribute to the legion of scholars, critics, reviewers, auditors, and comedy buffs whose work helped me to buttress my argument and keep from falling off the deep end. This has been a labor of love from which I learned as well—not perhaps as much as I should have. I have been forced to accept that, like Sut Lovingood, I am a "nat'ral born durned fool"; so all errors, oversights, and stupidities I might just as well own up to as my own poor children. If, as Mark Twain figured, there is no humor in heaven, there are probably no proofreaders waiting either—nor need for them.

I am grateful to so many—particularly to Dr. Everett Emerson, my former mentor at the University of Massachusetts who saw the book in its infant stages; to the entire library staff of Fitchburg State College who were so patient and helpful, especially Bob Foley, Bill Casey, and Jerry Greene, and to the many others who supported and encouraged me like Vin Mara, Bill Barker, Dan Flynn, Mike Shanley, and Didi Slattery; to Shaun O'Connell and Tom Gleason for their shrewd common sense and generosity; to Sam and Georgie Sailon and my many friends in Montserrat at the Village Place; to Kurt Vonnegut and to my old friend and helpmate Ken Stuart without whom this book would not have seen what light it does see and to my new friend and editor PJ Dempsey; and to my research assistant, Goldie Osuri, that loyal Pocahontas who saved my head on more than one occasion.

To all of you, and to all the other countless friends and family who bore with me through this long journey with so many detours and stopsigns, I can only recount Sebastian's words to his friend Antonio in Shakespeare's *Twelfth Night*, "Thanks, and thanks, and ever thanks." Thanks, guys, *thanks* from the bottom of my heart.

THE PRELIM

American humor is violent—and often sexist, racist, brutal, and disgusting as well. There I've said it, and as Huck says, "All right, then, I'll go to Hell." So any reader in search of tidy conclusions should stop right here, let me go to Hell in a hand-cart, and get on with his or her business. But (just *but*) there may be more to it than that; there is certainly more that has interested me, and I would like to begin with a couple of old stories.

As every schoolchild knows, Columbus sailed the ocean blue and discovered America in 1492. Except of course there were folks already *on* those sandy isles; Arawaks and Caribs, who could themselves put in some sort of claim for having discovered their own neighborhood even if they didn't raise flags or write letters home. So that's one ethnocentric joke. Another historical joke is Columbus' insistence he had come upon the westernmost fringes of India, as he would so claim to the end of his frustrated life. No doubt the natives, even earlier, were making jokes of their own—before, that is, they were caught up in the deadly roundelay of influenza, tuberculosis, and syphilis that became the legacy of their barter for baubles and beads. No joke there. But it was Columbus who made perhaps the first

truly American joke (the first *white* American joke at least)
when he dubbed the natives of these isles "Indians" and
called his find "the West Indies." If nothing is so but saying it
makes it so, let Ferdinand and Isabella understand that he had
reached the gold and spices of India—proof to follow. P. T.
Barnum, that old bunco artist, would have been mighty proud
of old Chris. Certainly, in its play on the doubleness of reality,
Columbus' "joke" presages much American humor-to-be—and
he got away with it, *almost,* back in Castille when he brought
back a few "Indians," though he was a bit short on the gold and
spices.

But it is wrong to single out Columbus as a bit of a fraud.
Many early explorers were frauds, as well as adventurers and
cutthroats. If you rewarded your monarch with new lands to
exploit, he or she rewarded you with a knighthood and an estate. The truth was often fudged. Amerigo Vespucci inspired an
uncharacteristic tirade by Ralph Waldo Emerson, who wrote in
English Traits in 1856: "Strange that broad America must wear
the name of a thief! Amerigo Vespucci, the pickle-dealer at
Seville, who went out in 1499, a subaltern with Hojeda, and
whose highest naval rank was boatswain's mate, in an expedi-
tion that never sailed, managed in this lying world to supplant
Columbus, and baptize half the earth with his own dishonest
name!" Vespucci, it must be granted, was not only a good PR
man, but a good navigator.

It was not only the discoverers who were dishonest however.
Just as they would later in Australia, the English used their
early American colonies as a dumping ground for convicts, dis-
affected Irish, and dissident religious sects like the Puritans.
Colonizing is never easy, and the colonizing of North America
was particularly perilous. Roanoke, the infamous "lost colony"
established in 1587 by the redoubtable Sir Walter Raleigh,
"disappeared" in the feverish fens of the Carolinas. Jamestown
was founded in 1607, but—despite the resourceful efforts of
that sympathetic third-world princess, Pocahontas—lost all but
seventy of its first 900 settlers from arrows, disease, and starvation in its first three years. So, by the time the Puritans landed
on Cape Cod in 1620, the dubious dream of America as a land
of milk and honey should have been apparent to all but the

most deluded or innocent souls. There *were* signs, blips of despair. On the *Arabella,* the Puritans' own flagship, Dorothy, William Bradford's young wife, brooded beside the gunwales as the ship wallowed in winter surf off Cape Cod's inhospitable dunes—and then quietly slipped overboard to end her life. How empty the promise of the New World or of any glorious "City on a Hill" must have seemed to her! Significantly, the intrepid Bradford, later first governor, saw no cause to mention his own wife's suicide in his magisterial chronicle, *History of the Massachusetts Bay Colony.* Again, the emphasis was on glory not sadness.

So there has always been this American business of claiming more than there really is (or omitting less) to suit one's purposes; and if it is a joke, it is a dark joke. Thomas Morton, who arrived in 1624 in the company of fur traders, may lay claim to being America's first comedian (though as much lie-down as stand-up); he certainly saw the joke. In 1627, Morton set up a commune where all "would be free from service, and we will converse, plant, trade, and live together as equals and support and protect one another." As Samuel Eliot Morison tells it:

> Thomas Morton, a gay gentleman with an eye for trade, gathered a knot of boon companions on Mount Wollaston, which he renamed, in conscious punning, Ma-re Mount; and well he lived up to its usual pronunciation. . . . Young squaws were particularly welcome, and young Pilgrims probably found an occasional surreptitious visit to Merrymount as stimulating, and ultimately exhausting, as their descendants do a trip to New York. . . . Morton and his friends "set up a May-pole," (according to Governor Bradford) "drinking and dancing aboute it many days togeather, inviting the Indean woman for their consorts, dancing and frisking togithir . . . and worse practices."

The maypole ("a goodly pine tree of eighty feet longe") served as "a beacon for mariners," Morton claimed, tongue-in-cheek; and he tacked up a mock-classical poem whose mythological and phallic allusions puzzled the Pilgrims. Around this pole, Morton and his fellow revelers gamboled and sang:

> Drink and be merry, merry, merry, boyes
> Let all your delight be in the Hymen's joys
> Io! to Hymen now the day is come,
> About the merry Maypole take a Roome.
>
> . . .
>
> Give to the Nymphe that's free from scorne
> No Irish stuff nor Scotch over worne.
> Lasses in beaver coats come away,
> Yee shall be welcome to us night and day.

As might be imagined, the dour Puritans frowned on the spectacle of drunken fellow Englishmen staggering around a maypole with beaver-coated "lasses." But, as Morison reminds us, it was Morton's free-trading antics which nettled even more, and inspired the Puritans, in 1628, to give Morton and Company the boot. That the moment of truth was serio-comic at best sifts through even Bradford's account:

> But they found him to stand stifly in his defence, having made fast his dors, armed his consorts, set diverse dishes of powder and bullets on the table; and if they had not been over armed with drinke, more hurt might have been done. They sommaned him to yeeld, but he kept his house, and they could get nothing but scofes and scornes from him; but at length, fearing they would doe some violence to the house, he and some of his crue came out, but not to yeeld, but to shoote; but they were so steeld with drinke as their peeces were too heavie for them; him selfe with a carbine (had) thought to have shot Captaine Standish; but he stept to him, and put by his peece, and tooke him. Neither was ther any hurte done to any of either side, save that one was so drunke that he rane his own nose upon the pointe of a sword that one held before him as he entred the house; but he lost but a little of his hott blood.

Thus were Morton and his entourage carted away to Plymouth by the redoubtable Miles Standish in an *opera bouffe* of overloaded pistols and loaded defenders, and shipped home. Morton returned the following year; but, when he persisted in striking his own bargains with the Indians, he had his maypole cut down and was sent packing again. Back in England, Morton published his *New England Canaan* (1637), which praised the richness of the New World but lampooned certain of the Puritans (Standish was "Captain Shrimpe"), causing Bradford to label it "an infamous and scurrilous booke." Morton returned in 1643, only to be thrown into irons; and in 1645 he finally died, in York, Maine, a broken man, half-mad, drinking only water.

As S. J. Perelman once observed, "Comedy is a hard dollar." Among other things, Morton's story is a cautionary tale which demonstrates that, in the 1620s at least, America was a real Palookaville for a comic, particularly one who insisted on playing up to the natives. It is intriguing (though ultimately futile of course) to ask, as Leslie Fiedler has: "What would have happened if it had survived, this beatnik colony in the 17th-century New England woods, presided over by University bohemians —full of classical quotation, fun, and devilry?" (Perhaps Harvard would have had a rival—or is Harvard Merry-mount reincarnate anyway as many would have it?) Be that as it may, we know that making a nation (and money) is serious business; and Morton was as much a casualty of early capitalist interests as of Puritan ethics. As self-proclaimed "Lord of Misrule," Morton may be blamed for bringing his own house down around him. But he might also be defended for having acted in democratic fashion—by inviting everyone, even Indians, to his party. The Puritans wanted the Indians' business; but they resolutely drew the line at frolicking with beaver-coated lasses, no matter how lissome; Thanksgiving turkey was one thing, "ma-re mounting" quite another.

. . .

Columbus and Morton are very old stories indeed. But what Columbus did and what happened to Morton are in many ways emblematic of the forces at work in America that create, or attempt to squash, our humor. What we see, when we really look, is that our jokes are often double-edged swords, signs and signals of complicated relationships and power struggles. Our urge to ridicule, for instance, is terribly strong, as well as our belief in the cleansing effects of its demonic powers. "No God

and no religion can survive ridicule," observed Mark Twain in
Connecticut Yankee. "No church, no nobility, no royalty or
other fraud, can face ridicule in a fair field and win." Ridicule,
however, is no Doomsday Machine. As Twain's sometime-
mentor Artemus Ward observed wryly, "The pen's more migh-
tier than the sword, but which, I'm afraid, would stand rather a
slim chance beside the needle gun."

Morton's japes certainly did not withstand the Puritans' superior firepower. But, whether as a chigger bite or a tigerish
assault, ridicule certainly is something every American has to
contend with, in some form or another, at an early age. In high
school, the girl with the forty-inch bust gets dubbed "Melons";
in a neat twist of the knife, the three-hundred-pound fat boy is
"Tiny." And if one can't "take a joke" (almost like "taking a
punch"), that unfortunate will quickly earn a reputation as a
"sorehead" and become the butt of even nastier jokes until he
or she is forced to fight—or learns to hurl his or her own jokes
back.

In a sense, the genesis of this book lies in my own youth,
when I first noticed something "passing strange" about this
ridicule business. My pals and I used jokes not only to attract
attention and "divvy" up friends and foes along ethnic or jock
versus wimp lines, but to wound. Jokes, we somehow understood, were weapons that could protect you from attack. If you
were slow on the uptake, you got "ranked on"; if you were fast
and nasty, you were left alone. It was that simple, and it made
little difference that many of the biggest jokers, including myself, were not necessarily happy about the process or themselves. Even then I was aware of the paradox involved in
laughter, which serves as such blessed relief, but often stems
from the observation of something embarrassing or painful. But
it was not until much later, when I came to read Mark Twain
and other American humorists and saw their deliberate working out of what we street-kids had improvised, that I could
discern a pattern.

·   ·   ·

I once intended this book to span the far fields of American
humor. But I now understand my reach cannot be that wide,

my brain that cavernous, nor the most patient reader that indulgent, to allow such encyclopedic urges. So, where I had projected a perfectly proportioned edifice (perhaps not so much an elegant Alhambra as a more American rough-hewn log cabin) I seem to have created something that wriggles like an eel. Perhaps, "that ain't no matter," as Huck would say. Maybe, in its sprawl, the book now better reflects the sprawling nature of American humor, which in fact mirrors and mocks the sprawling and cataclysmic nature of our history. One could, for instance, (and several have) make an entire book out of just Abe Lincoln and "Abe-olition" as butt and counter-butt of antebellum and Civil War humor. The Congressional Record itself, as Will Rogers pointed out, is its own humorous weekly. Many fine books have been written on the "literary comedians," and on film comics like the Marx Brothers, Laurel and Hardy, W. C. Fields, and on a host of stand-up comedians; and I have drawn on much of this material.

Violence, both as a concern and a methodology, has effected a kinship among many American comic artists. When one considers the fundamental nature of our humor, one sees the same conflicts and contradictions at the heart of the jokes, and these conflicts and contradictions have something to do with that old chestnut, the American Dream. Whose dream *is* it anyway, and who is entitled to dream? Thomas Morton or the Puritans? The Indians? "Gentilmen" or squatters? Whigs or Tories? Immigrants? *Only* men—or women too? What about blacks, Hispanics, the homeless, the disenfranchised? American humor reveals a complicated process—the powerful ridiculing the powerless (ethnic jokes, negative caricatures of women, etc.); the powerless fighting back with duplicity and masks (early "darky" entertainers, for example). Furthermore, American humor not only has a pecking order but political overtones and is not always in good, clean fun. When Thomas Morton ridiculed the Puritans, they had him arrested. When Dick Gregory and Richard Pryor pointed out the reality of racism, they lost bookings. When Lenny Bruce *spritzed* on dirty words, he was arrested for obscenity. In America, there has always been a quarrel going on as to *what* or *who* is really funny. Though it does not work itself out along Marxist lines (except perhaps in the spirit of Groucho, Chico and Harpo), there is (and always has been), a class struggle in America, despite our cherished democratic ideals; and our jokes (and jokesters) reflect this struggle. Bob Hope's quips (and his audience) are not the same as those of Lily Tomlin.

The arena in which our humorists have sported is indeed enormous and embraces the wilds of Bret Harte's goldfields, the Maine woods of Seba Smith's Yankee Jack Spaulding and J. R. Lowell's Birdofredum Sawin; it sweeps from the Irish saloons of Mister Dooley's Chicago to the pigsties of J. G. Baldwin's Simon Suggs, the blood-and-guts Georgia of Augustus Longstreet, and the swamp "hollers" of Al Capp's shiftless Yokum yokels, and includes as well the elegant drawing rooms of the Algonquin wits and the bloody battlefields of Kurt Vonnegut and Joseph Heller. And the run of that humor, stretching from Thomas Morton's lampooning of Puritan seriousness through the Texas-style bragging of Davy Crockett, Mike Fink, and Paul Bunyan to contemporary "attack comics" such as Sam Kinison, does indeed seem to straddle that delicate balance between comedy and violence so characteristic of the native strain. But the thrust of their work is hardly unique. Indeed, much of this humor has been cross-fertilized and mirrored by and in the popular culture—from the camp-meetings, minstrel shows and burlesques of the nineteenth-century to the nickelodeons that fostered early silent clowns like Chaplin and the depression era Rialtos and Tivolis that served up snarling clowns like W. C. Fields, and the smoky comedy clubs of the fifties and sixties that featured (and exposed) the likes of Bruce and Pryor. Popular culture has never stopped fostering new forms of humor, from the antiwar sentiment that encouraged war-comedies like *Doctor Strangelove* and "M*A*S*H," to daily newspapers that welcomed Herblock, Paul Szep, and satirical cartoons like *Pogo, Bloom County,* and *Doonesbury*; to television shows like "Laugh-In" which showcased the off-beat humor of Lily Tomlin and Goldie Hawn and "Saturday Night Live" which spawned self-styled whackos like Gilda Radner, John Belushi and Bill Murray.

American humor does provide an embarrassment of riches, and let me admit my own embarrassment in having to leave out so much and acknowledge here some of the omissions. I am only too ruefully aware that much has fallen through the cracks or sneaked out the back door.

First off, you will find little strictly ethnic humor in these pages, though it has a strong and virulent shelf life and certainly is often violent. Ethnic humor feasts upon difference and misunderstanding, stereotypes and the superiority of one's own tribe. There are two kinds of ethnic jokes: in-jokes among minorities themselves and outsider jokes about those very same minorities made at their expense. In the first case, it is clear that the purpose of the joke is *defensive*, that is, designed to recognize and joke about their very difference; in the second case, the thrust is *offensive*, to indicate how stupid Paddy or Sambo is, how venal Hymie. Jewish fathers may make Jewish-American-Princess jokes; but a JAP joke on the tongue of a Jewish father is a very different kettle of *gefilte* fish than one on a gentile tongue.

Ethnic jokes often depend upon accents, such as the joke about the irate Chinese father who looks upon his white baby and says, "Two Wongs don't make a white," only to have his wife protest, "Occidents will happen." Sometimes ethnic jokes are not in themselves offensive: "What do you get when an Irishman marries a Negro?—A guy they keep throwing out of the parade every St. Patrick's Day." But more typical is the spate of light bulb jokes that suggest the stupidity of the minority (usually Polish), or the racist jokes that emphasize their "un-American" habits: "Why did the Mexicans fight so hard to capture the Alamo?—So they would have four clean walls to write on."

Ethnic jokes (and ethnic humorists) came into their own when the first waves of European immigrants came to America before the Civil War. The camp meetings and minstrel shows usually included "Tambo and Bones" routines, "Pat-and-Mike" skits, and "Dutch" comics (either German or Jewish) who played an even larger role later in vaudeville and burlesque; and we can note echoes in Amos and Andy, in Chico Marx's "Eye-talian" immigrant, in Jackie Gleason and Art Carney's "Ralph and Ed" routines in "The Honeymooners," in the spate of Polish jokes which still flourish and multiply, and in the routines of Jewish comics like Lenny Bruce, Mel Brooks,

Woody Allen and Jackie Mason, who have spritzed their way across stage and screen in a flood of yiddishisms and *goyische* jokes. If we have less ethnic comedy today, it is perhaps because so many minorities have assimilated and assimilation is the death of ethnic comedy. Where *are* today's Irish comedians? George Carlin is Irish—he is not, however, an *Irish* comedian.

But ethnic humor is not exclusively, or even particularly, American. Czechs make fun of Slovaks, the Japanese ridicule the Chinese; no doubt the Hopi laugh at the Zuni. That most ethnic humor is violent in that it denigrates others seemed to me so obvious that I have not felt it necessary to make a big case for it.

Nor do I make a big case for sick jokes which we always seem to have with us. (Mommy, Mommy, why am I running around in circles? Shut up or I'll nail your other foot to the floor.) Recently, a rash of *Challenger* jokes ("How many astronauts can fit in a car?—Eleven: two in the front, two in the back, and seven in the ashtray"), some so tasteless they hardly bear repeating. Again, "sick" jokes are part of the world's humor, and the childish glee of such humor does not need much analysis. The political humor of Eastern Europe, for example, no doubt because of its awful history, is often darker than anything our "sickest" comedians can concoct. (One Roumanian story: A guy fed up with queues sets off to kill the president, only to come back crestfallen. His friends ask him what happened. He shrugs, "The line was too long.") We Americans also did not invent sick jokes.

I realize, too, that there are few women to be found in these pages, though that, I feel, is the subject of another book, one more attuned to the sociology of sexual politics than this. One thing is for sure: women, in the persons of Phyllis Diller, Joan Rivers, Bette Midler, and, of course, Lily Tomlin, have come out of the comedy closet—forever. Nor have I dealt at length with The *New Yorker* school of James Thurber, Robert Benchley, Dorothy Parker, and S. J. Perelman. This does *not* mean that I don't admire these writers; I most emphatically do. I read them and they make me laugh. But their work does not concern itself with the themes of this book. I also regret not finding more room for others I much admire—Flannery O'Connor, Nathanael West, and "black" humorists such as Heller, Thomas Pynchon, and Terry Southern, not to mention Melville and Faulkner whose humor often goes unappreciated. But these writers, though they can be screamingly funny, do not view themselves primarily as humorists.

I chose to begin with writers of the "heartland"—Mark Twain, Ambrose Bierce, Ring Lardner, and Kurt Vonnegut—all white, midwestern Protestants. These humorists were in no way outsiders. They spoke from within the mainstream tradition to people whose values and prejudices they knew; and if they began criticizing those values (as Bierce did and Vonnegut has), it came not as sniping but betrayal. Each of these writers took a different slant on violence, and their varied attacks expose much, not only about the nature of American humor, but about America herself. I move on to film comedians—Chaplin and Keaton, those sublime silent clowns; and those great talking clowns of the thirties, Laurel and Hardy, the Marx Brothers, and W. C. Fields. I then turn to the strange and undeniably violent world of stand-up comics; and I have singled out Lenny Bruce, Richard Pryor, George Carlin, and Lily Tomlin (whatever one cares to call her) because once again I find their work worthy of special notice. I also consider political satire (will it *ever* end?) and the thrust of such humor as it manifests itself in our newspapers, movies, and television. In sum, I chose the humorists I did because they seemed to me all significant figures who wrestled, in one fashion or another, with the greasy pig of violence and *that*, after all, is the subject of this book.

· · ·

A few final observations.

First off, one must be careful not to overstate any claim for this coupling of humor and violence as exclusively American property. The savage farces of Aristophanes, the pummeling of Don Quixote, the head-knocking of Punch and Judy come readily to mind. Laughter itself has violent roots. "As laughter emerges with man from the mists of antiquity it seems to hold a dagger in its hands," anthropologist J. C. Gregory has observed. "There is enough brutal triumph, enough contempt, enough striking down from superiority in the records of antiquity to presume that original laughter may have been wholly animosity." And this "baring of the fangs," Gregory claims, accounts for a great deal of what might be considered primitive or childish laughter. There seems to be something to this. Is there a child alive who does not delight in the *be-bop-bop-bop* antics of Tom and Jerry or the noisy nose-bonking of The Three Stooges? When Wile E. Coyote gets crushed by a five-ton boulder or smooshed like a pancake by the rambunctious Roadrunner, kids laugh—whether they are "corrupted" by such violent farce or not.

Humor itself is a will-of-the-wisp, most difficult to bottle or label. "Humor theories" breed like frogs in spring. Aristotle viewed the comic imp as one aspect of "the ugly," Hobbes emphasized the "sudden-glory" of superiority that laughter gives, Bergson found many useful clues in incongruity, and recently there has been an amusing melange of revenge theories, anger theories, etc. Behaviorists, too, have diligently studied risibility in primates and college students (perhaps the same genus); but they are concerned more with responses than with stimuli, the laughter rather than the jokes. The jokes, however, are what interest me. I most emphatically do not propose to tell you, dear reader, why either of us laughs (if we are so fortunate); on some matters, even the gods must be silent. But what I hope to do is show the kind of jokes Americans make and comment on what these jokes might suggest. This book is more a query than a study.

I deal with violence, also, in its myriad forms. Violence, in its etymological roots, suggests violation—not just of the body, but of rights and dignity as well. Violence always threatens, though not always physically. Invective and common insult are more pervasive and, on occasion, just as deadly. It may seem ironic that we often find our humorists employing a methodology of savage, comic deflation to attack the violence they see around them. But that has as much to do with the process, or psychology, of humor as anything else.

Freud cited three things necessary for a joke—a teller, a listener, *and* a target. He theorized that "tendentious jokes" provided outlets in the face of aggression or injustice, thereby serving as alternatives to actual physical violence. So, Freud suggests, there seems to be something to the old adage, "Sticks and stones may break my bones, but words will never hurt me." Observing such hostile mechanisms at work, American psychologist Rollo May asserts that frustration is not only at the root of most violence but most humor. Our comedians themselves certainly understand the function of humor is a safety valve. Abe Burroughs explains, "Other kids threw rocks. I made jokes." Mel Brooks puts it another way, "If your enemy is laughing, how can he bludgeon you to death?" So humor can be both an offensive and defensive weapon.

Thus, the working formula, then, might go:

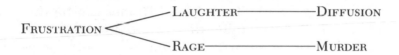

The greatest poets, too, tell us that laughter certainly does not signify happiness. "I laugh that I may not weep," says Byron's Don Juan. As Horace Walpole observed: "This world is a comedy to those who think, a tragedy to those who feel." To Charles Baudelaire, the source of laughter was "satanic," and he made a distinction between joy, which he viewed as "unity," and laughter, which he saw as "the expression of a double, or contradictory, feeling," which was "why a convulsion occurs." Baudelaire speculated that the "satanic laughter" bubbling out at odd moments springs from recognition of our flawed human condition and reveals an evil twin within who can joke openly about our mortality. Laughter, too, often has a debilitating effect—can render us, as Arthur Koestler has observed, equally incapable of killing or copulating.

Thus, the poets and psychologists suggest, if we laugh so that we do not weep, then we also laugh so that we do not explode or kill. But what can be said about our American humorists, who seldom seem incapacitated or humbled, but who so often go for the jugular without shame and wield their sharp jokes like razors? If violence has always been a part of the world's humor, but the special savagery of so much American humor does seem to point to a preoccupation, even a peculiarity. Why? From where does this impulse spring? What are its roots—its obsessions? These are the questions this book raises and, I hope, helps answer.

"Violence" and "humor" have become such catchalls for every sort of public and literary refuse that one must resist the temptation to try and pour twelve ounces of theory into a shot glass of fact. Unfortunately, as with Polonius and his Protean cloud, a writer is often able to see only what he wishes to see. I have tried to avoid overstating what has seemed at times a painfully obvious thesis: the particular and peculiar conjunction of humor and violence in America.

Writing about humor is tricky business. As Henry Nash Smith observed, criticism is notoriously helpless in the face of writing that is really funny. E. B. White agreed: "Humor can be dissected as a frog can, but something dies in the process." It is, of course, easier to write about writers. Film comics and comedians are especially hard to "catch" because nuance, often, is all. How *does* one do justice, on paper, to Chaplin's subtleties; or to Lenny Bruce's delivery and voice, which had the rasping precision of a steel drill; or to the quick-silver impersonations of a Lily Tomlin or a Richard Pryor? I have tried to gloss performances as I best remember them; and I hope the reader is equally glad that I have been less than exhaustive.

Finally, I have tried throughout to keep from poking the reader in the ribs, though I trust it will prove obvious that it is the humor that attracted me to these artists and that I have been most impressed (if at times terrified as well) when they have made me laugh. Oh, yes.

ROUND ONE

The Violence of American Humor

California's a great place to live—if you're an orange.
                                        —Fred Allen

*God is not evil. But the best you can say for Him is
that he's an underachiever.*   —Woody Allen

How to win at black jack?—Use a real blackjack.
                                        —Steve Allen

Allen—an interesting name. In *Roughing It*, Mark Twain relates how the "Allen" revolver served as a popular and "cheerful" weapon for those prone to mayhem in the Washoe
Territory during the 1860s. "Sometimes," he tells us, "all its six
barrels would go off at once, and there was no place in all the
region roundabout but behind it." A punch line there, too. It
may be overstatement, however, to claim all American humor
comes from "Allens"—whether Fred, Steve, Woody, or sometimes Gracie. But what we can say is that these "Allen" jokes,
like so many American jokes, are wisecracks packed with a
wallop.

We Americans enjoy making fun of sacred cows. Recall James
Thurber's parody of Ben Franklin's Poor Richard, "Early to rise
and early to bed make a man healthy, wealthy—and dead," or
Lyndon Johnson's jape that Gerry Ford's troubles stemmed
from his having played too much football without a helmet. But
not everybody gets—or appreciates—jokes like that. Humor
travels poorly and translates worse. Consider, for instance, this
Japanese joke: One woman praises another's nose, but the
owner drops her eyes to protest humbly, "Maybe on the outside, but inside it's really just full of snot." Now, to an Ameri-

can, there is nothing necessarily funny in this—but it cracks up many a Tokyo Toyota salesman. The Japanese get the joke because they understand their culture and can laugh at a modesty which disclaims beauty to deflect envy. It is a self-effacing joke appropriate to a people who value self-effacement. But you would be hard-pressed to find its like back in the U.S.A. More typical of the thrust of our humor is Rodney Dangerfield's mordant jest that sex after sixty is like playing pool with a rope. This punch line is darker and more jolting—deflating.

In this light, such caricatures as Chevy Chase's takeoff of Gerald "Stumbles" Ford and Gary Trudeau's portrayals of Ronnie "Headrest" Reagan and an "invisible" George Bush are typical. Making the president a fall guy is a clear attack on pomp and circumstance; and we not only applaud such "democratic" humor but expect it. This impulse, however, does not necessarily spring from radical or reformist roots; our humorists have included Whig conservatives as well as Jacksonian populists, and the upstart backwoodsman can be as much a figure of fun as the elegant "gentilmin." Any pompous popinjay who pats his own back is fair game for the guns of our American humorists who share this common deflationary humor. As Richard Hofstadter aptly observed, "Comic deflation is a kind of violence, usually at heart reductive though not necessarily incendiary." Thus the "put-on" and the "put-down," the hoax and the naked insult, are as much weapons in the arsenal of Mark Twain and Ring Lardner, as they are in those of Groucho Marx, Lenny Bruce, or Don Rickles. Our stand-up comedians have a lingo for what they do; they go out to "destroy" an audience—"knock 'em dead"—and if they don't, they "bomb." Since this language of death is one shared by our greatest literary comedians and film comics, and since violence, both as subject and method, is at the root of much American humor, it seems appropriate that we call the point of an American joke "the punch line."

· · ·

National humor does much to explain, or betray, a culture. German humor—or the lack of it—is itself a joke. Goethe insisted that one cannot have a sense of humor unless one is without conscience or responsibility (perhaps providing additional substance to the gibe that it takes a Prussian three days to understand a joke at which he will laugh for three days). One can make generalizations: Soviet bloc humor tends to be bleak and nihilistic, e.g., consider the dour political reality of *Krokodil;* French humor, full of double entendre and repartee; Italian humor, gargantuan and full of farce, and so on. But English humor deserves special mention since, as no less a "white savage" than Mark Twain once observed: "Americans are not Englishmen, and American humor is not English humor; but the American and his humor had their origin in England, and have merely undergone changes brought by changed conditions and environment."

In search, then, of origins, we might note that England has long maintained a distinguished tradition of "genteel" humor —one appreciative of wit and forgiving of foibles, which, in the skillful hands of an Austen or Thackeray, amuses but does not wound, and posits a stable society wherein redemption is not only possible but necessary. Within this tradition, "[c]ontempt," as George Meredith insisted, "is a sentiment that cannot be entertained by the comic intelligence." The English, too, have often expressed a wariness of the comic demon. "Frequent laughter, " Lord Chesterfield warned his son, "is the characteristic of ill manner in which the mob express their silly joy in silly things," Not all Englishmen, however, fall into this neat pattern. Swift and Pope created a jugular rather than jocular humor; and the humor of Monty Python, to cite one contemporary example, is certainly far from tame. Malcolm Muggeridge spoke up for this satirical tradition when he observed: "All great humor is in bad taste, anarchistic, and implies criticism of existing institutions [and] beliefs." But (*pace* Swift et al.) we must agree that the English sense of humor, on the whole, has been, as Harold Nicolson describes it, "kind, sentimental, reasonable and fanciful." We might also note that this genteel strain crossed the Atlantic with the early colonists and may be traced through such writers as Washington Irving, Oliver Wendell Holmes, and James Russell Lowell to The *New Yorker* school of E. B. White, Robert Benchley, and the like.

Even here, cavils crop up. In one sense, Irving's *Legend of Sleepy Hollow* is the ultimate torture story, anti-intellectual at base, as beefy Brom Bones torments the itinerant schoolteacher Ichabod Crane; and Benchley's vision, like Thurber's, is often dark and misogynistic. But these writers are still in the genteel tradition.

Whatever may be said about the parentage of America humor, something happened—and it happened in the nineteenth century. The child became unrecognizable to many English observers, became nasty, and was disowned. After their American sojourns, English novelists like Mrs. Trollope and Charles Dickens returned to England shaking their heads. The Americans went, *well*, simply too far. "There has always been something sui generis in the American comic spirit," speculated Christopher Morley, "a touch of brutality perhaps? Anger rather than humor? Sardonic, extravagant, macabre," And this "brutality"—often disguised by an edgy deadpan—has put off English critics. W. H. Auden, for instance, noted how remarkably stoical Huck Finn is (how unlike Oliver Twist!)in the face of the horrors he encounters, and confessed to finding Twain's novel "emotionally very sad." V. S. Pritchett professed similar astonishment, and some manner of disgust, at the frightening assortment of child-beaters, cowards, con men, and cutthroats who people Huck's world. What is interesting is not that Pritchett and Auden point out the violence (American critics have done that as well), but that they should be so shocked as to question the values of the society that can laugh at (and thereby appear to encourage) such antics. And many contemporary English writers have echoed this sense of a special American ferocity. Playwright Jonathan Miller remarked that his own *Beyond the Fringe* was a "pinprick" compared to "the bloodbath" of Lenny Bruce's act; and novelist Martin Amis judged the cynical wisecracking of the reporters covering Ronald Reagan's 1980 campaign all savage and sad, since "like so much American laughter, [it] did not express high spirits or amusement but a willed raucousness."

The debate continues. At the Oxford Student Union recently, American comedians Alan King and Steve Allen took on some students and British comedians to resolve the question of whether American humor is "funnier" than British humor. The approaches were strikingly different. The English humor was cerebral—one Oxfordian, for instance, mocking the Milwaukee cabdriver who thought Botticelli a new pizza topping. King, on the other hand, attacked—declaring war on England and the students with his let-it-all-hang-out Gonzo humor, spewing obscenities and insults along the way—and was rewarded with the biggest laughs. "Gorillas," concluded Allen, "prefer American humor." Gorillas maybe, but not gentlemen.

But it has not been only English observers who have expressed shock at the rawness, cruelty, and lack of restraint of American humor. As Madame Bentzon, a nineteenth-century French traveller, tutted, "there is something in the American spirit, an inclination to gross mirth, to pranks, which reveals that in certain respects this great people is still a childish people." Jean Charpentier referred to Twain as "a Homais dressed in the feathers of the redskin and dancing the scalp dance around the body of Pallas Athene." And high-toned American observers, like Columbia professor H. H. Boyesen and *Atlantic* essayist S. S. Cox, worried aloud as well. Boyesen complained about the "plague of jocularity" that infected us so that "instead of that interchange of thought which other civilized nations hold to be one of the highest social pleasures, we exchange jokes," while Cox insisted our "slashing humor" sacrificed "feeling, interest, sociability, philosophy, romance, art and morality for its joke." Even Josh Billings (himself a low-brow "phunny phellow") noted, "Americans prefer turpentine tew colone-water [and] must have [their] humor on the half-shell with cayenne."

. . .

There is no doubt that many of the professors and foreign observers were missing out on the "funning" part. Many of our early native humorists enjoyed "having on" the "dam furriners." If they expected crude, then, by gum, they would show them crude. "Some pranksters," Walter Blair and Hamlin Hill tell us, "put on shows for travellers; others cooked up elaborate lies. In Louisville, a gang of young bucks staged a fake free-for-

all with horrendous casualties for a genteel visiting man of letters, then enjoyed reading about the carnage in his book."
Washington Irving concocted a Maryland (which he never visited) peopled by a gunpowder race of men who lived on hoe-
cakes, drank gallons of mint juleps and brandy toddies, and
spent their days boxing, biting, gouging, and tar-and-feather-
ing. And the humor itself was not only crude but "gigantic,"
that is, it went beyond the possible. Davy Crockett claimed to
be able to "swallow a nigger whole if you but butter his head."
John Henry Jarvis's "Wildfire" prated that he was "half-horse,
half-alligator, a touch of earthquake, with a sprinkling of the
steamboat." Kentucky soil, Jarvis proclaimed, was "so rich that
if you but plant a crowbar over night perhaps it will sprout ten-
penny nails afore mornin'." Just planting in "Arkansaw" could
be plumb dangerous: "I had a good-sized sow killed in that
same bottom-land. The old thief stole an ear of corn, and took
it down where she slept at night to eat. Well, she left a grain or
two on the ground, and lay down on them: before morning the
corn shot up, and the percussion killed her dead."

But the violent exaggeration of much nineteenth-century
American humor was often the whole point. The Great American Joke, as Louis Rubin defines it, "arises out of the gap between the cultural ideal and the everyday fact, with the ideal
shown to be somewhat hollow and hypocritical, and the fact
crude and disgusting." This humor, Stephen Leacock notes,
also played off "sudden and startling contrasts as between
things as they are supposed to be—revered institutions, accepted traditions, established conventions—and things as they
are." In a sense, then, our humorists could be said to be poking
fun at the American Dream by sticking folks' noses in American
reality. "Like many other things this humor," as Leacock suggests, "came out of the west, beyond the plains. You had to get
clear away from civilization to start it." Beside the campfires
and out on lonely ranges of the old Southwest, the tall tale, the
humorous ghost story, and the raucous practical joke provided
welcome relief from the terrible and dangerous conditions of
the frontier. Maurice Breton described the humor of the Far
West thus: "If men must laugh together in order to forget their
hardships, the laughter is loud, nervous, and rough, with overtones of disillusionment and bitterness."

But this "frontier theory" still does not explain the continu-
ance of that tradition long after the disappearance of the actual
frontier. The myth persists and even some of our politicians
live it. Back in 1964, Ronald Reagan, then governor of California, said of Vietnam, "We could pave the whole country and
put parking strips on it, and still be home by Christmas." *Wha-
hoo!* Texans still wear cowboy boots and Stetsons (albeit from
Nieman-Marcus), and Boston as well as Houston has its urban
cowboys; Clint Eastwood continues to "hang'em high" on the
streets of twentieth-century Los Angeles as well as on the
crusty plains of the pseudo-West; and many Americans view
Bernard Goetz as a vigilante hero for his shooting of subway
thugs. American violence is certainly more than a Western phenomenon. Back in the 1930s, Nathanael West, that deft observer of folly, noted: "In America violence is idiomatic. Read
our newspapers. To make the front page a murderer has to use
his imagination, he has also to use a particularly hideous instrument. Take this morning's paper: FATHER CUTS SON'S THROAT IN
BASEBALL ARGUMENT. It appears on an inside page. To make the
first page he should have killed three sons and with a baseball
bat instead of a knife. Only liberality and symmetry could have
made this daily occurrence interesting." In the 1960s, Black
Power revolutionary H. Rap Brown said simply, "Violence is as
American as cherry pie."

The problem has, if anything, worsened. What are we now to
make of such box office heroes as the Popeye-muscled Sylvester Stallone and the steely-eyed Arnold Schwarzenegger, red-
white-and-blue heroes who simply blow away the bad guys—
to stand-up applause? Our cities are under siege from drug
dealers and the underclass. Homicide is the greater killer of
black males under twenty-five. We are all too accustomed to
newspaper front pages such as the one displaying a shadowy
photo of a seventeen-year-old who has admitted to keeping a
gun under his sweatpants because he liked the feel of it against
his skin. "I don't know if I'll ever be 30 years old," says
"George," "a lot of people I know don't make it to 30 years
old." And there are many "Georges" (certainly not all black)
prowling the streets with Magnums, Uzis, and sawed-off shot-
guns. But aren't these the typical scare tactics of the Fourth
Estate, some might argue—overkill—and playing up the ex-

ception rather than the rule? *Is* America all that violent? What
are the facts?

Well, there are some startling statistics. Between 1882 and
1927, 4,950 lynchings were recorded, lynchings, mind you, and
rough estimates double that figure. Further, a simple body
count suggests that American society has promoted a gun culture without parallel among all other nations. American domestic firearms fatalities during the twentieth century total more
than 265,000 homicides, 333,000 suicides, and 139,000 gun-
related accidents—a figure twice the number of Americans
killed in all this century's wars. Our homicide rate consistently
runs eight times that of Japan and four times that of any European country. In 1988, there were 900,000 Americans incarcer-
ated in prisons (the majority for violent crime) and 3.2 million
(one out of every 55 adult Americans) under some sort of cor-
rectional supervision; and experts are expecting this figure to
double in the next ten years. Sexist violence—date-rape, bedroom rape, just plain rape—abounds. Nationwide there are
hundreds of centers servicing the estimated 500,000 women
battered every year, as well as thousands of homes for abused
children—figures which suggest that the American home itself
is too often a battleground.

It is not, however, the figures themselves—horrifying as they
are—that shock many observers. It is the widespread procla-
mation of innocence in the face of such facts that they find most
remarkable and most ironic. David Brion Davis sums up the
case neatly:

> If we could formulate a generalized image of America in the
> eyes of foreign peoples from the eighteenth century to the pres-
> ent, it would surely include a phantasmagoria of violence, from
> the original Revolution and Indian wars to the sordid history of
> lynching; from the casual killings of the cowboy and bandit to
> the machine-gun murders of racketeers. [T]his sparkling, smil-
> ing domestic land of easygoing friendliness, where it is esti-
> mated that a new murder occurs every forty-five minutes, has
> also glorified personal whim and impulse and has ranked
> hardened killers with the greatest folk heroes. Founded and pre-
> served by acts of aggression and characterized by a continuing
> tradition of self-righteous violence against suspected subversion

and by a vigorous sense of personal freedom, usually involving the widespread possession of firearms, the United States has evidenced a unique tolerance of homicide.

Richard Hofstadter speculates that this "unique tolerance" is the result of "historical amnesia" which has granted us a history but not an awareness of domestic violence. It is our capacity for self-deception on the subject he finds most telling: "What is most exceptional about Americans is not the voluminous record of their violence, but their extraordinary ability, in the face of that record, to persuade themselves that they are among the best-behaved and best-regulated of peoples." In other words, we *think* we are nice, peaceful folks because we *say* we are.

Such self-deception has certainly not escaped the notice of our humorists, who often direct their barbs at just this hypocrisy in order to expose the violence and cruelty lurking under the mask of assumed goodness. In *Huckleberry Finn,* for instance, Twain ridicules the democratic pretensions of Pap Finn, Huck's reptilian Daddy-O. In "Haircut," Ring Lardner exposes Jim Kendall, the self-styled prankster, as morally debased— even as both Pap and Kendall insist on their own good natures and purest of motives. But there is obvious danger in satirizing such "varmints" if the humorist is also ridiculing the shared delusions of his audience; so we should not be surprised to see our humorists often skirting the issue of violence rather than facing it head on, and frequently masking their assault with some such device as the "poker face."

But often, in this other, distinctly "un-English" strain of American humor, which arose out on the frontiers and edges of civilization, we see no such sophisticated hanky-panky. Here the humor is at once more raucous in tone and concerned with unredeemable "low" types; the jokes come as swift and deadly as bullets, and the laughter is poised a hair's breadth from cosmic grief. This native humor reflects the more menacing aspects of American society, and lampoons certain of our most cherished assumptions, such as the natural goodness of man and the inevitability of progress. We see it in the work of such early humorists as A. B. Longstreet, J. J. Hooper, and George Washington Harris. They created shrewd backwoods rogues who speak "Amurrikan" and demonstrate a practically invincible instinct for survival. With these "crackers," there is no gallantry, no generosity of spirit, no "California dreamin'." In one of Longstreet's "Georgia Scenes," a young "cracker" just about kills himself in a one-man fight—with himself. Proclaiming "It's good to be shifty in a new country," Hooper's Simon Suggs sets out the manual for the con men and flimflammers we meet again in the Duke and Dauphin and in W. C. Fields.

But it is Harris's Sut Lovingood who is the best-conceived, most fascinating, and most frightening specimen of all these early versions of "white trash." *The Tales of Sut Lovingood*, as penned by Harris, a rabid Tennessean Democrat, are extraordinarily violent by any standard; and Sut himself manages, barely, to entertain as he appalls. Sut refuses to accept any insult or injury lying down—"By golly, no body can't tramp on me, wifout gittin thar foot bit." Revenge weighs heavily on Sut's scale of justice, as he sets a horse loose at a quilting bee or "re-decorates" a corpse at a funeral. Sut's victims include snotty old "widders" and sassy "gals" who look down on him and his family; "surkit riders" and other self-styled evangelists who threaten to cut in on any of his "fun"; any helpless blacks or Irishmen who just happen to get in his way.

The typical Sut Lovingood story begins with Sut sipping whiskey with his old friend "George" (played by Harris himself, the bemused observer) before breaking into a *by-the-way* tale of one of his prime escapades, all told in a racy, back-home dialect rich in metaphor and invective. Sut's philosophy is simple: If someone injures you in any way, get him or her and get him or her *good*. Sut's defenses, too, are simple; he makes use of his "durned foolishness" (which is "nat'ral born" and derives from his father "Hoss," who has come by his name honestly for having played horse so well pulling a plow he almost killed himself) and his long, spindly "laigs," which whisk him out of the path of a rampaging bull or an irate "widder." Sut's weapons are simple as well: *one*, his imagination, which thinks up the violent practical jokes; and *two*, his ruthless determination in carrying them out.

In one typical tale, "Parson John Bullen's Lizards," George comes upon a poster setting a reward for Sut:

AIT ($8) DULLARS REWARD
'TENSHUN BELEVERS AND KONSTABLES! KETCH 'IM!

THIS kash will be pade in korn, ur uther projuce, tu be kolected at ur about nex camp-meetin, ur thararter, by eny wun what ketches him, fur the karkus ove a sartin wun SUT LOVINGOOD, dead or alive, ur ailin, an' safely giv over to the purtectin care ove parson John Bullen, ur lef' well tied, at Squire Mackjunkins fur the raisin ove the devil pussonely, an permiskusly discum-furtin the wimen very powerful, an skerin ove folks generly a heap, an' bustin up a promisin, big warm meetin, an' a makin the wickid larf, an' wus, an' wus, insultin ove the passun orful.

Test, JEHU WETHERO

Sined by me,

JOHN BULLEN, the passun

When George asks what the commotion is all about, Sut ex-plains. It seems that when Bullen came upon Sut and a neigh-bor girl spooning in the bushes he told her mother, and the girl received an "overhandid stroppin." So Sut sets about sneaking into the next camp meeting of the good parson (or that "durnd infunel, hiperkritikal, pot-bellied, scaley-hided, whiskey was-tin, stinkin old groun'-hog," as Sut calls him) and looses lizards up Bullen's pants as he is preaching on "Hell-sarpints," where-upon Bullen is forced to slip out of his pants and run out of the camp meeting, losing a bit of respect along the way, as Sut observes proudly, especially among the womenfolk. So Bar-belly Bullen, as he is now known, has declared war on Sut, whom he views as "living proof ove the hell-desarvin nater ove man." But Sut is unafraid and promises that if he is not left alone he'll "lizzard him again." Sut recognizes he has con-cocted a kind of devious Old Testament justice. "Say George," he concludes, "didn't that ar Hell-sarpint sermon ove his'n, hev sumthin like a Hell-sarpint aplicashun? Hit looks sorter so tu me."

This pattern of insult and revenge runs through all the Sut Lovingood tales—along with an incredible assortment of may-hem involving bulls, horses, bee swarms, snakes, and other animals, including man. While fellow Southern writers such as William Faulkner and Flannery O'Connor have paid tribute to

Harris's art and Sut's vigor, not all readers have been equally charmed. After reading Harris's collection of Sut's tales, Edmund Wilson said, "It takes a pretty strong stomach to get through . . . it is by far the most repellent book of any real literary merit in American literature." Wilson is right as usual, but there is more to be said. If Sut's "univarsal onregenerit human nater" is repellent, his sense of life is pagan, based on the here and now. "Men were made a purpos jis' to eat, drink, an' fur stayin awake in the early part of the nites," says Sut, "an' women were made to cook vittles, mix the spirits, an' help the men do the stayin' awake. That's all an' nothin more." Sut has no sense of the transcendental, of life after death ("fur hits onpossibil fur me to hev a soul"); or if there be, Sut knows he is damned, as the Calvinists would have it.

Sut accepts that he is a "nat'ral born durned fool" with white trash poverty and craziness all around him. But what he refuses to accept is the hypocrisy of "sirkut riders" with their promises of heaven and their hands out, or that of "wimen-folk" who claim they want love when they are really looking for a farm; and he rails at them in story after story. Give old Sut a jug of moonshine and a sensible twenty-five-year-old "widder" with a nicely turned ankle who knows just how to move in the saddle, and he's happy. Of course Sut would like to go to heaven —anything to get him out of his dreadful hand-to-mouth existence—but he's never yet met a fit representative of the hereafter. Sut reminds us of what Lenny Bruce said often: "There was never the what-should-be, there is only what is."

In this sense Sut is in the grand tradition of American humorous characters who attack hypocrisy by deflating pretension. Sut has looked behind doorways, under skirts, and beneath frock coats, so he knows what is going on and uses that knowledge to expose hypocrites. As he says, "Folks in public don't look much like folks in private nohow, dus they, George?" Often Sut's revenge is ugly, his practical jokes cruel, his motives thin and spiteful; and the very idea of a world of Sut Livingoods is enough to make one shudder. But a Sut-less world would be lacking as well; Sut not only understands and speaks for his own underclass, he understands the losses of other underdogs as well. In the midst of one vituperative diatribe on the Puritans, Sut cries out that, when the *Mayflower* arrived, the Indians "should have carcumsized the head ove the las' durn'd one, burnt thar close, pack'd thar carkuses heads-and-tails, herrin fashun, in thar old ship, sot the sails, an' pinted her snout the way Ward's ducks went." From the Indian point of view, Sut's tirade makes sense, and Thomas Morton would have approved. "Durn them leather injuns," laments Sut, "they let the bes' chance slip ever injuns had to give everlastin comfort to a continent and to set hell back at leas' five hundred years."

But what does this all mean—what's its "puppus," as Sut would say? Well, Harris has Sut offer his own wish (and slight defense) in the preface to their "collaboration":

> "Ef any poor misfortunit devil hu's heart is onder a millstone, hu's ragged children am hungry, an' no bread in the dresser, hu is down in the mud, and the lucky ones a-trippin him every time he struggils to his all fours, hu hes fed the famishin an' now is hungry hissef, hu misfortins foller fas an' foller faster, hu is so foot-sore an' weak that he wishes he wer at the ferry—ef sich a one kin fine a laugh, jis' one, sich a laugh as is remembered wif his keerless boyhood atwixt these yere kivers—then I'll thank God that I hes made a book, an' feel that I hev got my pay in full.
>
> "Make me a Notey Beney, George. I wants to put sunwhar atween the eyebrows ove our book, in big winnin-lookin letters, the sarchin, meanin words, what sum pusson writ onto a 'oman's garter onst, long ago—
>
> "Evil be to him that evil thinks."
>
> "Them's em, by jingo. Hed em clost apas' yu, didn't yu? I want em fur a gineral skeer—speshully fur the wimen.
>
> "Now, George, grease it good, an' let hit slide down the hill hits own way."

Like so much American humor, Sut's *Tales* slid down "hits own way," and there were some who thought evil and saw evil and others who got "sich a laugh." There has always been a battle between those who say, "How dare you?" and others who say, "Thank God." Despite the sometimes impenetrable dialect and heavy doses of violence, Harris accomplished a great deal in defining (and refining) the terms of that important American comic formula by which a rough-hewn rogue with nothing to hide roams free and tells the truth; and he offered one example for Mark Twain to follow. But, as Kenneth Lynn has pointed out, through the narrative device of the "self-controlled gentlemen," Harris managed to distance himself from the violence and immorality of his comic creation and thus allowed us to peer safely at Sut as but a peculiar version of a backwoods troll. It would take Twain's substitution of victim's humor for spectatorial humor (and that in midcareer) to humanize the comic treatment of the American frontier. If Sut was not Pap Finn (whom he much resembles), he was kin of sort, just over-the-"holler," a crude uncle from whom Huck could learn much— but whom he would later repudiate.

ROUND TWO

The Painted Fire of Mark Twain

Words are only painted fire; a look is the fire itself.
—Hank Morgan, *A Connecticut Yankee*

The Early Years: Rough Draft of Genius

To begin with Mark Twain is to begin right smack in the middle because Twain is the fulcrum of american humor—the one writer early literary comedians seem to point toward and all later humorists look back to and are judged by. More than any other artist, Twain seemed (and still seems) the measuring rod, the artist most attuned by temperament to the violent paradoxes of his America. Though he borrowed much from the Southwestern tradition, Twain's real accomplishment was to take what had been a mostly local lode, alchemize it, and mint it as a truly national—even international—currency.

But to invoke the figure of Mark Twain today is to conjure up a host of conflicting images—boyish Sam Clemens/Tom Sawyer sauntering out in search of fresh fences to whitewash and new hoaxes to play; Hal Holbrook's white-suited philosopher with the deceptive drawl and laughing eyes joking about cigar-smoking and Presbyterian heaven; and the old rapscallion himself winking in his doctoral robes, fresh from having put one over on the Oxford dons.

Such are the popular views, though critics and scholars who have turned over stone after stone of Twain's life know better the torment and confusion underlying the jokes. But they disagree. Where Van Wyck Brooks sees a backwoods boy scarred by lack of cultural amenities, Bernard DeVoto defends—even proclaims—Twain's "Western" brashness and intuitive vision. Where Henry Nash Smith details Twain's conscious craftsmanship, Robert Wiggins finds him but a spontaneous "jackleg" novelist. James Cox discovers a struggling humorist, Pascal Covici, a grand hoaxer with a magic box. Like a will-o'-the wisp, the man continues to change shape. Behold the "Washoe wild man" of Paul Fatout, the foolish businessman of Justin Kaplan, the true friend of gentle William Dean Howells, the broken figure of the Angelfish Club, the . . .

But *stop*—we must stop. Criticism hardly matters when you're dealing with a national institution, the "Lincoln of our literature" as Howells dubbed him. Sam Clemens might have created a largely fictional Mark Twain, and, in his autobiography gotten his own back by inventing a largely fictional Sam Clemens, but tain't no matter. Our Mark Twain today is sealed up firmly in the marble vault of our national regard, locked in as solid as Fort Knox, where no degree of revisionism may tarnish him. Maker of myths, Twain has himself become a myth, his "reality" clouded by the same sort of sentimental nostalgia that infested his own notoriously unreliable memory.

But myth-making, wonderful as it is, tends to wink at truth. So our Mark Twain, tolerant and wryly funny, finely polished by time and sentiment, has become—well, everyone's favorite uncle; and perhaps because of the myth, certain unpleasant or unsavory elements of his work get ignored or suppressed. Stage and film versions of *Huckleberry Finn* have typically played down the novel's violent elements. In the 1935 movie, for instance, Mickey Rooney's Huck is more like a cute Tom Sawyer, and the action centers around swimming holes and mid-American nostalgia. In the 1975 ABC–TV production, Ron Howard's Huck is a nice, freckle-faced kid out for a lark with his buddy Jim, who in turn is just a victim of unfortunate circumstances— a "nigger" in the wrong neighborhood, say. In both versions, the story line concentrates on the broader farce, the situation comedy of the Duke and Dauphin. Perhaps, we have too much of our own violence, our own petty wars and daily outrage, to want Twain's, and so might well prefer a romanticized Huck to serve as another etiolated leaf of pastoral innocence on the American psychic tree. But this kind of transformation—this *rewriting*—is troubling for several reasons. It is a kind of castration and lobotomy. Look at what it does to political figures like Washington, Jefferson, Kennedy—even Reagan; it makes them out to be gods, not men. Mark Twain may not always have been a great artist, but he *was* a great reactor. The cataclysms of the nineteenth century were reflected in his life and work, so that Mark Twain, warts and all, reflects a kind of bone-truth. And his *real* story *is* a great story.

Twain bore witness to much violence, which may help to account for the catalog of horrors we discover in his work—the casual heaping up of corpses; the specters of dead cats, starving Indians, open coffins, and endless graveyards; the pig-guttings, child-beatings, whippings . . . an impressively terrifying list. We may note how this experience infused his humor with a particularly violent methodology of comic deflation, which included invective, parody, travesty, burlesque, and hoaxing, and also how Twain's attitude toward violence shifted from amusement to passionate disgust and how, as he "got class," he came to have misgivings about such crudities as the practical joke. Thus, we can see an evolution from a no-holds-barred japing into that of a societally approved "good humor" (much like that of Bill Cosby today) and, finally, into a misanthropic despair.

Before stepping into Twain's world, I might offer one last caution—to myself as much as to the reader. One has to be very careful in talking about "evolution," as if Twain moved logically from one clearly definable plateau to another; he rarely operated that way. He was a chameleon with a mercurial temperament, a humorist, not a thinker with a clearly defined philosophy. So he is apt to end a stricture against violence by admitting to a desire to strangle the idiot with his own hands. Rather than claim that Twain "solved" the problem of violence *(who has?)*, one might more fairly observe that all his life he wrestled with the violent urges he found, not only within society but within himself. As with Jacob wrestling with his dream of God, the bout was often interesting—even valiant; and we stand to learn from that struggle.

To sift out the "truth" about Sam Clemens's boyhood is difficult. That it was of vivid and particular importance to Twain the writer seems beyond question. He made constant reference to that boyhood in conversations and letters and drew on his memory of it, not only for *Tom Sawyer* and *Huckleberry Finn*, but also for the setting of *Pudd'nhead Wilson* and much of the paraphernalia of *A Connecticut Yankee*. His wife Livy called him "Youth," which Howells found particularly appropriate to his boyish charm; and it seems clear that youth maintained a particular hold over his imagination. Youth meant energy and hope, and when he came to feel he had lost his own he turned almost desperately to that of others. For his own daughters, his "girls of summer," Twain was an enthusiastic storyteller, game player, and scribbler of vile but amusing sketches of cats and dogs; he also entertained many of his friends' children with picnics and plays. Often, even in his declining years, Twain could be found bouncing on his knee one or more members of the "Angelfish Club" he created for favorite young girls; and his letters to prepubescent Mary Rogers, the daughter of an industrialist friend, are a strange melange of adolescent gush and anguished complaint about old age and bodily decrepitude.

But Twain's own childhood in Hannibal, however fondly remembered, was far from Eden. His parents were of stern, fundamentalist stock, not given to outward shows of emotion. The only time he could recall a Clemens kissing, Twain noted in his autobiography was when his father lay dying and put his arm around his sister's neck and drew her down and kissed her, saying, "Let me die." A chill lingers in such reminiscence. And after a lapse of almost seventy years Twain could still recall the fifteen-year-old girl who had made fun of him the first day of school because he couldn't "chaw tobacco." Twain's comment is aptly laconic, "Children have but little charity for one another's defects."

Twain also recalled with particular clarity the scenes of violence he saw in Hannibal—the abortive lynching of an abolitionist, a death by fire, a hanging, an attempted rape, two drownings, two attempted homicides, and four murders. A frightening litany for any child. There was also the black man he saw struck down with a chunk of slag, the young Californian emigrant stabbed with a bowie knife by a drunken companion, and another young man gunned down by a widow he was threatening. One important memory (important because it served as the basis for the Boggs–Sherburn scene in *Huckleberry Finn* was that of seeing "poor old Smarr" shot down in the streets and his family laying a Bible like an anvil on his heaving chest.

Perhaps too much can be made of this. Twain did not express shock at the violence he witnessed. And young Sam Clemens, despite Van Wyck Brooks's claims, was certainly no Holden Caulfield. Twain himself looked back at his boyhood fondly, and his judgment of the people of Hannibal is kind: "There were no hard-hearted people in our town—I mean there were no more than would be found in any other town of the same size in any other country; and in my experience hard-hearted people are very rare everywhere." But there are certain qualities that should be noted about the Hannibal violence because they also occur in Twain's work. First, almost all the violence he mentions is of the quick, emotional brand—no poisonings or vindictive tortures. Thus there is a casualness about violence which, while terrifying, softens it and argues against deliberate cruelty. Secondly, Twain does not suggest a natural depravity —unlike, for instance, William Golding in his *Lord of the Flies*. Thirdly, Twain offers no excuses nor does he call for reform; the tone is laconic, the events recounted with terse stoicism. What he tells us, simply, is that these things happened and that he remembers them vividly.

One other important fact emerges from Twain's own portrait of his childhood: its brevity. When Judge Clemens died (that "strange, austere, loveless man," as Kenneth Lynn calls him), young Sam was only twelve. So he was forced to work, and by the age of fifteen he was putting in twelve-hour days as an apprentice printer. As a boy thrust into an adult world, young Sam Clemens's first instinct, not surprisingly, was for foolery. In "My First Literary Venture," Twain recalls the hot water he got into while substituting for the editor of The *Weekly Hannibal Journal*. As Twain tells it, Higgins, the editor of a rival paper, who had been jilted and so went to a nearby river to commit suicide, was soon seen returning after losing his nerve. Sam, all of thirteen, then "wrote an elaborately wretched account of the whole matter, and illustrated it with villainous cuts engraved on the bottoms of wooden type with a jack-knife— one of them a picture of Higgins wading out into the creek in his shirt with a lantern, sounding the depth of the water with a walking stick." He then went on to slander a local agricultural

editor and a foppish journeyman tailor and to lampoon "promi-
nent citizens—not because they had done anything to deserve
it, but merely because I thought it was my duty to make the
paper lively." The upshot of Twain's "first literary venture"
was to drive poor Higgins out of town and to make his pub-
lisher-uncle "hopping mad." The paper, however, according to
Twain, sold well; new accounts poured in, mollifying his uncle
and offering Twain a wry lesson in human nature.

So, as printer's devil and apprentice-everything, Twain
found himself rudely dropped into the world of early American
journalism, a world notorious for a climate of competitive invective and casual slander. In a later piece, "Journalism in Tennessee," Twain satirized the violent working conditions of his
youth. The young reporter was with his editor when a shot
came through the open window, "and marred the symmetry of
my ear" and a grenade came down the stovepipe and "a vagrant
piece knocked a couple of my teeth out." Later, his chief instructs him on the art of "the Tennessee rewrite": "The innocuous John W. Blossom, Esq., the able editor of the Higginsville
Thunderbolt and Battle-Cry of Freedom arrived in the city yesterday. He is stopping at the Van Buren house," becomes "That
ass, Blossom of the Higginsville Thunderbolt and Battle-Cry of
Freedom, is down here again sponging at the Van Buren." His
editor exults: "Now that is the way to write—peppery and to
the point. Mush-and-milk journalism gives me the fan-tods."

But violence breeds violence. An angry colonel arrives with
his pistol as calling card:

> "Sir, have I the honor of addressing the poltroon who edits
> this mangy sheet."
> "You have . . . . I believe I have the honor of addressing the
> putrid liar, Colonel Blatherskite Tecumseh."

As he steps out, the editor's instructions invite mayhem: "Jones
will be here at three—cowhide him. Gillespie will call earlier
perhaps—throw him out the window. Ferguson will be along
about four—kill him." Later the chief returns with "a rabble of
charmed and enthusiastic friends, and people are shot, probed,
dismembered, blown up, thrown out the window. There was a
brief tornado of murky blasphemy, with a confused and frantic

war-dance, and the gory chief and I sat alone and surveyed the sanguinary ruin that strewed the floor around us." Twain's last word is tongue-in-cheek but cautionary: "Tennessee journalism is too stirring for me."

In another account, "How I Edited an Agricultural Paper," a young subeditor with no knowledge of farming takes over a farmer's weekly only to commit howler after howler, at one point even suggesting they send young boys up trees to shake the turnips off. Confronted by the angry editor upon his return, the young man says, "Sir, I have been through the newspaper business from Alpha to Omega, and I tell you that the less a man knows the bigger noise he makes and the higher the salary he commands."

Another sketch, "Nicodemus Dodge—Printer," portrays the casual cruelty enacted by town boys against a country bumpkin. But each time the boys play practical jokes on Nicodemus—giving him an exploding cigar, putting ice water over the door, tying his clothes at the swimming hole—he slyly turns the tables. When they place a skeleton in his bed, he sells it for three dollars. But the broad humor cannot entirely gloss over the rather frightening world it reveals. What, we might ask, would have happened had Nicodemus not been so clever?

Admittedly, Twain wrote these veiled memoirs at least ten years after the events they purport to sketch, and they are certainly decorated by his colorful imagination, but there seems some justice to the picture. The pre-Civil War press was, in fact, full of high-blown tomfoolery, smears and hoaxes; and Twain's own first genuine literary venture, the "Snodgrass Letters," published in the *Keokuk Post* (1856–57), employs similar elements of crude humor. The letters purport to be Thomas Jefferson Snodgrass's account of having been tricked into taking a basket with a mulatto baby in it and then having been thrown into jail for trying to drown it. He is released, far from regenerate: "I promised—No, sir, I swar I won't tell what I promised them sharks. It 'pears to me that that baby'll larn to swim yit afor it's six weeks older,—(pervided it don't perish in the attempt.)" Though the cruelty is somewhat deflected by the device of using Snodgrass as narrator, this is still a rather morally obtuse joke.

. . .

Most of Twain's earliest attempts were characterized by an instinct for the jugular; and in 1862, as a young man with a talent for crude satire, Clemens was fortunate to make it to the Washoe Territory, to a Nevada aglow with the glitter of speculation and peopled by desperadoes and dreamers, where he latched onto a job with the *Virginia City Enterprise*, one of the wildest and wooliest of the "silver rags." Here, too, his imagination was to come alive; and here too, Sam Clemens became Mark Twain, in person and on paper.

In Virginia City, liquor was the only currency other than silver; fortunes made overnight were sometimes lost by the following evening, and citizens walked the streets at their peril. In fact, the first twenty-six inhabitants of the Virginia City graveyard were victims of homicide, a fact which led Twain to comment sardonically on the frequency of murder and the rarity of conviction:

> We average about four murders in the first degree a month . . . but we never convict anybody. The murder of Abel, by his brother Cain, would rank as an eminently justifiable homicide up here in Storey county. When a man merely attempts to kill another and fails in his object, our Police Judge handles him with pitiless severity. He has him instantly arrested, gives him some good advice, and requests him to leave the county. This has been found to have a very salutary effect. The criminal goes home and thinks the matter over profoundly, and concludes to stay with us. But he feels badly—he feels very badly, for days and days together.

In that last sentence we can hear the pause, a favorite Twain platform technique; and the entire account drips with sarcasm.

In the Washoe Territory, Mark Twain killed off a lot of people with his pen. In one particularly grisly hoax, the "Empire City Massacre," he detailed the mass murder of a wife and nine children by a man named Hopkins, and concluded: "About 10 o'clock on Monday evening Hopkins dashed into Carson on horseback, with his throat cut from ear to ear, and bearing in his hand a reeking scalp from which the warm, smoking blood was still dripping and fell in a dying condition in front of the Magnolia saloon." This story, though filled with obvious howlers, was picked up and reprinted by major dailies such as the *San Francisco Bulletin*. The editors were furious when they realized they had been taken in; and one trenchant rebuke came from the *Virginia City Evening Bulletin*: "The man who could pen such a story, with all its horrors depicted in such infernal detail, and which to our knowledge sent a pang of terror to the hearts of many persons, as a joke, in fun can have but a very indefinite idea of the elements of a joke." Humph-humph.

This scolding from a rival Virginia City paper may seem predictable, but it does point to what many (not only in Washoe, but later in Hartford and Boston) were to see as Twain's fatal flaw: his irreverence. But at this point, for Twain, no cow was sacred, not even a Brahmin bull, and he found the gullibility of the public bottomless. As he observed, "To write a burlesque so wild that its pretended facts will not be accepted in perfect good faith by somebody, is very nearly an impossible thing to do." Another hoax, "The Petrified Mummy," an even more patent fraud, was also picked up by San Francisco newspapers as a news item. The description of the mummy is hilariously precise:

> Every limb and feature of the stone mummy was perfect, not even excepting the left leg, which had evidently been a wooden one during the lifetime of the owner—which lifetime, by the way, came to a close about a century ago, in the opinion of a savant who has examined the defunct. The body was in a sitting posture, and leaning against a huge mass of croppings; the attitude was pensive, the right thumb rested against the side of the nose; the left finger pressing the inner corner of the left eye, and drawing it partly open; the right eye was closed, the fingers of the right hand spread out. This strange freak of nature created a profound sensation in the vicinity.

Anyone who might try out the posture would see quickly that the mummy is not only winking but thumbing his nose at the sky, like Bokonon at the end of Vonnegut's *Cat's Cradle*. The mummy's wooden leg was not the only one that Twain was pulling.

Besides dreaming up such elaborate hoaxes, Twain worked diligently on assaying reports and rumors of rich strikes out on the hills. He also wrote ghost stories and satirical pieces for the *Virginia City Enterprise* which became, as chronicler Ivan Benson describes it, "a journal of comradery—a lively, fresh, rugged, vigorous, fearless, picturesque, distinctive, masculine expression of the energetic life on the Comstock Lode." But even among these roughened spirits, Twain was notable for his ferocity. "Aurelia's Unfortunate Young Man," depicts a young gentleman with smallpox, who has fractured a leg falling down a well, lost an arm to a Fourth of July cannon and another to a cording machine, suffered from erysipelas, and finally been scalped by Indians. At the end, Twain asks drolly: "What should [Aurelia] do? This delicate question involves a lifelong happiness of a woman and that of nearly two-thirds of a man." Twain's resolution, parodying the do-gooder instinct he found so ridiculous, is that "she can build him again." Admittedly, this is bachelor humor (more cleverly executed by Voltaire in *Candide* and Nathanael West in *A Cool Million*); but it displays Twain's instinct for the jugular. Just as later, through Tom and Huck, he was to parody the goody-goody lads so prevalent in the popular literature of the nineteenth century, so he parodied the insipid sentimentalities he saw around the Washoe.

He was, of course, not without critics. "Meriden" of the *Virginia City Union* rebuked him sternly:

> "A true satirist will ridicule the follies of the times, in direct and polished terms, and will separate his subjects from harsh and flippant expressions. He will never attempt to affect a neuralgic contempt for himself and all human relations, that he may succeed in bringing a matter into contempt or assert a privilege of playing loosely with moral or serious points or exhibit a noticeable style of peculiar wit."

A haughty injunction indeed for Virginia City, and Twain and his cronies no doubt enjoyed a hearty laugh at such high-handedness. Such prescriptions might produce the tolerant, genteel (and unsellable) smile of a George Meredith, rather than the guffaw and whinny necessary to draw attention. No critic was to change Twain—that would come later, at his own hand, as the events of his life deepened and broadened his humor.

But a series of incidents did occur that affected one aspect of his own disposition and character. He eventually found himself a victim of practical jokes. Confederates stole in to take the candle he worked beside at night; a meerschaum pipe he had been given as a gift suddenly crumbled in his hands. Twain's temper and gift for invective made him an enticing victim. As Alf Doten, an old pal, reminisced, "It was well understood by all who knew him best that although he liked practical jokes on others, he did not seem to enjoy one upon himself."

Who, one might ask, ever does?

But it was the backfiring of one of his own hoaxes that eventually forced Twain to leave Virginia City. In the spring of 1864, Union supporters had been raising large sums of money in the Washoe Territory by auctioning off a flour sack in town after town. Competition had risen to fever pitch; and the townspeople of Virginia City were anxious to go over $20,000, thereby topping the other towns of the territory and laying to rest once and for all accusations of Confederate sympathies. Put off by the hooplah, Twain decided to have a little fun. As temporary editor of the *Enterprise,* he ran a column entitled "The Flour Sack Scandal," in which he said, "The reason the Flour Sack was not taken from Dayton to Carson was because the money raised at the Sanitary Fancy Dress Ball, recently held in Carson had been diverted from its legitimate course, and was to be sent to aid a Misecegenation Society somewhere in the East; and it was feared the proceeds of the sack might be similarly disposed of." The column caused an immediate hue and cry. By invoking the specter of Copperhead support, Twain had "insulted" the motives and character of the high-minded ladies who had organized the ball; and this time he had gone too far. Though he argued that any idiot could see the joke, he gritted his teeth and apologized.

But the incident was far from closed. Delighted at the chance to humiliate Twain at last, certain rival newspapers laid into him with a vengeance. There was a rough exchange of letters between Twain and James L. Laird of the *Virginia City Union,* which led to Twain's challenging Laird to a duel. However, before the duel, Twain left Virginia City, ostensibly because he was liable to imprisonment under a recent antidueling law that made it an illegal offense even to issue a challenge. It was certainly one of the more ignominious events of his life; and the picture of Twain lighting out for San Francisco, his tail between his legs, is chastening.

The *Gold Hills Daily News* of May 30, 1864 could hardly restrain its glee:

> Among the immortal names of the departed we notice that of Mark Twain. We don't wonder. Mark Twain's beard is full of dirt, and his face black before the people of Washoe. Giving way to the idiosyncratic eccentricities of an erratic mind, Mark has indulged in the game infernal—in short, "played hell." Shifting the locale of his tales of fiction from the forest of Dutch Nick's to Carson City; the dramatis personae thereof from the Hopkins family to the fair Ladies of the Sanitary Fair; and the plot thereof from murder to miscegenation—he slopped. The indignation aroused by his enormities has been too crushing to be borne by living man, though sheathed with the brass and triple cheek of Mark Twain. . . . He has vamoosed, cut stick, absquatulated.

The *Daily News* was not alone in its spirit of happy revenge. As Twain's "friend" Art McEwen remarked some years afterward, "Not many people liked Mark Twain, if one may judge by the tone of depreciation in which he is spoken of on the Comstock to this day." An ebullient, irreverent young man like Twain, we might well imagine, will never lack for detractors.

That Twain was hurt by the incident may be evinced by the several versions of the story he offered later. In *Roughing It*, he claimed he left because he could not bear to be demoted. In "How I Escaped Being Killed in a Duel," which appeared in *Tom Hood's Comic Annual for 1873*, he made another lame effort to laugh it off:

> I was young and foolish when I challenged that gentleman, and I thought it was very fine and very grand to be a duelist, and stand upon the "field of honor." But I am older and more experienced now, and am inflexibly opposed to the dreadful custom. If a man were to challenge me now—now that I can fully appreciate the iniquity of that practice—I would go to that man, and take him by the hand, and lead him to a quiet, retired room— and kill him.

In his autobiography, he offers a tall tale of a fictitious duel in which his second shoots birds and thereby scares off Laird's party under the misapprehension that it is Twain himself practicing his shot. But try as he might (and he tried often), Twain could not wipe out the memory of his disgrace.

When Mark Twain did return once again to Washoe, in the autumn of 1866, for a speaking engagement, "the boys" were waiting for him. One bitterly cold November night, Twain and Denis McCarthy, his manager, were returning to Virginia City from a lecture in Gold Hill when they were held up. The highwaymen took little, though they forced Twain and McCarthy to remain for hours in the cold looking down a gun barrel. In a whimsical open letter to the bandits, Twain said, "You know you got all the money Mac had—and Mac is an orphan—and besides, the money he had belonged to me. Adieu, my romantic young friends." Dan DeQuille (in on the joke as was McCarthy) penned a mock-earnest editorial: "This is no joke, but it is downright sober earnest. There should be a little hanging done among these rascals." When he finally learned of the conspiracy, Twain reacted with predictable anger. "No practical joke," he wrote, "is anything more than a spoken or acted deception." And his resentment surfaced in a bitter fare-thee-well in the *Alta Californian:* "Good-bye, felons, good-bye. I bear you no malice. And I sincerely pray that when you appear finally before a delighted and appreciative audience to be hanged that it will be a ray of sunshine to call to mind that you never got a cent out of me."

But though Twain might still make use of practical jokes and elaborate hoaxes in his own work, from then on he was to condemn the practical joker in the harshest of terms. In his *Autobiography,* he apologizes for his youthful predilection and heaps scorn on the unregenerate:

In those extremely youthful days I was not aware that practical joking was a thing which aside from being as a rule witless, is a base pastime and disreputable. In those early days I indulged freely in practical joking without stopping to consider its moral aspects. During three-fourths of my life I have held the practical joker in limitless contempt and detestation, I have despised him

as I have despised no other criminal, and when I am delivering
my opinion about him the reflection that I have been a practical
joker myself seems to increase my bitterness rather than to mod-
ify it. When a person of mature age perpetrates a practical joke
it is fair evidence, I think, that he is weak in the head and hasn't
enough heart to signify.

Later Twain concludes: "There were many practical jokers in
the new Territory. I wish I could say a kindlier thing about
them instead . . . that they were burglars or hatrack thieves."
Elsewhere he averred, "Their equipment is always the same: a
vulgar mind, a puerile wit, a cruel disposition—and the spirit
of treachery."

Just as his own victimization changed him, Twain also came
to recognize the hostility and the cruelty at the heart of such
jokes. Certainly his tale of Nicodemus Dodge coolly deflecting
the hoaxsters indicates a more mature outlook. But if one looks
for signs of this chastened philosophy in his work, there is less
consistency than one might expect. For instance, the persecution of Nigger Jim in *Huckleberry Finn* is a cruel practical joke
played upon the helpless Jim. Little Satan too, Twain's late
creation, is a devilish practical joker, yet he does not get his
comeuppance. So Twain's instinct for practical joking and
hoaxes, frustrated in real life by his better judgment, continued
to find outlets in his writing.

·   ·   ·

Twain was far from resolving any of these difficulties when he
"absquatulated." But he did manage to land a job as a police
reporter and general gadabout for the *San Francisco Call* during the summer of 1864; and even within the formulaic columns detailing brawls and arrests, his "peculiar wit" managed
to poke through. The unmistakable Twain thumbprint is clearly
visible in articles such as "Amazonian Pastimes":

Mollie Livingston and two friends of hers, Terese and Jessie,
none of whom are of at all doubtful reputations, cast aside their
superfluous clothing and engaged in a splendid triangular fist
fight in Sofford Alley about seven o'clock yesterday evening. It
was a shiftless row, however, without aim or object, and for this

reason officers Evrard and McCormick broke it up and confined the parties to it in the City Prison. It originated in whiskey.

In another piece, "Mayhem," his laconic tone adds a touch of humor to the account of routine violence:

"Gentle Julia," who spends eleven months of every year in the County Jail, on the average, bit a joint clear off one of the fingers of Joanna O'Hara, (an old offender—chicken thief,) in the "dark cell," in the station-house yesterday. The other women confined there say that it's the way Gentle Julia always fights.

Though Twain usually refrained from moralizing, there were times when the excesses of California's "new society" drove him to satire. In an item headed "Accommodating Witness," the irony is heavy: "A man was summoned to testify in the Police Court yesterday, and simply because he said he would swear a jackass was a canary, if necessary, his services were declined. It was not generous to crush a liberal spirit like that." In another piece, Twain has a graveyard digger explain the proper "planting" of Democrats:

I always plant them foreign Democrats in that manner, sir, be-cause, damn their souls, if you plant'em any other way they'll dig out and vote the first time there's an election—but look at that fellow now—you put'em in head first and face down and the more they dig the deeper they'll go into the hill.

But Twain's snipings at the injustices he saw around him were often censored by the *Call*'s editorial policy, which catered to its Irish readership. The Irish shared the low end of the eco-nomic totem pole with the Chinese, whom they battled for railroad jobs and general day laboring, so the subject of the abuse and persecution of the "heathen Chinee" by the Irish was considered off-limits. One of Twain's censored pieces, "Disgraceful Persecution of a Boy," attacked this two-faced-ness by describing how "common citizens" were outraged at the "despicable" incarceration of a young white boy for stoning Chinese. As Twain recalled, it was a common sight for police-men to turn their backs as several young toughs beat up the Chinese or cut off their pigtails.

Twain never forgot this cruelty, and afterward, with William

Dean Howells, he attempted to set up a scholarship fund for worthy Chinese youths. He also collaborated with Bret Harte on a "Chinese" play, *Ah-Sin*, but it proved to be no more than broad farce. Twain's most ambitious protest piece, "Goldsmith's Friend Abroad Again," was a series of increasingly disillusioned letters purportedly written by a Chinese immigrant in the land of the "great-hearted people" and serialized in *The Galaxy* (1870–71). One Irishman, objecting to the "yellow wave," says: "The Ching devil comes till Ameriky to take the bread out o' dacent intilligent white men's mouths, and whin they try to defend their rights there's a dale of fuss made about it." Without condoning prejudice, Twain understood its economic roots.

But the racism and violence of San Francisco weighed heavily on him, and he was later to recall his stint as depressing:

> By nine in the morning I had to be at the police court for an hour and make a brief history of the squabbles of the night before. They were usually between Irishmen and Irishmen, and Chinamen and Chinamen, with now and then a squabble between the two races for a change. Each day's evidence was substantially a duplicate of the evidence of the day before, therefore the daily performance was killingly monotonous and wearisome.

So in the dreary winter of 1864–1865 Twain left to try his hand at prospecting around Jackass Hill. But he continued to write odd columns which were occasionally reprinted by the New York press and which helped maintain his reputation as the "Washoe Wild Man." "Advice to Little Girls" instructs young girls on the proper treatment of a little brother: "Never, on any account, throw mud at him because it will spoil his clothes. It is better to scald him a little, for then you obtain desirable results." Elsewhere he writes: "And so you think a baby is a thing of beauty and joy forever? Well, the idea is pleasing, but not original; every cow thinks the same of its own calf." In a parody of fashion articles, "After Jenkins," Twain took off again after "society":

> Mrs. W. M. was attired in an elegant pate de foi gras made expressly for her and was much admired. Miss. R. P., with that repugnance to ostentation in dress which is so peculiar to her,

was attired in a simple white lace collar, fastened with a neat pearl-button solitaire. The fine contrast between the sparkling vivacity of her natural optic, and the steadfast attentiveness of her placid glass eye, was the subject of general and enthusiastic remark.

Perhaps Twain knew he was again getting ready to leave. Surely he could not expect a welcome in many San Francisco homes after that particular nose-thumbing.

And there does seem not only a lack of focus but a manic disdain in his work of this time. Ever restless, Twain, in letters home, had already expressed a desire to strike out for the East; and he had been encouraged by Artemus Ward, who had made the move himself with success. Ironically, it was to be "The Celebrated Jumping Frog of Calaveras County," another hoax, which was to provide him with the needed impetus. Encouraged by Ward, Twain wrote up this tale, which appeared in the *New York Saturday Press* on November 18, 1865 and brought him fresh fame in the East. Twain himself alternated his opinion of "The Jumping Frog," referring to it as "that villainous backwoods sketch," and then at other times claiming it to be the finest tale of its type. Spurred by this popular success, Mark Twain headed East—his formative years, those years he was so consistently to draw on in his works, behind him, and his fame and fortune ahead.

· · ·

What was the legacy that journalism and the West bequeathed to Twain? Certainly, there is much to be said for the kind of journalism Twain did in Hannibal and Keokuk, Virginia City and San Francisco. First, and perhaps most importantly, it brought him into close contact with many of the forces that were forming the "new" America. For an intuitive and instinctive writer like Twain, it thus provided a valuable firsthand experience of frontier life and its hardships and violence that was to be the subject of much of his best work. Also, it seems a heartier and more democratic education than reading German philosophy or Indian Veda in Concord and Cambridge or poring over "Old Masters" in Rome. These ragtag newspapers and journals afforded Twain space and time to perfect his style and master dialects and prodded him to invent a new language with which to talk to his fellow "Amurikans."

The legacy, however, was admittedly spotty. The day-to-day battle for circulation rewarded sensationalism; and Twain was perhaps too comfortable in that gunpowder atmosphere of outrage and invective. The pen, after all, is not supposed to be a gun. But Twain was certainly no helpless victim; if anything, the evidence suggests that his editors had to tone *him* down. Though many of his pieces can still make us laugh out loud, their excessive venom and satirical overkill suggest a crudeness and narrowness about not only the world they portray but the man portraying them.

Mark Twain's early world does seem a violent place. From the streets of Hannibal to the graveyards of Virginia City and the jails of San Francisco, death did not simply stalk its victims, but jumped and clawed them in moments of passion or negligence. Yet Twain offers little comment on the legal or moral aspects of this violence. Perhaps it is not the humorist's job to offer answers; perhaps recognition of the problem, (and the sharp finger of ridicule) is the first step toward solution. Still, despite his youth and the nature of early American journalism, Twain's stoicism seems oppressive, even heartless.

. . .

One thing that civilized man tries to do is to defuse violence. Freud pointed out that "tendentious jokes" were often veiled assaults against mighty figures—and he speculated that, since a joke requires less psychic effort than murder, the fiercer the joke, the less reason for murder. In *The Ordeal of Mark Twain*, Van Wyck Brooks cited Freud to suggest how Twain defused his own rage by a humor of "singular ferocity," and there seems something to this. Certainly the mystique of the Wild West— its open lands and rough-and-ready democracy—includes a legacy of blood in the streets and freewheeling frontier justice. Twain's channeling of his own frustration into ridicule seems a healthy reaction to the dominant violence around him; and he did, in fact, direct many of his jokes against that spirit.

Also, it is worth noting that Twain's own instinct at the close of the Civil War (which he skillfully avoided) was to light out from the Washoe Territory—to opt, in other words, for civilization; and it seems clear that Mark Twain would not be as important to us as he is today if he had not made that move. To be sure, he continued to feel torn between the "Wild" West and the "Genteel" East (misleading as these adjectives often were); and his courtship of civilization continued to be stormy, with flashes of the old anger often lighting up the muted sky. If Mark Twain was never to become entirely "civilized," his encounter with the genteel East would inform his humor with a deeper resonance. But his struggle, always, was to reflect that particularly American dilemma: Can freedom and civilization, like the lion and the lamb, ever really peacefully lie down together?

The Middle Years: Maturity and Glory

Though he could not then know it (and was often to look back wistfully), when he left the West Twain was "absquatulating" for good. In fact, his first real book, *The Innocents Abroad* (1869), turns eastward and is that hoariest type of all, the travel book, and chronicles the journey of a group of upper-middle-class Americans to the Old World and the Holy Land. Shifting his irreverence to the lips of "rough" Blucher from the Far West, Twain serves as intermediary between Blucher and his genteel fellow passengers, such as "The Oracle" and "The Pilgrim." Blucher is now the "Wild Man," and Twain has fun with that. If Twain himself can still be a bit crude, the image of himself as a rough pearl is one he enjoys polishing before his new readership. Here he directs his jokes at clearly unpopular targets, such as ignorant guides and pompous frauds and offers "facts" to corroborate American superiority, the River Jordan, he smirks, is really only a trickle. The reductive humor of *The Innocents Abroad* throws paint on the dusty relics of the past; and an American reads the book with a feeling of pride because this no-nonsense fellow Mark Twain was *there* and says *here* is better. Twain treats his readers as companions rather than opponents—and this tactic was a smashing popular success.

But it was with *Roughing It* (1872) that Twain perfected this happy conspiracy; and his original title, *The Innocents At Home,* offers an additional clue to his awareness of this new partnership. The Mark Twain of *Roughing It* is, in fact, more genteel and boyish than the genuine article; his "innocent eye" regards that rough pioneer society with wonder. In his preface, he insists, "It is a record of several years of variegated vagabonizing, and its object is rather to help the resting reader while away an idle hour than afflict him with metaphysics, or goad him with science." In other words, Twain intended *Roughing It* to serve as what Graham Greene calls an "entertainment." Like *The Innocents, Roughing It* comprises another journey through time (in this case the recent past of a still-growing America) in a setting as exotic to most of its readership as the pyramids of Egypt.

There is a fresh realism in Twain's description of the landscape and actual (not Fenimore Cooper) Indians, and Twain purports to tell the truth behind the beards and the swaggers. But *Roughing It* is really a work of fantasy. We do not really come to know these "wild" men; we learn little of their day-to-day lives or of what they do when they are not swapping yarns or murdering each other. What Twain does give us is an account of their daydreams of striking it rich and their nightmares of violence. In fact, *Roughing It* is well-varnished truth throughout. By the time of its writing, many of Twain's own recollections had been "dis-remembered"—he even had to ask his brother Orion for an account of their stagecoach trip from St. Joseph to the Washoe Territory because he could remember next to nothing about it himself. Nor does he (perhaps understandably) tell the truth about his infamous challenge of Laird; and he elides the all-night drinking bouts with cronies such as Dan DeQuille and the Unreliable—probably because of their practical joke at his expense.

But *Roughing It* is one of the finest of those long, quasi-autobiographical anecdotes that Twain was always inventing about himself, and as such it provides an amusing and readable version of the truth. We encounter Twain speaking and dealing with other men; and the rambling stories, the tall tales, and the local color all have the unmistakable twang and character of his voice. The flavor of frontier life is all there, attractively packaged, boisterous rather than crude, its anecdotes a bunch of rough beads held together by the string of Twain's charm.

Roughing It, in the end, is an account of a masculine Wonderland told by a chastened Alice just up from the rabbit hole.

Novelist Paul Bowles has made an interesting distinction between the tourist and traveler. "The difference," he points out, "is partly one of time. Whereas the tourist generally hurries home at the end of a few weeks or months, the traveler belongs no more to one place than to the next, moves slowly, over periods of years, from one part of the earth to another." In this sense, Mark Twain was certainly a "traveler," passing through slowly, adopting the ways and means of the people around him. Facts bored him anyway, and he was always to insist on "the absorption of the heart" over mere detail. Twain was fond of describing himself as "a sponge who leaked truth," and his several years out West had him filled to capacity. Leak, he did indeed.

The picture of frontier society Twain limns is an ambiguous one. One the one hand, he seems to sympathize with the broad masculine urges of these men, their tall tales and exuberance; on the other, he expresses disgust with the deliberate killings and the too-constant cruelties. He insists on distinctions: "No Californian gentleman or lady ever abuses or oppresses a Chinaman under any circumstances. Only the scum of the population do it—they and their children; they, and naturally and consistently, the policemen and politicians, likewise, for these are the dust-licking pimps and slaves of the scum, there as well as elsewhere in America." Twain's outrage here as elsewhere is sincere; and his contempt argues for a moral courage to raise men and women above racism and towards a kind of "natural" humanity. But his real struggle lies in the attempt to come to terms with the endemic violence of the frontier. Often, as in the case of the mass murderer Jim Slade, he opts for simple reporting, figuring shrewdly that the facts are sensational enough to shock his Eastern audience; but still he displays a certain ambiguity:

> Violence was the rule. Force was the only recognized authority. The commonest misunderstandings were settled on the spot with the revolver or the knife. Murders were done in open day, and with sparkling frequency, and nobody thought of inquiring into them. After a murder all that Rocky Mountain etiquette

required of a spectator was that he should help the gentleman
bury his game—otherwise his churlishness would surely be remembered against him the first time he killed a man himself and
needed a neighborly turn in interring him.

Thus, through the hyperbole of "Rocky Mountain etiquette,"
Twain transforms a rather ugly story into a tall tale that amuses
as well as horrifies.

Throughout *Roughing It,* we see Twain deflating (or deflecting) many other spectacles of violence through humor. Just
after detailing the murder of a man whose ears Slade is carrying
in his vest pocket, Twain regales us with an account of dining
with him. "Here was romance," Twain declares, but declines a
second cup of coffee because Slade has not killed anybody that
morning and "might be needing diversion." Twain describes
Slade as "most gentlemanly-appearing, quiet and affable"; and
his mock innocence seems to distance him from the violence.

But, as we learn, frontier violence is symptomatically sudden, and that suddenness contributes to the horror. At the station where a stagecoach driver has been ambushed and
murdered, Twain dwells on the terror of being out on a dark
night in such wild parts. The entreaties of the victim, the cries
and shots in the night, the stagecoach clattering off into the
darkness—all contribute to a sense of helplessness and fear.
The climate, too, is cruel in this unknown terrain. The snowstorm in which Twain and his friends almost lose their lives
reminds us that nature can strike out at a man at any moment.
Thus the natural world echoes the sudden violence of men and
is an apt setting for the human drama.

Throughout the Washoe Territory, Twain notes, the gun is as
common as mud. After a year in the Washoe, Twain himself has
"degenerated" into going coatless with a

slough hat, blue woolen shirt, pantaloons stuffed into boot tops,
whiskered half to the waist, and the universal navy revolver
slung to my belt. But I discarded the revolver. I had never any
occasion to kill anybody, nor ever felt a desire to do so, but had
worn the thing in deference to popular sentiment, and in order
that I might not, by its absence, be offensively conspicuous and
the subject of remark.

But, though his objections are usually couched in irony, Twain in places does treat violence as more than simply humorous. He presents several newspaper extracts detailing common homicides as "an instance of how, in new countries, murders breed murders." But in respect to common justice, he is flatly cynical:

> Trial by jury is the palladium of our liberties. I do not know what a palladium is, having never seen a palladium, but it is a good thing no doubt at any rate. Not less than a hundred men have been murdered in Nevada—perhaps I would be within bounds if I said three hundred—and as far as I can learn, only two persons have suffered the death penalty there. However, four or five who had no money and no political influence have been punished by imprisonment—one languished in prison as much as eight months, I think. However, I do not desire to be extravagant—it may have been less.

Twain follows this attack on the jury system with an account of Captain Ned Blakely's frontier vigilantism. Frustrated by the slow hand of the law, Captain Ned, "a rough honest creature full of pluck," has taken it upon himself to hang a murderer; and Twain cites Blakely's act as "straightforward justice unencumbered with nonsense." Characteristically, his admiration for "the man" could override any legal or moral concerns.

This inconsistency reveals sitself in the implicit violence of his humor. The much-anthologized story of Jim Blaine, for instance, includes Miss Jefferson's "wandering" glass eye, missionaries eaten by cannibals, the three-ply carpet containing William Wheeler's remains; and the humor springs from the grisliness of itemized horrors so casually presented. The wandering nature of the tale does deflect some of the horror. Also by telling the story through the viewpoint of Jim Blaine, Twain manages to remain outside, like an amused onlooker. Much of the additional anecdotal humor of *Roughing It*, especially "Bemis's Buffalo Hunt" and "Buck Fanshaw's Funeral," depends on jokes and one-liners, the broader the better; and the humor is not so much part of the overall texture (as in, say, *Huckleberry Finn*), as a series of ribald baubles dangling from the tough rawhide of frontier life. Here Twain's manic humor, in its heaping up of absurdity after absurdity, invites the reader to laugh at spectacles of sheer horror. This "humor of horror" (as in Bierce, Vonnegut, and, later, Heller) mingles disgust and defiance, death and laughter. Twain recounts cosy nights spent listening to Mormons telling "thrilling evening stories about assassinations of intractable Gentiles." Death seems a kind of joke—the ultimate one-liner. For instance, he works up the hoary Horace Greeley story so that the invalid "in trying to retain the anecdote in his system strained himself and died in our arms." All mock deaths—and there are many in Twain— parody real death, of course, and aim to take away the sting.

But, on the whole, the humor of *Roughing It* does involve a creative evolution. The invective and crude satire of Twain's early journalism has been toned down for popular consumption. Consider, for instance, Twain's handling of the "Arkansaw Incident." Arkansaw, "who carried two revolvers in his belt and a bowie knife projecting from his boot, and who was always drunk and always suffering for a fight," taunts and humiliates his landlord before being faced down by the landlord's wife with a pair of scissors. This tale, inspired perhaps by Twain's own memory of the Hannibal widow facing down the drunken Californian, exposes Arkansaw as a coward; and the reader is invited to applaud this comeuppance. But there is another version, which Twain chose not to include, in which six ruffians led by "Arkansaw Chief" beat up two helpless tramps:

> ARK: Out with your weapons like a man! Nothin' won't do you
>   but a fight, and by geewhillikins you can have it.
> BILL: Oh, please don't, Arkansaw!
> ARK: I don't fear no man!. I'm on it—bigger'n an Injun. I'm
>   chief! I tell you I'm the worst man in 17 states!—I'm all
>   fight! I don't stand back for Buck Fanshaw nor Scotty
>   Briggs, nor no man! I can lick seven men that ever was
>   spawned! Draw, you linen-livered thieves—both of you!

The brutality here is more obvious, right down to the quaking victims; and there is no resolution. Twain wisely used the more palatable version.

In the world of *Roughing It*, we see life played out in the face of sudden death, and the wild hyperbole of the most fan-

ciful anecdotes seems to refract its deadlier realities. Twain's
humor, as Charles Neider has observed, helps us laugh at terror
and death and humanizes by reaching "down into the bomb-
cellars where man huddles, tear-stained, fearful." And the
sneer of the early Twain is gone; his humor now demonstrates
a more sympathetic awareness. He can now laugh at himself (as
he does with Slade for instance) and bear the brunt of his own
joke; and his discovery, and use, of victim-humor is an important achievement.

Yet, for all of this, in *Roughing It*, Twain does not always
succeed in making frontier life seem humorous or even bear-
able. Having begun in a spirit of exuberance, Twain seems to
become increasingly dispirited and weary along the way. It is
not just that he runs out of material and thrusts the Sandwich
Islands and several tiresome appendices about the Mormons at
us (a compulsive word-counter, he was no doubt thinking of his
subscription market); the real problem lies at the heart of the
book. *Roughing It*, like so many of Twain's works, is a kind of
crazy quilt of facts and figures, tales, anecdotes, landscapes, and
jokes. Held together by the warp of Twain's own mercurial
personality, the product is an odd woof, liable to any and all
changes that affect him. The chastened Twain who soberly reflects on the fake robbery is a far cry from the brash youth who
went West with Orion. "Since then," he says, "I play no practical jokes on people and generally lose my temper when one
is played on me." Twain revisits the Washoe only to note the
particular cruelty of time: "I found home a dreary place after
my long absence; for half the children I had known were now
wearing whiskers or waterfalls, and few of the grown people I
had been acquainted with remained at their hearthstones prosperous and happy—some of them had wandered to other
scenes, some were in jail, and the rest had been hanged." The
moral of the book itself betrays a wry disillusionment: "If you
are of any account, stay at home and make your way in faithful
diligence; but if you are of 'no account,' go away from home,
and then you will have to go to work, whether you want to or
not."

At the end, it is as if Twain's contemplation of the vain
dreams and endemic violence of the frontier has caused the
jokes to wear thin. Despite its vigor, Washoe society, based as

it was on speculation and greed and rife with violence, was doomed to waste away as soon as the lodes of gold and silver ran out. It never was to produce a "civilized" society. Encased in a kind of perpetual and bloody adolescence, the frontiersmen played out their violent lives in places like Virginia City and Gold Hill—now just ghost towns close by contemporary playlands like Reno and Las Vegas that raise their own flickering neon come-hithers. *Roughing It* is an elegy to a life that Twain understood was over almost as soon as it began. In this light, Twain's humor is not just the saving grace but the only grace, the legacy of the dream.

If in *Roughing It* (1872) Twain detailed the violence of the American outback without judging, in *Huckleberry Finn* (1884) he was to make a frontal assault on that violence with Huck as his point man. But even in his work during those intervening years, we can note increasing concern. Bits and pieces prepare us—almost—for Huck's world. *The Gilded Age* (1873) satirizes political corruption. *A Tramp Abroad* (1880) parodies the machismo of Austrian dueling societies and introduces Nicodemus Dodge, Huck's brother-under-the-skin. In *Life on the Mississippi* (1883), Twain returns to the lost world of rafters and pilots and plumbs the Mississippi, that "Great River God" of Eliot. (These latter works are, in a very real sense, both "travel" books—flights in space and time, excursions in "lighting out.") *The Prince and the Pauper* (1882) also presages many of the themes of *Huckleberry Finn*. Twain's citation is culled from Portia's speech on "the quality of mercy," and the detailing of tortures such as boiling in oil, flaying, and drawing and quartering, and the spectacle of piked heads on London Bridge are unusual in a book ostensibly for children, even one "for the young of all ages." To be sure, this was foreign violence, and old foreign violence at that, that Twain was railing about; but it signals an important shift in emphasis.

The most important book of this pre-*Huckleberry Finn* period is of course *Tom Sawyer* (1876), set in the dreamy antebellum world of St. Petersburg and, of course, introduces us to Tom and Huck. The central event, we sometimes forget, is the murder of Doc Robinson; and the figure of Injun Joe hovers like a dark cloud over the idyllic landscape. But here the forces of society band together to root out evil and punish violence;

and at the end, Injun Joe is but one more dead Injun, all is again right in St. Petersburg—and the boys are six thousand dollars richer. Except for Injun Joe, there is no evil in *Tom Sawyer*; and he is a stock villain—a wooden Indian. Nor are we terribly disturbed by Tom's fights with the new boy in town nor by the occasional canings he receives, which seem but the by-products of boyish exuberance. Tom, the leader of the pack, is portrayed as a likeable lad with a head for mischief. Also, though a murder is at the heart of the novel, we more easily recall the comic whitewashing of the fence, the invention of the pirate gang, the romance with Becky.

Huck Finn, however, lives beyond the pale of St. Petersburg society—literally on the outskirts. Though Tom and the other lads admire Huck because he doesn't have to wash or attend church and school, the mothers look down on him because he is "idle and lawless and vulgar and bad." In the bright, morning world of Tom Sawyer, Huck's outcast state may occasion pity on our part; but Huck most decidedly is not the hero—Tom is, and he is a caution.

At once tolerant of the practical jokes of boyhood and the foibles of adults, *Tom Sawyer* is a boy's book that anyone can safely read. But this is not true of *Huckleberry Finn*, which is not only an adult book but a subversive one. That Concord (Mass.) library committee, which banned the book in 1887, judging it immoral and corrosive, was perspicacious; the Congress of Racial Equality (CORE), which sued successfully during the late 1950s to have *Huckleberry Finn* banned in Brooklyn (New York) schools because of the use of the word "nigger" was, sadly, less so. For *Huckleberry Finn* is a book CORE and all African-Americans should insist on; it is a book to make white Americans blush.

Huckleberry Finn still shocks and dazzles. Though he conceived of a "companion piece" shortly after *Tom Sawyer*, this was not an easy book for Twain to write. He worked in fits and starts and struggled with the ending (how *should* it end?) which remains controversial and ultimately unsatisfactory. *Huckleberry Finn* is certainly not a book without flaws; but as a portrait of frontier American society, warts and all, it has no peer.

Certainly, Huck's confrontation with violence is one of the major themes. As V.S. Pritchett has observed: "If this is a great comic book it is also a book of terror and brutality. . . . Marvelous as it all is as picaresque episode and as a description of the mess of frontier life, it is strong meat." And the strong meat is as much in attitudes as in incidents—it comprises much of the fabric of Huck's world. Why then are we not more horrified? Part of the answer lies in the stoical nature of Huck himself. Time after time, Huck is able to escape—from the Widow Douglas, from Pap, from pursuers and con men like the Duke and King—and we applaud his narrow escapes. Huck is necessarily shrewd; he cannot afford boyish innocence—and, as we watch him outwit the bad guys, his shrewdness becomes part of the novel's humor. Huck's casual acceptance of death also helps to deflect much of the horror. In the first chapter, he tells us straight off he, "don't take no stock in dead people," and goes on about ghosts and deadly superstitions. We are at the outset, then, offered a graveyard humor which seems, in Huck, natural rather than ghoulish.

We learn of Tom Sawyer's gang. To avenge a wrong, members must kill the offender and his family and "hack a cross on their breasts." Any boy who reveals club secrets "must have his throat cut, and then have his carcass burnt up and all the ashes scattered all around." But when little Tommy Barnes wakes up frightened and begins to cry (he is tired of being a robber), we are reminded that these are, after all, just boys, and this imagined violence is not to be taken seriously. Twain is satirizing the romantic notions of violence that Tom picks up from his reading. Like Don Quixote, Tom has been much misled by books—something that later is to have painful, almost fatal, consequences for Jim and for himself. Significantly, Huck plays along with the mock tortures reluctantly. For Huck, violence is only too real.

Twain's introduction of death may be humorous, but a real body soon turns up. A bloated corpse is discovered, at first thought to be Pap; but Huck correctly reckons it to be a woman dressed up in man's clothes because "I knowed mighty well that a drownded man don't float on his back but on his face." But after Huck realizes it is not Pap, he says starkly, "So I was uncomfortable again." Uncomfortable?—because Pap is *not* dead! A chilling thought that invites us to look more closely at this quasi-orphan who fears his own father. But this first anonymous death demands no sentiment on our part. Shortly after, Huck decides to resign as a robber because "we hadn't robbed nobody, we hadn't killed any people, just pretended." He then elaborates on the gang's raid in which they invaded a grammar school picnic disguised as Arab pirates. Fake death, in St. Petersburg, is vastly more interesting than the real thing.

At home, Huck shrugs off the widow's canings: "Whenever I got uncommon tired I played hookey, and the hiding I got next day done me good and cheered me up." Even about Pap's beatings, Huck remains strangely detached. Pap whacks Huck because he can read and locks him up before going to town for whiskey. For Huck, it seems to be a case of the frying pan or the fire. To escape civilization and old Miss Watson pecking at him all the time, he is willing to suffer Pap. But things get too much, even for Huck, when Pap, in the throes of a bout of delirium tremens, takes him for "the Angel of Death" and chases him around the cabin with a knife.

In a very real sense, Huck *is* the Angel of Death. Death haunts his tracks. To mask his escape, he is forced to kill a pig and spread blood over the cabin, and with this sacrifice, the "civilized" Huck Finn dies. But omens of Huck's own mock death follow him. He is awakened by the shot of cannon attempting to raise his body, then finds baker's bread intended to "locate" his corpse and eats it calmly. Greeting Huck on Jackson Island, Jim cries out lamely, "I awluz liked dead people." Ironically, it is Huck, this ragamuffin "Angel of Death," who will dedicate himself to saving Jim. Even Jim, now with Huck, is stalked by death. He discovers Pap's corpse in a floating "house of sin," but conceals that fact from Huck. (Twain also withholds this information from the reader, for to see Huck at this point confronted with Pap's bloated carcass would jolt us in a very unfunny way.) So, once again, death is presented anonymously. Jim's malapropism ("Come in, Huck, but doan' look at his face—it's too gashly.") is a grisly joke. After breakfast, when Huck wants to "talk about the dead man," Jim discourages that line by reminding him that "a man that warn't buried was more likely to go a' ha'nting." (Particularly if he is your father, we might add.) So this death, then, is all but forgotten, and Huck, like us, is not to know until the end that, with Jim, Huck too is free.

A few days later Huck finds himself on a shipwreck with a gang of murderers. Huck escapes but, by stealing the only boat, causes the desperadoes' death. Huck does have a ferry sent out, but it returns after a fruitless search. He says, "I felt a little heavy-hearted about the gang, but not much, for I reckoned if they could stand it, I could." Again we ask: *Stand what?* The silence of death seems the only possible answer. The death toll is now up to five, and Huck and Jim turn in to sleep "like dead people."

But Jim himself, amid this litany of death, offers a sharp corrective to a certain callousness in Huck. Jim's interpretation of the parable of Solomon reasserts the worth of each and every human life: "But you take a man dat's got 'bout five million chillen runnin' roun' de house, en it's diff'unt. He as soon chop a chile in two as a cat." Later, Huck gets lost in "the solid white fog" in which he "hadn't no more idea which way I was going than a dead man," but he sights Jim at last and pretends to be a ghost. After catching on, Jim scolds Huck, "Dat truck dah is trash." Similarly, Jim's remorse over having struck his deaf daughter offers another parable of common decency.

But when Twain resumed writing *Huckleberry Finn* in 1879, his handling of death was markedly different. When Huck actually witnesses the treacherous ambush of Buck Grangerford and Cousin Joe, he is sick at heart: "I ain't agoing to tell all that happened—it would make me sick again if I was to do that. I wished I hadn't ever come ashore that night, to see such things. I ain't ever going to get shut of them—lots of times I dream about them." He tenderly covers up Buck's face, "for he was mighty good to me." In this scene, Twain clearly invites the reader to be revolted by the stupidity of blood feuds; the deaths of these two boys engage our sympathies fully.

But by far the most moving death (based on an incident Twain witnessed in Hannibal) is Colonel Sherburn's gunning down of the drunken Boggs. Here the pathos is heightened by the description of Boggs's bereaved daughter ("very sweet and gentle-looking, but awful pale and scared") placing the heavy Bible on Boggs's heaving chest. As the people of the town reenact the crime, relishing the details, Huck stands aside, recalling Sherburn's laugh as "not the pleasant kind, but the kind that makes you feel like when you're eating bread that's got sand in it"—and we are left with a bad taste in our mouths as well. Significantly, this murder, which occurs slightly more than half-way through, is the eighth and last of the violent deaths and is followed by Huck's going to the circus. It is as if Twain caught himself and returned to his stock-in-trade. Too much Sherburn, too much real death, and the book can no longer be funny. To be sure, Wilkes's funeral provides us with another corpse, but he has died naturally and is already two days cold when we meet up with him. Here, too, Twain's treatment of the funeral, as with Emmeline Grangerford's poetry, is a travesty of funerary rites. With the murder of Boggs, Twain is through with violent death.

But the climate of debasement and cruelty that comprises the rest of the novel is even more disturbing than the litany of corpses. Huck arrives at Bricksville, Arkansas—a town of callow idlers whose chief pleasures lie in "putting turpentine on a stray dog and setting fire to him, or tying a tin pail to his tail and see him run himself to death." Later, the King and the Duke are tarred and feathered, causing Huck to observe wearily, "Human beings can be awful cruel to one another." At the Phelps's farm at the end, only the doctor's intercession prevents the farmers from lynching Jim as an example to other runaway slaves.

Twain also resurrects his old standby, the hoax. By definition, the hoax is a double-edged knife in that it preys upon people's greed. Those who can so easily be taken in by such patent frauds as the Duke and the King lack the necessary skepticism of intelligence; and since the victims of a hoax have only themselves to blame, the violence of their reaction is easy to predict. The Royal Nonesuch rapscallions are masters of deception— bilking revivalist camp meetings, staging pseudo-Shakespearean come-ons, taking in advertisements for nonexistent newspapers. Their cruelest hoax is their attempt to steal the Wilkes girls' inheritance by impersonating their long-lost uncles. This is what finally spurs Huck into action, and there is an appropriate Old Testament justice in Huck's out-hoaxing the hoaxers by hiding the money in the coffin. By his own mock death and his faking of smallpox to protect Jim, Huck has already proved to be no slouch at hoaxing. In Twain, good people or bad can be the perpetrators or the butts of a hoax—the ultimate purpose determines its virtue. In other words, the end can justify the means; and often Twain seems to slip back and forth between enjoyment and condemnation.

But the hoax that Tom Sawyer plays on Jim (with Huck's compliance) at the Phelps's farm is the cruelest and least defensible hoax; and it has marred the book for many readers. As Ralph Ellison has complained, "Too often what is presented as the American Negro emerges as an oversimplified clown, a beast, or an angel." In fact, Jim is free because Miss Watson has died; but Tom plans an elaborate escape/ordeal for Jim—and Huck goes along. After all he and Jim have gone through, Huck's explanation seems lame: Tom's plan "would make Jim just as free as mine would, and maybe get us all killed besides." Tom defends his elaborate scheme, for "Jim's a nigger and wouldn't understand the reasons for it." Despite the ambience of boyish adventure, we are shocked to hear Huck tell us, "[t]he shirt was sent in early, in a pie, and every time a rat bit Jim he would get up and write a little in his journal whilst the ink was fresh." The burlesque and travesty of the ending reduce Jim to the simplicity of a minstrel show "darky," and what hurts is that by this time, Jim is far, far from being an anonymous "darky." As Huck's friend, Jim has not only shown genuine affection but has stood fast against violence and thereby grown in dignity. Twain's treatment of Jim seems a serious mistake. We can either care about a character—in which case we do not want to see him suffer or die; or we may not care—in which case almost anything can happen to him without engaging our sympathies. We should care about Jim; and his suffering destroys the book's moral balance. The mock torture of Jim is a blunder of Twain's heart. As for Tom, he deserves to be shot in the leg.

Huck's reaction at the end, when told of his father's death, is also odd. Huck says—*nothing*! Where Dickens would have given us several pages of heaving sentiment, Twain offers a shrug. To be sure, Pap isn't much to mourn over; but we *are* left with the final picture of Huck, a fatherless child like Twain himself, about to "light out for the Territory ahead of the rest, because Aunt Sally she's going to adopt me and sivilize me and I can't stand it. I been there before."

That's it . . . lights out. . . . Huck is gone.

.   .   .

But what *will* happen to Huck in "the Territory"? What *could* happen to him? It is an interesting question, one that Twain attempted to answer in two unpublished sequels. In one, Huck blacks his face to change places with Jim—that "ole black magic" of the minstrel show just won't die, Lawdy no! The intent here seems obvious; in the manner of John Howard Griffen's *Black Like Me,* Twain would have them swap roles (as later he was to swap black and white babies in *Pudd'nhead Wilson*), so the book would provide a plea for compassion for the black man. In another sketch, Twain imagined Huck resurfacing as an aged but hopelessly insane derelict. It is perhaps fortunate that we do not have a sequel—the open-endedness is part of *Huckleberry Finn*'s freshness. After rejecting the genteel hypocrisy of St. Petersburg and fleeing the debased towns he has encountered along the river, Huck is "lighting out" for the fresh dream of the Territory. We cannot be altogether sanguine about his future, however. We might *hope* that Huck will "pan out" in the Territory; but, with *Roughing It* in mind, we also have to suspect that, in that topsy-turvy world of wild hopes and boondoggling hoaxes, he will probably not find any pot of gold tucked under a rainbow.

Twain's treatment of lynching, dueling, and feuding in *Huckleberry Finn* provides a clear brief against violence. But there seems also a deepening skepticism about man's ability to live without it. The outlaw society of cutthroats and con men that Huck and Jim encounter provides ample evidence of lawlessness. Even the apparently sunny world of St. Petersburg is repressive. Widow Douglas, that staunch pillar of this most conventional society, insists on imposing her way on Huck—a way full of "do nots" and "must nots." So, besides satirizing the degeneracy of frontier society, Twain seems also to be suggesting that the good habits and Christian morals of the "sivilized" are often a straitjacket. The problem is complicated. Thwarted in his attempts to "rescue" Pap, the judge says "he reckoned a body could reform the ole man with a shot-gun maybe, but he didn't know no other way." When nothing else seems to stop them, the King and the Duke are tarred and feathered. How *are* we to prevent violence without force? Twain, in *Huckleberry Finn*, offers no easy answer. Faced by the Scylla of civilization on the one hand and the Charybdis of outlaw life on the other, Huck . . . runs away.

Huck himself, interestingly, is never violent. Twain's own customary reaction was to try to laugh violence out of town. But the laughter in *Huckleberry Finn* does not defeat evil or vio-lence—would that it could. The depressing reality will remain long after Huck has fled this America of "Huck-sters" and hoaxsters who prey on each other. Though much of the comedy lies in seeing through the deceptions, only Huck really amuses; and he laughs only once—at the spectacle of the Royal None-such, and that, after all, is a vision of naked fraud. Despite this grimness, there are many light moments—Emmeline Granger-ford's poems, the Shakespeare travesty, the undertaker; but these are generally moments of burlesque. In *Huckleberry Finn*, the humor is not, as it is in so much of Twain, a series of jokes or anecdotes; here, the comic episodes overlie a venom-ous and more ominous subsurface. But it is in *Huckleberry Finn* that Twain came closest to what he thought great humor should entail: "Humor is only a fragrance, a decoration. Humor must not professedly teach and it must not professedly preach, but it must do both if it would live forever. By forever, I mean thirty years."

Despite the joke, this is certainly true. *Huckleberry Finn*, despite the jokes, is also true—and the jokes are part of the truth. The cruel loafers of Bricksville, the foolish Shepherdsons and Grangerfords, the Duke and the Dauphin, Pap, and even the Phelps, seem to nullify any positive claim for a "great soci-ety." We may come away liking Huck, but we must be appalled by the prevailing violence of the America Twain has shown us —that worm in the apple of freedom—and be forced to ques-tion the value of a liberty that leads to such moral debasement.

The Last Years: Darkness and Smithereens

*The very reason I speak from the grave is that I want
the satisfaction of sometimes saying everything that
is in me instead of bottling the pleasantest of it up for
home consumption. . . . Annihilation has no terrors
for me, because I have already tried it before I was
born—a hundred million years—and I have suffered
more in an hour in this life, than I remember to have
suffered in the whole million years put together.*
                                    —Mark Twain, *Autobiography*

*French people should be wary of taking too seriously
the pervasive gloom in American humorous fiction.
Isn't the morbid pose the favorite trick healthy people use to hoax the insecure sucker?*   —Daniel Royat

Twain indicted democracy and the New World, but he was too
much the American—too much the democrat—to let other
sleeping dogs lie. In *A Connecticut Yankee in King Arthur's
Court* (1891), he turned to the past—to England, to monarchy
and "order"—and he judged that world worse. Sixth-century
England, as Twain saw it, provided all the elements of intolerable autocracy, with the Catholic church, King Arthur himself,
and an oligarchy of nobles ministering over a suppressed populace. Lest anyone think of bringing it back, Twain set about
reminding us that it was a world ripe for reform—something he
was willing to offer through the imagined revolution of a displaced Connecticut Yankee. On the face of it, this seems a
happy and promising conception. But the Yank's revolution
proves neither successful nor happy, and at the end all is, sadly,
ashes.

   A Connecticut Yankee darkens slowly. In the early going,
Twain seems most interested in the comic implications of his
subject, and his tone is light. In Hank's confrontation with "a
bedecked knight fresh out of a picture book," for example, the
misunderstanding is linguistic:

   "Fair sir, will ye just?" said this fellow.
   "Will I which?"

"Will ye try a passage of arms for land or lady or for—"
"What are you giving me?" I said. "Get along back to your
circus, or I'll report you."

This is the same sort of humor which made us laugh at the
brush between Scotty Briggs and the minister in *Roughing It*.
Hank Morgan has no time for "fol-de-rol"; his disdain is the
springboard for much of the humor—and his reductive japes
are vintage Twain. Hank meets a page ("an airy slim boy in
shrimp-colored tights that made him look like a forked carrot")
and says, "Go 'long, you ain't more than a paragraph." Hank
shares Huck's unerring eye for absurdity, but his observations
reveal as much about him as they do about King Arthur's Court.
Like most people away from home, Hank misses what he
knows—sugar, tea, coffee, soap, the "chromos" that decorated
his rooms. He sees little worth in Arthurian society and is only
comfortable when he can finally tag these people as no more
than "white Indians." The descriptions of pastoral bliss, which
dot the early pages, drift into travesty or burlesque. Knight's
armor, he vouches, is a most impractical arrangement, making
it impossible to scratch and causing a deadly sweat in the summer heat. Sandy, his maiden friend, turns out to be a blather-
skite "with no more ideas than a frog"; and the tales she and
others tell are verbose and pointless.

The violence of the court is a kind of cruel slapstick. When a
page bumps into Morgan le Fay, she slips "a dirk into him in
as matter-of-course a way as another person would have har-
pooned a rat." The Queen has a troubadour hanged for compos-
ing a bad song. Hank catches on quickly. After hearing the same
song, he gives the Queen permission to have the whole band
hanged; and later, after another of Sir Dinadan's bad jokes, he
orders him hanged as well. But underlying the jokes there is
something troubling about this casual violence. Though Hank's
own priorities are openly republican ("The first thing you want
in a new country is a patent office; then a school system; and
after that, out with your paper"), and he talks about starting up
a "teacher-factory" and encouraging a "complete variety of
Protestant congregations all in a prosperous and growing condition," he also observes ominously that "all revolutions that
will succeed must begin in blood."

The irony is that our Connecticut Yankee, despite his declared democratic sympathies, becomes a dictator with tragic
consequences. As the "Boss," he brags, "I was no shadow of a
king, I was the substance." To Hank the populace are "rabbits"
and "modified savages," degraded by a Catholic Church which
has "in two or three little centuries . . . converted a nation of
men to a nation of worms"; and he insists "any kind of aristoc-
racy, howsoever pruned, is rightly an insult." But Hank himself
seems blithely oblivious to his own contradictions; and as his
reformist sympathies become gradually and grotesquely
warped, he exercises his powers with tragic consequences. If *A
Connecticut Yankee* is a satire on the stupidity and institution-
alized violence of Arthurian England, it is also an attack on the
well-intentioned American reformer and the intolerance that
often lurks beneath his cheerful and "well-meaning" countenance.

A Connecticut Yankee, however, does not quite come full
circle. Twain's own outrage at the abuses of feudal society is
genuine; and, despite its inconsistencies, the novel still manages to stump for "progress." "In a country where they have
ranks and castes," Hank says, "a man isn't ever a man, he is
only part of a man, he can't ever get his full growth." Using a
favorite device (that of reversal of estate), Twain causes the
King and Hank to be sold as slaves to make the rather obvious
but still telling point that a king "is just a cheap and hollow
artificiality when you don't know he is a king." Hank's repub-
licanism is heartfelt.

But Twain's handling of violence is, once again, ambivalent.
On the one hand, the violence of the Court is clearly satirized
in the duels, the torture of poor criminals, and the hangings. In
Sir Dinadan, who ties metal mugs to dogs' tails to watch them
run themselves to death, the town of Bricksville, Arkansas, discovers a true forebear. On the other hand, Hank himself often
wins through executing simple force. He cuts down the brave
Sir Sagramour with a pistol and bombs hostile knights: "Yes, it
was a neat thing, very neat and pretty to see. It resembled a
steamboat explosion on the Mississippi; and during the next
fifteen minutes we stood under a steady drizzle of microscopic
fragments of knights and hardware and horse-flesh." (When
Twain's own brother Henry died in a steamboat explosion,

Twain was not to recall that event quite so picturesquely.) The point is that too often it is just Hank's more sophisticated knowledge of weaponry which enforces his reforms.

Hank's reductive humor attacks the mighty—and takes few prisoners. After demolishing Merlin's tower, he smirks, "I had the Government rebuild it for him, and advised him to take boarders; but he was too high-toned for that." Later Hank convinces Sir Ozana le Cure Hardy to sell shiny stovepipe hats to the knights, "another of [his] surreptitious schemes for extinguishing knighthood by making it grotesque and absurd." He campaigns to abolish the Catholic church and reform the entire apparatus of feudalism by replacing kings with cats and offering a qualified women's suffrage in which mothers have to prove they know as much as their twenty-one-year-old sons.

But perhaps his most effective debunking is the series of elaborate hoaxes Hank gets up to put down Merlin and superstition. His "miracles" include his staging of an eclipse—like Twain, Hank loves to show off. As he says proudly, "Every time the magic of fol-de-rol tried conclusions with the magic of science, the magic of fol-de-rol got left." But Hank as hoaxer is scarcely less absurd than his rigid but bumbling victims. James Cox calls him "the unmasked demon—the practical joker and compulsive showman—so much a part of Mark Twain's humor," and sees the novel as "a great comedian's nightmare vision of himself, grotesquely exposing the secret manipulator behind the mechanism of the comic performance." Twain's utopian vision, we must agree, is marred by the crude jokes, and Hank's mean joy throws the novel out of comic balance. His last "effect" (turning the Gatling gun on the medieval knights until he is trapped in a ring of heaped corpses) reveals the homicidal and suicidal nature of the comic demon. Once the "pen warmed up in hell" gets going, it scorches everything; and it does seem that, with the bloody slaughter, Twain was sweeping not only civilization but hope into the bonfire.

Twain elsewhere often defended the violence necessary to overthrow an unjust state. After listening to a lecture on the excesses of czarist Russia, he exclaimed, "If such a government cannot be overthrown otherwise than by dynamite, then thank God for dynamite." In *A Connecticut Yankee*, Hank boasts,

"Name the day and I would take fifty assistants and stand up against the massed chivalry of the whole world and destroy it." Yet Hank extracts a terrible price in carrying out his boast, and the final holocaust seems the exclamation point of a very bad argument. (More recently, Norman Mailer has proposed his own plan to replace war by having world leaders, like gladiators, engage in one-on-one combat in a coliseum. Despite an element of adolescent machismo—would we then see Sylvester Stallone as President?—there is something attractive in Mailer's fantasy, just as there is in Hank's exploits. Sadly, for both, solutions are not that simple—or that satisfying.) So, with *A Connecticut Yankee*, Twain seems to be clanging shut the door on hopeful change. If civilization is not regenerate, he seems to be suggesting, then reform is just another myth, violence inevitable, maybe even desirable. After the holocaust, we may perhaps start afresh, though the violent nature of man argues against optimism. One thing is for sure: the joke is over.

. . .

But the trumpeting of apocalypse signals a kind of artistic suicide. So, after *A Connecticut Yankee* we should not be surprised by the deepening pessimism in Twain's work, as the wild extravagance of the early journalism and the rollicking anecdotal humor of his middle period yield to a darker and more jaundiced spirit. Thereafter, the voice is more acerbic, the jokes often bitter parables, and his major characters "mysterious strangers" such as Pudd'nhead Wilson, The Man Who Corrupted Hadleyburg, and Little Satan. And Twain's own persona changes; the "bomulchus" and the "agriokos" (the entertaining clown and the humorous rustic) give way to the "eiron" (the ironist). Part of the problem, of course, was age. As Twain himself observed, "At fifty a man be an ass without being an optimist but not an optimist without being an ass." And misfortune, as it has a way of doing, found him. After the failure of the Morgenthaler typesetting machine, he was dogged by pressure from creditors. The deaths of his daughter Susy and wife Livy further haunted him with a sense of guilt. Also, the determinism he came increasingly to adopt offered him no easy joy.

Not surprisingly, Mark Twain as humorist began to fail. It is hard to tell fresh jokes when one feels old and tired.

But this darker side, his own Mister Hyde, had been there all along, under wraps. Earlier, as his letters and notebooks testify, he often welcomed the censorship of Livy and Howells. Despite his genius, Twain was a very uneven critical judge—particularly of his own work. Grateful to Howells after a good review of *Roughing It,* Twain wrote him, "I am as uplifted and reassured as a mother who has given birth to a white baby when she was awfully afraid it was going to be a mulatto." Twain feared being not quite "white" enough for civilized society— of being "found out" and rejected. He never altogether trusted, though he certainly recognized, the comic demon in himself, and he often felt a need for the approval of genteel critics. Only occasionally did Twain strike out at censorship. His "Washoe Wild Man" image was as much pose as anything—a brilliant stroke of public relations that appealed to the Walter Mitty element in his genteel readership. In fact, Twain felt that Livy and Howells embodied the ingrained prurience of the "civilized," and he admired their "smiling" view of human nature —a view he himself lacked. He also knew that his audience, that vast host of subscription buyers who were his bread and butter, shared these values and strictures; and he employed Livy and Howells as weathervanes. In short, Twain allowed himself to be tamed.

A strong argument can be made that the success of Twain's middle years was the result of this deliberate conspiracy to please and the toning down of his own natural instinct for ridicule. It accounts for much of the popular work—*Tom Sawyer, Life on the Mississippi, A Tramp Abroad.* It helped disguise *Huckleberry Finn* as a boy's book. Yet Twain's double was at work all along, and he exercised (without exorcizing) this demon secretly in "1601," *The Adam Family Papers*, and *Letters to the Earth.* But it was Twain's own nature, coupled with the reverses of fate, that finally came to defeat the conspiracy, and, in a sense, the explosion at the end of *A Connecticut Yankee* signaled the end of his public geniality.

Yet when Twain decided to take off the gloves and bare-knuckle his audience, they continued to laugh. The last wry joke was on Twain because, as with the boy who cries "Wolf!" the public refused to take him seriously. Even Twain's pessimism was generally dismissed, like that of W.C. Fields, as "part of the act"—just another joke. There is a further ironic twist in Twain's insistence, in letters and interviews, that the real truth could not be told until he was dead. Of course, the truth could be told, and Twain often told it during his last years; he just was not believed.

Upon returning home from England in the autumn of 1900, Twain complained to reporters that the English had taken everything he said as a big joke. Looking back over the years (he was then sixty-five), he tried to explain his own formula for "fabricating" truth; "Most liars lie for the love of the lie; I lie for the love of truth. I disseminate my true views by means of a series of apparently humorous and mendacious stories." But as we have seen, this had by no means always been true. Starting off as "God's fool" and happy in his ability to excite the laughter of God's creatures (as he had written Orion from the Washoe), Twain's philosophy had darkened under assault by "truths" he felt he could no longer ignore. As Pudd'nhead Wilson, another Twain alter ego, observed starkly: "Everything human is pathetic. The secret of humor itself is not joy but sorrow. There is no humor in heaven."

In his declining years Twain took to newspapers to air his views about society. Despairing of effecting change in the individual violence he had so long satirized, Twain launched attacks on imperialism and racism. America had crushed Aguinaldo in the Philippines and set its sights on the rich tropical isles of the Caribbean, but Twain ridiculed the fulsome public praise heaped upon Generals Wood and Funston for actions which Twain felt better demonstrated "the taste of Christian butchers." He said tartly, "I am opposed to having the eagle put its talons on any other land." In "The United States of Lyncherdom," he lit out after lynchers and called for the "kind and compassionate missionaries" in China to "come home and convert these Christians." But Twain's "solution" invokes the ghost of Colonel Sherburn—"I believe that if anything can stop this epidemic of bloody insanities it is martial personalities that can face mobs without flinching." Twain also heaped scorn on white supremacists. "There are many humorous things in the world," he commented in *Following the Equator* (1897), "among them the white man's notion that he is less savage than the other savages." Of the Australian aborigine, he commented wryly: "He diligently and deliberately kept the population down by infanticide—largely; but mainly by certain other methods. He did not need to practice these artificialities any more after the white man came. The white man knew ways of reducing a native population eighty per cent in twenty years. The native had never seen anything as fine as that before."

Twain included the exesses of certain European dictators in his indictments; and his outrage grew in the face of their colonialism and oppression of subject peoples: "I have been reading the morning paper," he wrote Howells, "I do it every morning—well-knowing that I shall find in it the usual depravities & basenesses & hypocrisies & cruelties that make up Civilization, & cause me to put in the rest of the day pleading for the damnation of the human race." One of the major themes of *A Connecticut Yankee* had been that of man's troubling accession to, and therefore complicity in, tyranny. Now, Twain protested, the czar of Russia would be an impossibility if men were really men. In "King Leopold's Soliloquy" (1905), he portrayed the king as a heartless hypocrite kissing the crucifix effusively as he counted the gold he had milked from the Congo while crying out, "Blister these meddlesome missionaries." Twain asked his readers to imagine the corpses of the estimated 15,000,000 Africans that Leopold's minions had exterminated laid out in a line from New York to San Francisco; and he observed acidly that the moral coffers of Europe were too often empty. But Twain could see no moral alternative in the exuberant expansionist America of Teddy Roosevelt. The message was clear: In the race for wealth and land, devil take the hindmost. It was such pessimism that motivated Twain's "War Prayer" (1900), a satire indicting the mutual righteousness of warring factions.

But, if nationalism, prejudice, and sectarianism could not be countermanded, and the only constants seemed war and greed, then just what *was* the answer? Twain's frustration drove him increasingly toward a kind of solipsistic despair, and his two most impressive late works, *Pudd'nhead Wilson* (1894) and *The*

Mysterious Stranger (1897–1905), are both infested with a dark view of human nature. "Be good," as Pudd'nhead says in the frontispiece, "and you will be lonesome."

In *Pudd'nhead Wilson,* Twain returned to the pre-Civil-War South and the disease of racism which, in robbing "dark" men of liberty in order to allow "light" men to live well, is pictured as a cancer eating away at the soul of the societies that depend upon it. But, though racism is attacked as a terrible and powerful curse, one of the frustrations of the novel is that there is no true resolution. The final irony, in which Thomas à Beckett/Valet de Chambre is sold down the river, is a nose-thumbing of sorts. But the racist society of Dawson's Landing remains intact—malevolent and inflexible. Nothing has really changed. The people of Dawson's Landing, conditioned to accept slavery, have in effect learned nothing. "Training is everything," Pudd'nhead observes, "a cauliflower is nothing but a cabbage with a college education." Dawson's Landing is a society of cabbage-heads disguised as cauliflowers; and Twain's despair is genuine.

The pessimism of *The Mysterious Stranger* is even darker. Little Satan notes that man "begins as dirt and ends as stench" and is the only creature to "inflict pain for the pleasure of inflicting it." It is man's tolerance of violence that is truly intolerable: "The vast majority of the race, whether savage or civilized, are secretly kind-hearted and shrink from inflicting pain, but in the presence of the aggressive and pitiless minority they don't dare to assert themselves." Man is a worm, and existence itself generally a bane. Little Satan's last message suggests the cruelest hoax of all: "It is true, that which I have revealed to you; there is no God, no universe, no human life, no earthly life, no heaven, no hell. It is all a dream—a grotesque and foolish dream. Nothing exists but you. And you are but a Thought—a vagrant thought, a useless thought, a homeless thought, wandering forlorn among the empty eternities!"

Twain had given signs of increasing pessimism in an earlier piece, "Wandering Photographs," in which he made up mock answers to a series of stock questions. (Sample: "What would you like to be?—The Wandering Jew with an annuity.") One entry is particularly interesting. To the query, "What is your dream?" Twain's riposte was, "Nightmare as a general thing."

In *The Mysterious Stranger*, this quip has become a terrifying
reality. But despite the fact that Little Satan insists on the
power of man's laughter as a weapon ("Power, money, persua-
sion, supplication, persecution—these can lift at a colossal
humbug—push it a little—weaken it a little, century by century, but only laughter can blow it to rags and atoms at a
blast."), Twain has stopped joking.

Haunted by a sense of unreality, Twain now saw his work
transformed by—and into—nightmare. Unable to bring himself
to believe in his childhood Presbyterianism and equally incapable of happiness within a mechanistic determinism he could
not refute, Twain took to raging against that "Great Dark" he
felt coming down over him. Never a successful stoic, his letters
to Howells detail his grief at heart-rending length. Toward the
end, life seemed too painful to be "real." If life were only a
dream, however, then terror and pain might be mere phantoms
of "vagrant thought"—and the nightmare, then, would soon be
over.

But there is scant consolation within such a philosophy. It
brings to mind the Chinese tale of the man who awakens after
having dreamed of being a butterfly and thereafter never is sure
whether he is a man dreaming he is a butterfly or a butterfly
dreaming he is a man. But the Chinese tale is mute and open-
ended; we are not told what the man then did. Solipsism, by
definition, does not lead to solutions. For Twain, the corollary
was just as troubling: If all were *not* just a dream, then life with
its absurdities was a hoax unworthy of a benevolent deity.
"Damn these human beings," he exploded to Howells, "if I
had invented them I would go hide my head in a bag." Himself
a creator and hoaxster of no mean talent, he came to recognize
in the Creator only a Grand Hoaxster nonpareil.

Buried within the spirit of the late Twain, then, is a streak of
violent nihilism that seeks to blow the world to smithereens
because it hurts so. If only it *were* a dream! In these last years,
Twain turned his withering gaze upon the duplicity of govern-
ments and the sham of custom, upon the cowardice of lynchers
and the officious pietism of smug missionaries, upon the hum-
buggery of Polyanna and the deceitful grin of "progress," upon
all irrationalism, up to and including the cruel hoax of a benev-

olent deity; and he came increasingly to despair and turned back to scorn and ridicule.

Twain's dilemma suggests the limits of comedy. There is a land that all humorists—even great ones like Mark Twain—must not enter, and that is the country of tragedy. The dilemma is, life cannot be laughed off because, to paraphrase Horace Walpole, it is both a comedy to those who think and a tragedy to those who feel. If King Lear earns our tears, Little Satan, that vile, extraterrestrial visitor, maddens us. Even if he is right about our stupidities, we still despise him because he is inhuman. The grotesque comic demon is a *memento mori*, an excrescence like the gargoyle upon the Gothic spire of tragedy; but he is the gargoyle, not the spire. By employing Little Satan as his spokesman, Twain sacrificed not only humor, but pity.

American humor relies upon a certain pretense of innocence—the poker face is its own defense. In his later work, Mark Twain dropped his guard, thereby unmasking himself and sacrificing his humor. The comic writer must be careful not to spill over into sheer vituperation. The springboard of Twain's most successful humor was his sense of violation and outrage, and the success of that humor depended upon his sometimes precarious control over his natural ferocity. The miracle is that Twain, who so often walked a high-wire, fell off so rarely.

.   .   .

Some critics have seen in Twain only the full flowering of a very poor cactus. Underneath his braggadoccio, Twain himself was sensitive to such criticism. "I have always catered for the Belly and the Members," he wrote Andrew Lang, "but have been criticized from the culture-standard—to my sorrow and pain; because, honestly, I never cared what became of the cultured classes; they could go to the theatre and the opera, they had no use for me and the melodion." Mark Twain was more than Belly and Members. No less an arbiter than H. L Mencken proclaimed Twain "the one authentic giant of our literature . . . the full equal of Cervantes and Moliere, Swift and Defoe." In the man and in his work, there is a sense of a common bond with flawed humanity. He disapproved of those who put them-

selves outside of the human fold, frowning on Swift, for instance, whom he found "void of every tender grace, every
kindly humanizing element—a bare, glittering iceberg," and
Bret Harte for the excessive negativism of his humor, which
"consisted solely of sneers and sarcasms." Twain himself, of
course, was not above glittering and sneering on occasion; but
he wished to give, and usually gave, something more. As he
said to Opie Read, "Laughter without tinge of philosophy is
but a sneeze of humor. Genuine humor is replete with wisdom."

It has become fashionable to consider Mark Twain as but
another example of spectacular failure—of the American artist,
of American civilization itself. But the facts argue for a greater
complexity. Perhaps Mark Twain, the Wild Man of the Washoe,
did die in despair, no jest on his lips. But how many men die
well? It is important to recall the rich life Twain enjoyed and
his contribution to American—and world—literature. True, he
embodied many paradoxes and contradictions. He was violently opposed to violence, for instance, and in many ways his
career is both a warning and an exemplum. But Twain fought
valiantly to keep his own violent nature in check; his instincts
were generous, and, most especially, his heart—like Huck's—
was sound. There is much to be said for Howells's claim for
him as the "Lincoln of our literature," in that he remained, like
Lincoln, fundamentally democratic and inimitably American.
The frontier humorists numbered many "phunny phellows,"
but only one Mark Twain.

Twain's legacy includes, finally, a plea for peace. In a world
racked by continuous and increasingly sophisticated violence,
Huck's words, "It is lovely to live on a raft," take on additional
poignancy. The raft, that symbol of a difficult earned peace, is
the heart and soul of Mark Twain's humor; and he directed
much of his "painted fire" at the violent excesses of our society
in a fierce effort to have them laughed out of town and to arrive
at that earned peace. Like Sisyphus, he failed again and again;
but his example continues to inspire others to push that same
boulder up the same mountain—along the same tortuous path.

ROUND THREE

The Bottled Bile of Ambrose Bierce

Nearly all Americans are born humorous. If any are born witty, heaven help them emigrate!
— Ambrose Bierce

May you live as long as you want to, and then pass smilingly into the darkness—the good, kind darkness.
— Ambrose Bierce in a letter to Jo McCrackin,
September 13, 1913

Less than four months after his wry fare-thee-well to Jo Mc-Crackin, Ambrose Bierce himself passed into the "good, kind darkness"—perhaps in Mexico—perhaps even smilingly. Not many mourned.

As devil's lexicographer and self-appointed gadfly to three generations of political thieves and literary poseurs, Bierce had stood practically alone on the outermost crags of misanthropy. Yet he was also a man of high idealism and ruthless honesty who well knew the price one paid for telling uncomfortable truths. The cynic, as he once observed in *The Devil's Dictionary,* is "a blackguard whose faulty vision sees things as they are, not as they ought to be. Hence the custom among the Scythians of plucking out a cynic's eyes to improve his vision."

Born in 1842 at the backwoods settlement of Horse Creek Cave in Meigs County, Ohio, Bierce was the tenth child of parents he later referred to as "unwashed savages." He scorned the rudimentary education offered by intinerant schoolmasters and, like Huck Finn, ran wild on the nearby shores of the Tippecanoe River. Like Sam Clemens, seven years his junior, Bierce drifted into journalism in his teens, working as "printer's devil" (how apt a phrase for Bierce!) on the *Northern In-dianan,* but after being accused of theft he "absquatulated" to the Kentucky Military Academy.

His military schooling was to be short-lived. On April 19, 1861, in a burst of patriotism, Bierce volunteered for the Ninth Indiana Volunteer Infantry of the Union Army. His service during the Civil War was the key event of his life; and he later recalled, almost with relish, the many grotesque scenes he witnessed in it. After the battle of Cheat Mountain he saw pigs eating dead soldiers: "They had eaten our fallen," he later wrote, "but—touching magnanimity!—we did not eat theirs." Bierce distinguished himself in battle, but sustained "a dangerous and complicated" head wound while directing a charge at Kenesaw Mountain. Later, Bierce was to recall feeling "broken like a walnut." His brother Albert agreed: "He was never the same after that. Some of the iron of that shell seemed to stick in his brain, and he became bitter and suspicious, especially of his close friends. He would remember each failing and slight, fancied or otherwise . . . say nothing of it at the time, and then, many years afterward, release the stored-up poison in a flood." Though he took pride in having been the only American writer of importance to have fought for the Union cause, he came out of the war with no illusions about the United States which he later defined as "a great, broad blackness with two or three small points of light struggling and flickering in the universal blank of ignorance, crudity, conceit, tobacco-chewing, ill-dressing, unmannerly manners, and general barbarity." (Certainly not as many points of light as George Bush has seen, alas.)

But besides becoming prone to long, withering silences and explosions that frightened friend and family alike, Bierce came out of the war with an admiration for clear-cut, life-and-death decisions. Death was constantly on his mind, and often on his lips. For this ex-soldier, the struggle for survival was no metaphor; and his ramrod-straight military bearing and "extraordinary vitality" inspired respect, even fear. After a distasteful term as a federal administrator in Alabama, Bierce joined General Hazen's 1866 campaign against the Western Indians—a "master-stroke of military humor" as he later put it. But the one-sided savagery quickly disgusted him, and he continued on to San Francisco, where he took up work as a staff writer.

His crisp venom found ready outlets in the newspapers of the
Far West which, as we have seen, often delighted in invective.
"In the evolution of the comic spirit," as Bertha Clark Pope,
editor of Bierce's letters, has noted, "the lowest stage, that of
delight in inflicting pain on others, is clearly manifest in savages, small boys, and early American journalism." Bierce was
as much at home in the cockpits of San Francisco as on the
battlefield, and he described their daily horrors with relish.
"The Italians continue their cheerful national recreation of
stabbing one another," he wrote in one of his columns. "On
Monday evening one was found badly gashed in the stomach
going about his business with his entrails thrown over his arm."

Like Twain, Bierce was fond of drunken hijinks. After one
memorable drinking bout, Bierce and two of his buddies tried
to remove a cross atop a hillside in Golden Gate Park, but
somehow got themselves enmeshed in ropes and had to be
rescued. But even among fellow journalists, Bierce, despite his
high spirits, was regarded as something of a "lizard," only too
willing to deal with the darker side of man's nature. "All is
worms," he proclaimed; the joke was on any fool who thought
differently, and he wielded his pen like a cleaver. To be sure,
Reconstructionist America afforded Bierce a host of tempting
targets, and he attacked with relish. "To say of a man," he
growled, "that he is like his contemporaries is to say that he is
a scoundrel without excuse. The virtues are accessible to all.
Athens was vicious, yet Socrates was virtuous." He wanted
men to stand up—and keep standing. "Christians and camels,"
he scoffed, "receive their burdens kneeling."

For Bierce, wit, not "vile humor," was of value; and he cham-
pioned wit despite the unpopularity of his position: "Vituperation—Satire, as understood by dunces and all such as suffer
from an impediment in their wit." To a reviewer who critized
him for the indelicacy of his humor, he replied:

O certainly humor should be "delicate." Every man of correct
literary taste will tell you that it should be delicate; and so will
every scoundrel that fears it. A man who is exposed to satire
must not be made unhappy—O dear, no! Don't mangle the man
like that coarse Juvenal, and that horrid Swift, but touch him up
neatly, like Horace or a modern magazinist.

Bierce insisted on going for the jugular rather than the funny bone, and he defended the violent underpinnings of his basic comic mode:

> The wittiest man that we ever knew never said but one funny thing in his life, and that killed him—of which we were very glad. We hold that the true function of wit is not to make one writhe with merriment, but with anguish; it is not a sportive cow gamboling absurdly in a pasture, but a vicious horse latent in a stall, who kicks you in the bowels as you pass unconsciously behind him. Somebody has said that humor was but pathos masquerading. That is our idea of it; it is something to make a man cry.

Bierce sneered at Howells's suggestion that American authors should concentrate on "the more smiling aspects of life" and called Howells and Henry James "two eminent triflers and cameo-cutters-in-chief to Her Littleness the Bostonese small virgin . . . complacently enamored of their own invirility and pouring like sponges the vocal incense of a valleyful of idiots." For Bierce, a writer was "sinner, saint, hero and wretch"; and he opposed the genteel tradition by hurling insults at the motley mass of Panglosses he saw spreading across the land like rancid butter from Beacon Street to the Napa Valley. For Bierce, wit was a useful scourge. "Humor is tolerant, tender; its ridicule caresses. Wit stabs, begs pardon—and turns the weapon in the wound. Invective, a secular curse, consists of direct assault to obliterate its object through abuse. I am not a poet but an abuser." Of one local hoodlum he wrote:

> Chuck him overboard! Let him suffocate in slime and stenches, the riddances of sewers and the wash of slums. Give his carcass to the crabs utterly, and let the restless shrimp embed its body in his eye-socket, or wave its delicate antennae from his pale nostril. Let globes and tangles of eels replace his bowels, and the muscular squid lay coils of clammy tentacles about the legs of him. Over with him!

A Juvenal among Horaces as he saw it, Bierce also disdained the camp of native humorists—Twain and Artemus Ward in particular. He regarded what he called the "dialect industry"

as "the grunt of the human hog with an audible memory." As
for American satire, it was a fantastic and imaginary beast, which

> never had more than a sickly and uncertain existence, for the
> soul of it is wit, wherein we are dolefully deficient, the humor
> that we mistake for it being tolerant and sympathetic. Moreover,
> although Americans are "endowed by the Creator" with abun-
> dant vice and folly, it is not generally known that these are re-
> prehensible   qualities,   wherefore   the   satirist   is   popularly
> regarded as a sour-spirited knave, and his every victim's outcry
> for codefendants evokes a national assent.

At every opportunity Bierce disdained the poker face of American humor and called for "savage indignation." Stylistically,
too, Bierce declared war. Where Twain insisted that the success of American humor depended upon the teller's seeming to
lose the point and wander about, Bierce found such tomfoolery
not only insufferable but sloppy. He offered to match his "leth-
iferous" (i.e., lethal) wit against Twain's "bovine humor" and
belabored Twain, Petroleum V. Nasby, and Bret Harte for their
long-windedness; and he contended that native reading habits
consisted usually of "Indian novels, stories in dialect, and
humor in slang." Bierce bowed his own head toward Rome and
"Augustan" England, and took as models Juvenal, Catullus,
Tacitus, and Marcus Aurelius; also Swift, Gibbon, and Macau-
lay. Like Irving, Cooper, and Hawthorne before him, Bierce
took the "high road" of English. (Which may account for the
stilted quality of much of his dialogue. Americans, after all, do
not speak "English.")

For a man of these predilections, there was little room in the
literary establishment of late-nineteenth-century America, but
Bierce courted his unpopularity assiduously. Rejecting the genteel practitioners and the "phunny phellows" both, Bierce was
doomed to be an outsider. But he enjoyed his outcast state, and
he relished personal invective. After hearing of Twain's fortui-
tous marriage to Olivia Langdon, Bierce wrote:

> It was not the act of a desperate man—it was not committed
> while laboring under temporary insanity; his insanity is not of
> that type. It was the cool, methodical culmination of human na-

ture working in the heart of an orphan hankering for someone
with a fortune to love—someone with a bank account to caress.

Eventually he came under the wing (or talon, as the case may
be) of William Randolph Hearst, and wrote for several Hearst
publications and such quasi-literary journals as *The Wasp* and
The Prattle, where he was encouraged to attack whatever prevailing foolishness caught his eye. There, with his poison pen
and black ink in endless supply, Bitter Bierce, as many called
him, came into his element. Though he wrote too much (over
eight million words) and never did quite manage to free himself from the journalistic yoke, there is a bristly integrity to his
best work. No Frostian lover's quarrel, Bierce's relationship
with the world can more fairly be described as a long divorce
proceeding, and much of what he wrote has fallen into deserved limbo. Yet there still is much of worth. Bierce might
have been a casualty, but he was no man's fool.

Bierce's wit is probably his most enduring legacy. His serious stories, *Tales of Soldiers* and *Tales of Civilians,* praised for
technical excellence and economy, seem now overly depen-
dent on plot and coincidence. His one novel, a collaboration
cum translation of a German Gothic tale, *The Monk and the
Hangman's Daughter,* is an overwrought and inadvertent parody of the genre, notable for its curious preoccupation with
female purity. His longer pieces, too, in *Tangential Tales* and
Shadow on the Dial, now seem repetitious and tedious.

Bierce excelled in the short form, and his "ante-mortem"
epitaphs and terse newspaper items testify to his mordant wit.
Many a Bierce neologism, 'futilitarianism" or "femininnies,"
sparkles like an epigram. Many pithy entries to his *Devil's
Dictionary* offer ample evidence of his quirky genius:

> **Bride,**   a woman with a fine prospect
>   of happiness behind her.
> **Brute,**   see husband.
> **Novel,**   a short story padded.

Within the short form, only Mark Twain and Dorothy Parker
rival Bierce, but neither of them was able to invent so aptly or
consistently. Typically, Bierce worked through inversion. He

reverses an old saw, for example, to give it a new twist: "To forgive is to err, to be human divine." Absurdity is "the argument of an opponent"; Christmas, "a day set apart and consecrated to gluttony, drunkenness, maudlin sentiment, gift-taking, public dullness, and domestic behavior."

Bierce viewed any notion of the natural goodness of man or the providential integrity of the state as naive and hypocritical. Optimism was but "the doctrine that everything is beautiful, including what is ugly, everything good, especially the bad, and everything right that is wrong"; cheerfulness was "the religion of the little." Bierce saw his own pessimism corroborated in racist California laws and in the hypocrisies of corrupt capitalists such as railroad baron Collis P. Huntington. As Bierce understood the function of wit to be the unmasking of society's crimes, he intended his *Devil's Dictionary* to expose injustice through the topicality of its definitions:

Amnesty,   The state's magnaminity to those offenders it would be too expensive to punish.
Beggar,   A pest unkindly inflicted upon the suffering rich.
Compulsion, The eloquence of power.
Love,   Temporary insanity curable by marriage.
Recreation, Stoning Chinamen.

Unlike Twain or other humorists, "Almighty God" Bierce refused to pull his punches. He wrote purposely to shock, and those he most wanted to shock were the smug and self-certain, or the stupid, his pet aversion. Bierce did shock, sometimes in Swiftian fashion:

Last week was the best week for dead babies we have ever had. Of the seventy-four deaths occurring in the city, more than half were of infants under two years of age. Thirty were under one year. Whom the gods love die young, particularly if their parents get drunk and neglect them.

Such joking is strong meat, and not for every taste.

Bierce worried little about offending the soft-throated public with his jugular humor. As a coat of arms for American letters, he proposed an illiterate hoodlum rampant on a field of dead

authors with the motto, "To Hell with Literature." Bierce dedicated his *Dictionary* to "those enlightened souls who prefer
dry wines to sweet, sense to sentiment, wit to humor and clean
English to slang." He also predicted "it will have no sale, for it
has no slang, no dialect, and no grinning through a horse-col-
lar," and therefore would not appeal to the common reader who
was a Philistine "sometimes learned, frequently prosperous,
commonly clean and always solemn."

Not all of Bierce's jests still glow; some chestnuts have indeed staled, and as a kind of perverse Pangloss he can be cantankerous to a fault. Even the *Devil's Dictionary* is very uneven work. His techniques—invective, rhetorical overkill, and
comic deflation—become repetitive, and as the subjects of his
invective have passed on, their crimes sealed up in the petty-
cash box of time, we are left with merely the blue streaks. Also,
as one becomes acquainted with the Bierce philosophy, his
quips and witticisms, unfailingly pessimistic, seem not only
formulaic but a bit oppressive:

Defenseless,	Unable to attack.
Noncombatant,	A dead Quaker.
Congratulation,	The civility of envy.
Birth,	First and direst of all disasters.
Year,	A period of three-hundred and sixty-five disappointments.

Yet, for all the cavils, there is, as Mrs. Pope has said, "enough
audacity to startle, enough paradox to charm."

Bierce's fiercest thunderbolts were reserved for the political
system around him; and as the Gilded Age began to tarnish,
many Americans came to doubt the providential implications
of the New Zion. California politics in particular inspired many
of Bierce's most cynical entries:

Bribe,	That which enables a member of the California legislature to live on his pay without any dishonest economies.
Presidency,	The greased pig in the field of American politics.
Diplomacy,	The patriotic art of lying for one's country.

The law seemed but a matter of caprice. The legal, Bierce rued, was that which was "compatible with the will of a judge having jurisdiction" and a lawyer but "one skilled in circumvention of the law." As Richard O'Connor observes, "In their treatment of the Western frontier Bret Harte made the prevalent contempt for the law picturesque and Mark Twain found it humorous, but Bierce labelled it for what it was—murder, armed robbery, and intent to kill." Indeed, Bierce sneered at the grand legend of the West as "bosh." Juries were the greatest joke of all: "In the McFarland case the defendant set up the plea of insanity, and succeeded in proving himself a fool. And he was acquitted by a jury of his peers." Bierce went on to compose his own "Rational Anthem":

> My country, 'tis of thee,
> Sweet land of felony,
>   Of thee I sing—
> Land where my fathers fried
> Young witches and applied
> Whips to the Quaker's hide
>   And made him spring.
>
> My knavish country, thee,
> Land where the thief is free,
>   Thy laws I love;
> I love thy thieving bills
> That top the people's tills;
> I love thy mob whose will's
>   All laws above.

Bierce was also a hard-liner on crime, and he advocated harsh prison discipline and the death penalty to keep the rabble in line. Strict adherence to Roman law, he argued, would cauterize society and help sweep the rabble from the streets. Anarchists incensed him: "I favor mutilation for anarchists convicted of killing or inciting to kill," he wrote, "mutilation followed by death."

Bierce was no admirer of the so-called "common man." Once, looking out at a crowd, he remarked, "Wouldn't it be fun to turn loose a machine gun into that?" And he was scornful of optimistic claims for the "voice of the people":

Sum up the intelligence of the country and divide it by the number of inhabitants: the quotient represents the intelligence of the average man. It would be found to be considerably greater than that of a soft-shelled crab, and considerably less than that of a hippopotamus. Its expression in bad English is "vox populi," and calling this "vox Dei" is besetting blasphemy.

Bierce proposed "a despotism of brains to save civilization from the mob," but he was not sanguine about its prospects. Democracy was an illusion, and equality "an imaginary condition in which skulls are counted, instead of brains, and merit determined by lot and punished by preferment." Of a "republic," Bierce expected only "the foundation of public order in the ever-lessening habit of submission."

Bierce was a defender of classicism in art, honesty in human dealings, and high-mindedness in government. However (always, with Bierce, a however), though he knew the crimes of capitalists only too well, he also hated socialists and reformers; though he insisted on (and practiced) chivalry toward women, he reviled the sex in print; and though defending the rights of the common man vigorously, he attacked the common man's stupidity constantly. One can, of course, find many glaring contradictions in his writings, but Bierce's attacks do seem a healthy antidote to that ostrich mentality which refuses to recognize problems or register alarm.

·   ·   ·

Bierce also excelled at the humor of horror. As Clifton Fadiman has noted, "Bierce's morbidity was exceptionally fertile—he made it produce humor as well as chills. I should say in this extremely narrow field of the sardonic, of the ludicrous ghost story, and the comical murder, he is unrivalled. He begins by somehow making you accept his basic premise: death is a joke." And murder high comedy, we might add. We have seen something of this in *Roughing It*, where Twain uses such stories for change of pace, but in Bierce it is the ghoulishness which seems the entire point.

In *Negligible Tales*, Bierce's humor is not without a touch of grisly zaniness, and the absurdity set off by the flat style. "A Revolt of the Gods" begins calmly: "My father was a deodorizer of dead dogs, my mother kept the only shop for the sale of cat's-meat in my native city. They did not live happily; the difference in social rank was a chasm which would not be bridged by the vows of marriage." Other stories are spiced with similarly gratuitous observations, such as this from "A Bottomless Grave": "I was immediately arrested and thrown into jail, where I passed a most uncomfortable night, being unable to sleep because of the profanity of my fellow-prisoners, two clergymen, whose theological training had given them a fertility of impious ideas and a command of blasphemous language altogether unparalleled." Blithely thumbing his nose—at realism, at any and all offended sensibilities—Bierce seems to be offering these tales as catchbasins of graveyard humor; and they seem the most relaxed, the least tendentious of his works.

The humor of another volume of tales, *The Parenticide Club*, however, borders on the pathological. "Oil of Dog," for instance, starts off deceptively, suggesting Dickens—for a sentence and a half: "My name is Boiffer Bings. I was born of honest parents in one of the humbler walks of life, my father being a manufacturer of dog-oil and my mother having a small studio in the shadow of the village-church, where she disposed of unwelcome babes." Again, the style lulls, though underneath lingers a wormy ghoulishness. "An Imperfect Conflagration" begins, "Early one June morning in 1872 I murdered my father—an act which made a deep impression on me at the time." Another tale, "My Favorite Murder" recounts the torture of an unloved uncle at inordinate length, and is sheer sadism. In these stories we again confront the Bierce who is only too happy to shock or repulse; and (perhaps appropriately) these tales were awarded the first "Prix de l'Humeur Noir" in 1956.

Bierce's obsession with death (an obsession he shared with the late Twain, who could rip off one-liners such as, "Pity is for the living, envy is for the dead.") remained with him throughout his life. For Bierce, death was "the greatest good for the greatest number" and suicide was "courageous"; and he courted danger with an unnatural fondness. Just as, as a young soldier, he had distinguished himself for bravery (some said foolhardiness), later, as a civilian and a journalist, he insulted rival after rival, avoiding challenge only because of his reputation as a crack marksman. It was even rumored that he had acquired the asthma that plagued him by sleeping off his hangovers in graveyards after drinking bouts with the likes of Jack London.

But Bierce claimed that his preoccupation was essentially moral in that death was the final leveler and thus the thought of death should, he felt, encourage modesty. He regarded war as the righteous sword of the Avenging Angel cutting through the mess and fat of civilian life. Certainly, his own life had its share of tragedy. In 1888, Bierce himself left his faithful (and no doubt long-suffering) wife Molly after finding a love-letter to her from an amorous Dane. In 1889, Day, his teenage son, killed his wife's suitor and turned the gun on himself. In 1901 his son Leigh, a reporter, died at twenty-seven in New York. Bierce did not complain; it was as if he expected nothing more from life. Death, on the other hand, he seemed to view as an amiable companion; and he spoke admiringly of the little death-skull cookies Mexican children are given, *memento mori*.

Late in life Bierce took to wearing a suit of black—as naturally, it seems, as Twain took to his famous white suit; and one fellow newspaperman described his forlorn figure, "dressed in black from head to foot [with] a walking cane, black as ebony and unrelieved by gold or silver," like a Puritan minister or Poe's raven, wandering from one Civil War battlefield to another, squatting on gravestones, the sounds of distant thunder awash in his inner ear, the battle sites now quiet and empty except for an occasional cow. Bierce confessed to some remorse about his own role in the war. "They found a Confederate soldier the other day with his rifle alongside," he once said to a friend, "and I'm going over to beg his pardon." With his two sons and estranged wife dead, Bierce became ever more morbid and found the twentieth century even less to his liking. "Why should I remain in this country," he wrote his daughter Helen in 1913, "that is on the eve of prohibition and woman's suffrage? In America you can't go east or west any more, or north; the only avenue of escape is south . . . I want to go down and see if these Mexicans shoot straight."

Go south he did—right into the teeth of the political hurricane that was Mexico torn by a bloody civil war. In his "last piece of humor" as Jay Martin puts it, Bierce crossed over at Ciudad Juárez in November carrying $1500 in American currency and bearing credentials as an observer to Pancho Villa's rebel army, and disappeared into the chaos. On December 16, he arrived in Chihuahua as General Huerta fled; and in his last letter to Connie Christiansen (dated December 26, 1913) Bierce spoke of going to Ojinaga by rail. But nothing more was heard of the old man—the rest is silence, as they say.

But not quite.

The mystery of Bierce's disappearance has never been solved—though theories abound. One theory has it that Bierce died at the hands of Pancho Villa's henchmen; another that he was shot while fighting for Villa at the battle of Ojinaga; still another has him executed by General Urbina farther south. One Charles Fort, who devoted his life to strange phenomena, has noted that an Ambrose Small disappeared at the same time and theorized that some "demonic force" was collecting Ambroses. But by far the most bizarre theory is that of Sibley S. Morrill in *Ambrose Bierce, F.A. Mitchell-Hedges, and the Crystal Skull*. Morrill posits a melange of spies, intrigue, and primitive Indian tribes to explain Bierce's disappearance. Because Bierce worked as a journalist in Washington and was carrying a money belt, Morrill lumps him together with three other foreign "spies" in the Yalbic area of Guatemala, and concludes that Bierce, like the others, must have been "disappeared" because he had seen "the Crystal Skull" in a sacred cave used by the Charro Indians. Morrill's final "proof" is that a British businessman, Mitchell-Hedges, has refused to tell where he found the Crystal Skull, thereby confirming that he was also a spy unable to breach the British Official Secrets Act.

Morrill's odd conspiracy theories extend to Bierce's final letter: "What seems more likely is that if it did, in fact, mention that he was going to Ojinaga, the letter was designed to throw anyone off the scent of where he did go." Morrill's logic, in effect, argues that two plus two must equal five because four is such an obvious answer. *Ambrose Bierce, F.A. Mitchell-Hedges, and the Crystal Skull* is a marvelously absurdist book, amortizing two thousand years of Central American history, an erstwhile British adventurer, a second-string crystal skull, and a lost American satirist into a hilarious concoction of the completely impalpable. Bierce, needless to say, would have delighted in this extra idiocy. Even final ironies, it seems, have final ironies.

The truth seems far less fanciful. Elias Torres, who served with Pancho Villa, says that Villa had Bierce shot before remarking, "Let's see if this damned American tells his last joke to the buzzards on the mountain."

More recently, Mexican novelist Carlos Fuentes has "imagined" Bierce's fate in *The Old Gringo*, a dark and moving novel in which Bierce, "an erect old man, stiff as a ramrod," crosses the border because, as the Mexicans all understand, he has "come to die." Bierce involves himself in the protection of a young, idealistic American woman, Harriet Winslow, to whom he reveals himself as "Old Bitters . . . a contemptible muckraking reporter" whose name is "synonymous with coldness, with anti-sentimentality." Our man, all right.

Fuentes's Bierce speculates about his family, who feared him

[because] he had mocked God, his Homeland, Money; for God's sake, then, when would it be their turn? They must have asked themselves then: when will it be our turn? When will our accursed father turn against us, judging us, telling us you're no exception, you prove the rule, and you, too, wife and you, my beautiful daughter, and you, my sons, you are all a part of the ludicrous filth, the farts of God, we call humanity.

I shall destroy you all with my ridicule. I shall bury you all beneath my poisonous laughter. I shall laugh at you as I laugh at the United States, at its ridiculous army and flag," the old man said breathlessly, choking with asthma.

He offers the commandments of a New Decalogue:

Adore no images save those the coinage of the country shows;
Kill not, for death liberates your foe from persecution's constant woe;
   Honor thy parents, and perchance their wills thy fortune may advance.

But, as he also admits, he might have betrayed his ideals by allowing himself to be used:

> I saw myself as a kind of avenging angel, you see. I was the bitter and sardonic disciple of the devil because I was trying to be as sanctimonious as the people I scorned.
>
> I stoutly insisted I was the friend of Truth, not of Plato while my lord and master of the press [Hearst] cannibalized my anger for the greater glory of his political interests and his massive circulation and his massive bank accounts. Oh, what a fool I was, Miss Harriet. But that's what they paid me for, for being the idiot, the buffoon, in the pay of my lord and master on this earth.

This is an interesting observation—one echoed more recently by Kurt Vonnegut and editorial cartoonist Herblock, who also come to question if, in fact, humor does more than just serve as a safety valve for righteous anger against the powerful.

Later, Bierce mutters, with a smile, "To be a gringo in Mexico . . . ah, that is euthanasia." Eventually, he is granted his wish to be "a good-looking corpse." Betrayed and shot in the back, he is then dug up and shot in the front for appearance's sake.

So, even in his grave it seems, wherever that might be, Bierce continues to intrigue. The themes of *The Old Gringo* include the misuse of anger, the apparent futility of goodness, and the sorrow of our imperfections: all of Bierce's darkest and most heartfelt themes. Yet, interestingly, Fuentes has managed to soften—to humanize—some of the edges to create an appealing Bierce.

· · ·

Bierce continues to occupy a niche, albeit narrow, in the American literary grotto; and there are those who find refreshment in the cutting edge of his satire. "Bierce is good," James Agee wrote Father Flye, "Irony and savage anger and even certain planes of cynicism are, used right, nearly as good instruments as love, and not by any means incompatible with it; good lens wipers and good auxiliaries. . . . I care a lot for smaller, sharp

intelligent sore-heads like Bierce." We must agree that there is
a hard, thorny sincerity to the man. H. L. Mencken, a tough
hombre himself, admires his ferocity and fearlessness:

> His disbelief in man went even further than Mark Twain's; he
> was quite unable to imagine the heroic in any ordinary sense.
> . . . Man, to him, was the most stupid and ignoble of animals. But
> at the same time the most amusing. Out of the spectacle of life
> about him he got an unflagging and Gargantuan joy. The obscene
> farce of politics delighted him. He was an almost amorous con-
> noisseur of theology and theologians. He howled with mirth
> whenever he thought of a professor, a doctor, or a husband.
>   His stories are not a transcript of life. The people in them
> simply do not live or breathe. Ring Lardner, whose manner Am-
> brose Bierce would have detested, did a hundred times better in
> that direction. . . . The timorousness of Mark Twain was not in
> him; no head was lofty enough to escape his furious thwack.
> Such berserk men have been rare in history; the normal Ameri-
> cano shows considerable discretion.

Bierce was a dutiful "town crier," faithful to his calling, raising
a loud hue and cry at the crimes he saw. And Bierce was proud
of what he was. As he wrote Walter Neale: "My independence
is my wealth; it is my literature. I have written to please myself,
no matter who should be hurt." Convinced that the image of
reality around him was false, Bierce tried to preserve his own
mind by ridiculing the crazed world that questioned his sense
and sensibility. His grotesque humor presages Nathanael
West's extravagant satire, Mencken's own attacks on the "boo-
boisee," and the work of such black humorists as Terry Southern, Joseph Heller, and Thomas Pynchon. In many ways, too,
Bierce stands as a precursor to contemporary comedians like
Lenny Bruce and Don Rickles, who assault their audiences. By
deliberately flinging away the restraint of manners, Bierce
pointed a finger at naked human fraud; and his insults offer the
release of truth.

But no matter how much one "explains" Bierce, there is still
something unsavory about him. Perhaps it is simply that we
don't wish our jokes quite that raw. Bierce seems too much the
wolf, excessively diabolical. If, in his sardonic couplet, "For-

give, O Lord, the little jokes I play on Thee,/And I'll forgive Thy great big one on me," Robert Frost implies a wry acceptance. Bierce, on the other hand, could never bring himself to forgive or forget that "great big joke." Life, to Bierce, seemed but an empty parenthesis upon the black sheet of eternity.

Since no flower could flourish under the withering gaze of his basilisk eye, Bierce's garden grew only cacti, and thus he seems destined to remain a cult figure. His contribution to the grand concert of American humor may best be summed up as a catcall from the balcony. Though such writers as Hemingway, Mencken, and Stephen Crane (whom he detested) have praised him, no important American writer has claimed Bierce as mentor. Clifton Fadiman has called him "a Swift minus true intellectual powers, Rochefoucauld with a bludgeon, Voltaire with stomach ulcers." Edmund Wilson branded him a "fascist."

Whatever his "value," Bierce is proof-positive of the comic dilemma. As a gleeful paymaster of invective, Bierce attacked his violent society violently; his is the comic mask stripped of pretense, ugly and accusatory. If Mark Twain often shone as the blazing sun of American humor, Bierce seems more its dark shadow. Even if the humorist or satirist, on pain of blandness, must not pull his punches, he must also provide his audience with some tentative comfort, some possible joy. "The danger," as Kurt Vonnegut has shrewdly noted, "is spilling over into misanthropy like Bierce and the late Twain."

Yet the extreme has value. Bierce's critical comments on the general run of American humor do much to illuminate its special nature. Praising the "crank and curio," Bierce might well have been writing his own epitaph: "What would life be without its mullahs and its dervishes? A matter of merchants and camel-drivers—no one to laugh with and at." A harsh, frowning mullah in ministerial black, Bierce reminds us of the limits of humor—even American humor. He stands poised, like a fierce and implacable eagle, on the edge of the abyss. On the very edge.

ROUND FOUR

Ring Lardner:
Sad Sack in the Fun House

If he got stewed and fell in the gutter he'd catch a fish.
— Ring Lardner, "The Big Town"

Lardner was that rare beast—a writer who professes to a happy childhood. Indeed, it does seem idyllic, if a bit sheltered, with Ring home till the age of twelve, tutored and watched over by an adoring mother in a house full of music, literature, and good cheer. As Lardner later reminisced in his self-mocking manner: "Us 3 youngest members of the family was too fragile to mix with the tough eggs from the West Side and the Dickereel. We had a private tutor that came to the house every morning at 9 and stayed till noon and on acct. of it taking him 2 and a ½ hrs to get us to stop giggling why they was only a ½ hr left for work and this was generally always spent on penmanship which was his passion." Despite such joking, what emerges is a sense of a genteel environment of genuine affection and common sense —qualities, he was later to learn, often sadly lacking in the world at large.

For Lardner, his early life was a subject of fun:

I was born at Niles, Michigan on the 6th of March, 1885, and soon entered the high school. . . . I wanted to go to the University of Michigan and take football and dentistry, so I was sent to Armour Institute, Chicago, to study mechanical engineering. At the end of the first semester, I passed in rhetoric and out of Armour.

During the next year and a half I took part in two minstrel shows, and then came an opening as bookkeeper at the gas-office. I felt exhausted and didn't want to take it, but my father

coaxed me into it in a few well-chosen words. I learned one
thing on this job—that there's a lot of cheating done in the gas
business, and it's all done by the consumers. The company
doesn't have to cheat.

Soon afterward Lardner drifted into journalism, first with the
South Bend Times as sporting editor and dramatic critic, society
and courthouse reporter, and banquet hound, then as sports
reporter for various Chicago papers. There, Lardner first exper-
imented with the quirky vernacular style which was to become
his trademark; and the often amusing contrast between the
tight, hard rules of baseball and the loose, flaky young men who
played it provided him with a rough diamond to polish. In
January 1914, Lardner published his first baseball story, one of
the "Busher" letters later incorporated into *You Know Me Al*.
The *Saturday Evening Post* was besieged by readers demanding more of Jack Keefe—and Lardner was off and running. But,
by 1919, Lardner felt boxed in, and signed on as a columnist for
the Bell Syndicate, centered in New York. He was a hit, too, in
"The Big Apple"; and, after publishing "The Young Immigrunts" (1920) and "The Big Town" (1921), he received as
much as $3,000 a story, had a weekly column syndicated in
over 150 newspapers a week, and was earning $50,000 a year
in pre-Depression dollars. With his beloved wife Ellis and
their growing family, he settled on Great Neck, Long Island,
where he drank with Fitzgerald, Grantland Rice, and others
who visited him at "The Old Mange," as he referred to his
homestead.
    Yet even then there were signs of his peculiar gravity and
loneliness which contributed to the depressions of his later
years. Josephine Herbst described Lardner as he appeared in
1926: "A tall, thin, slightly stooping man, with a grave, beautiful smile, high cheekbones, and enormous, alive dark eyes that
could look out at an interlocutor with melancholy attentiveness,
he stood out in any gathering, where he gave the impression of
being detached, silent, and peculiarly alone." The eyes caught
the attention of many observers; Walter Tittle described them
as "hypnotic and suggestive of Svengali," and the Chicago

White Sox dubbed him "Old Owl Eyes" and "Rameses II."
Sherwood Anderson, after a night of drinking with Lardner in
New Orleans, said of him, "A long, solemn-faced man. The face
was wonderful. It was a mask. All the time, when you were
with him, you kept wondering 'what is going on back there?'
There was a feeling, if anyone hurts this man I'd like to punch
him on the jaw."

Lardner wore many masks, not the least of which was that of
invisibility. All of Lardner's devices—the vernacular, the
"wise-boob" narrator, the foolish puns—seem designed to contribute to this mask. Often, in the ceaseless patter of his narrator's wisecracks, Lardner simply drifts out of our view. Even
his nonsense seems a smoke screen to divert attention. But
there seems deliberation in the mask: If the truth as you see it
is cruel, you may well wish to veil it with nonsense—or disap-
pear.

Lardner's life and work also present many paradoxes. A witty
and humorous writer, he was profoundly melancholic. A facile
psychologizing might suggest that any ideal childhood must
lead to disillusionment. But I think a stronger argument can be
made that the roots of Lardner's melancholia lay in his refusal
(not his inability) to come to terms with the Jazz Age society
around him. Underneath Lardner's party lampshade their
brooded a Puritan spirit at odds with the frantic hustle and
mindless boosterism around him—he was, in many ways, truly
a sad sack in the fun house of the twenties. But he inspired
great affection among family, friends, and colleagues; and you
find no nasty gossip about him (surely a strange phenomenon
in Grub Street). F. Scott Fitzgerald wrote a moving epitaph:
"Ring made no enemies, because he was kind, and to many
readers he gave release and delight."

.   .   .

Lardner wrote a lot of nonsense, and nonsense creates confusion. Is it just frivolous fun, or is it rather, as Freud argued, a
sign of psychic turmoil? If Lardner's sardonic stories suggest
the dark side of the moon, his lighter pieces show off his silly
Oliver Hardyish moon face. Lardner always liked to clown. In

an early letter to Ellis upon her graduation from Smith College, he offered her his "Commencement Tips":

1. Don't commence too young.

2. Don't stay in the east too long. The west needs you.

It was characteristic of Lardner to disguise his affection in clowning.

Lardner also enjoyed parodies. In one column he evoked *HAMLET* to commemorate Heinie Zimmerman, a ball player threatened with a hundred-dollar fine for fighting umpires:

> The C or not the C, that is the question—
> Whether 'tis nobler for the tough to suffer
> Mistakes and errors of outrageous umpires,
> Or to cut loose against a band of robbers,
> And, by protesting, lose it? To kick—to beef—
> To beef! Perchance to scream—
> Yes, I'll keep still,
> Thus money does make cowards of us all.

Clever stuff, nonseditious, good for a chuckle.

Lardner's first book, *Bib Ballads* (1915) is a collection of verse dedicated to his son and illustrated with cutesy-marmsy plates. At the expense, perhaps, of the remnant of his reputation, I quote "His Sense of Humor," to illustrate Lardner's penchant for mawkish jokes:

> Perhaps in some respects its true
>   That you resemble dad;
> To be informed I look like you
>   Would never make me mad.
> But one thing I am sure of, son,
>   You have a different line
> Of humor, your idea of fun
>   Is not a bit like mine.
>
> You drop my slippers in the sink
>   And leave them there to soak.

> That's very laughable, you think,
>   But I can't see the joke.
> You take my hat outdoors with you
>   And fill it full of earth;
> You seem to think that's witty too,
>   But I'm not moved to mirth.
>
> You open up the chicken-yard;
>   Its inmates run a mile.
> You giggle, but I find it hard
>   To force one half-smile.
> No, kid, I fear your funny-stuff,
>   Though runny it may be,
> Is not quite delicate enough
>   To make a hit with me.

But not all of Lardner's nonsense is so innocuous. His 1925 collection *What of It?* contains more pointed material. In "The Other Side," the narrator describes Europe through a series of pet gripes and addresses us in that same humorous/reductive manner Twain utilized in *The Innocents Abroad:* "I suppose you people wants to hear about my trip acrost the old pond. When I say the old pond, I mean the Atlantic Ocean. Old Pond is what I call it in a kind of joking way." Even Paris has been tainted: "All the music was American jazz and all the conversation was American and English, though one of the newspapermen told me they's some old time Parisians that still speaks French." The idiom is perfect, right down to the Anglicizing of "Parisiennes" and the distinction Lardner makes between English and "our" language.

Lardner professes a harsh realism which refuses to be bamboozled by old-world glitter:

> If anybody can sleep late on a Sunday morning in Edinburgh they are a wonder. I never heard so many chimes in my life. We got up early and drove to the Firth of Forth which sounds like it was named by a lisper. Our driver knew Edinburgh and Scotland like a book and every little while he would stop the car and point out a house where Mary had once et breakfast or a fence that whoever it was had set on when he wrote the Blue Laws of Scotland.

The humor is broad—with the Old World the butt of the joke: "Theys an old saw to the effect that the sun never sets on the British Empire. While we was there, it never even rose." And there are traces of Lardner's tough moralism. One wonders if Hemingway could have appreciated this description of a bull-fight: "Then it was the last horse's turn, but the bull wasn't satisfied with his job on the last horse and attacked him after he was down. It was the first time I had ever studied a horse's anatomy from the inside. It was a pretty sight, and no wonder the Spaniards cheered." Even his friends did not escape his needle: "Mr. Fitzgerald is a novelist and Mrs. Fitzgerald a novelty. They left the United States last May because New Yorkers kept mistaking their Long Island home for a roadhouse."

"The Other Side," is nonsense—Europe is not, after all, what Lardner's narrator insists it is. But he himself is interesting. Like Blucher, Twain's "rough" Westerner in *Innocents Abroad,* the Lardner narrator is ignorant of the past, suspicious of the present, and doubtful of the future. He also expects the amenities of home wrapped in a little local color—in fact, he can hardly wait to get home, which as Lardner hints, is where he belongs.

"The Young Immigrunts," a tale purportedly told by Lardner's three-year-old son, is a companion piece detailing a family trip from the Midwest to New York. The reader is invited to inspect the Lardner caravan:

> My parents are both married and ½ of them are very good-looking. The balance is tall and skinny and has a swarthy complexion with moles but you hardly ever notice them on account of your gaze being rapped up in his feet which would be funny if brevity wasn't the soul. Everybody says I have his eyes and I am glad it didn't have to be something else tho Rollie Zeider the ball player calls him Owl Eyes for a nick name but if I was Rollie Zeider and his nose I wouldn't pick on somebodys else features.

Lardner here walks a high-wire between bedlam and mockery, and it is his "highly manured prose" (as Artemus Ward would say) which is the balancing pole:

What have you been doing since 3 o'clock as it was now
nerly 5.
Having a high ball my father replied.
I thought Detroit was dry said my mother shyly.
Did you said my father with a rye smile.

Are you lost daddy I arsked tenderly.
Shut up he explained.
We got lost mudder I said brokenly.
We did not screamed my father and accidentally cracked me
in the shins with a stray foot.

The harassed and bumbling father careens on:

Soon my father had paid the check and gave the waiter a lordly
bribe and once more we sprang into the machine and was on our
way. The lease said about the results of my fathers great idear
the soonest mended, in a word it turned out to be a holycast of
the first water as after we had covered miles and miles of ribald
roads we suddenly come to a abrupt conclusion vs. the side of a
stagnant freight train that was stone deef to honks. My father sat
there for nerly ½ a hour reciting the 4 Horses of the Apoplex in
a undertone but finley my mother mustard up her courage and
said affectedly why don't we turn around and go back some-
wheres. I can't spell what my father replied.

The use of the child-narrator is a sophisticated device, and the
reader laughs (when he doesn't wince) at what he is told, literally, through "the mouth of a babe." "The Young Immigrunts"
is a wacky comic-lament. Lardner was good at this sort of mock
essay—perhaps too good, in that in such pieces he never had
to come to "real" grips with anything.
    In "Symptoms of Being 35," he took a run at our obsession
with age and the aging process:

When a man has got a legal wife and 4 and no one hundredths
children what does he care if he is 35 or double that amt. Besides
which they claim that 35 is about the average of all the grown
ups in the world. If I was above the average would I keep it a
secret? Don't be silly.

Lardner's spoof of such actuarial figures implies we are both an overly analyzed and absurdly analytic people to whom facts mean nothing and everything. His observations on "home" are shrewd, reminiscent of Frost's dictum that home is where, when you go, they have to take you in:

> But at 35 you spell it with a big H. Its where you can take off your shoes. Its where you can have more soup. Its where you don't half to say nothing when they's nothing to say. Its where they don't wait till the meal is all over and then give you an eye dropper full of coffee raw. Its where they don't smear everything with cheese dressing. Its where you can pan everybody without it going no further. Its where they know you like doughnuts and what you think about a banana.

In most of Lardner's "low" humor, the nonsense is burlesque. But some of the pieces in *What of It?*, contain humor which is darker, edgier. He offers a purported interview with artist Domba Splew in his "Italian garden with "all the Italian dishes in bloom—ravioli, spaghetti, garlic, Aida, and citrous fruits." Domba tells of his wife who "has got what is called chronic paralysis. She has a stroke every day, but it is never quite enough." Such oddly hostile jokes continue to pop up in the lightest of Lardner's nonsense. But in *What of It?* Lardner's strangest and most unsettling offerings are his surrealistic plays. Act I of *The Water Lilies* opens with people on the outskirts of a Parchesi board wondering what has become of the playing pieces. Acts II and III having been thrown out because "nothing seems to happen," Act IV begins in a silo and is pure Becket: "Two rats have got in there by mistake. One of them seems diseased. The other looks at him. They go out. Both rats come in again and wait for a laugh. They don't get it, and go out. *I Gaspari* opens in a bathroom: "A man named Tupper has evidently just taken a bath. A man named Brindle is now taking a bath. A man named Newburn comes out of the faucet which has been left running. He exits through the exhaust." *Taxidea Americana* ends on the following exchange:

> DR. BONIFACE: "Well, do you have luck with your hogs?"
> HOOKLE: "Oh, we never play for money."

Whether the plays are serious or not, Lardner's surrealism seems like a blip rising to the surface from a certain subaquatic despair. They certainly jolt anyone who feels he has a "handle" on the old Ring.

Lardner never outgrew his penchant for nonsense, and continued to throw such Dadaist parentheses into his books. *The Story of a Wonder Man*, his own mock autobiography, appeared when he was forty-two and already enmeshed in the depression that plagued his last years. The foreword by Sarah E. Spoondripper (another Lardner mask, this time a maid at "The Mange") is another self-parody. Says Sarah/Ring:

> The publication of this autobiography is entirely without the late Master's sanction. He wrote it as a pastime and burnt up each chapter as soon as it was written; the salvaging was accomplished by ghouls who haunted the Lardner ash bbl. during my tenure as night nurse to this dromedary.

In light of Fitzgerald and Edmund Wilson's constant chastising of Lardner for never keeping copies of his stories, the humor is chilly.

Lardner, in fact, reveals little in *Wonder Man* and remains an elusive self-mocker. Not wanting to hurt Ellis (how does one make fun of someone one loves?), Lardner invents a wife:

> We now come to my first marriage. The girl was a born Laplander and landed in my lap during the course of a quiet weekend party at the Curley estate on Long Island. I suppose I was fascinated by the music of her broken English as much as by the blonde perfection of her 212 pounds of bubbling youth.

Everything is a joke: "I got up one morning and after my customary plunge down the staircase, I took my finger exercises, consisting of pointing first one finger and then the other at my wife."

We may laugh, but we also still wonder about the Wonder Man. Indeed, most of the book is a series of one-liners, humorous footnotes, and asides:

The chief difficulty about the Spanish war lay in finding out
where it was being held.
  It was at a petting party at the White House that I first met
Jane Austen.

Q. Where is your appendix located?
A. In Washington Park Hospital, Chicago—unless
   the cleaning lady has been in.
Q. How does the stomach act when you eat regularly?
A. Surprised.

The two doctors made me strip to my night-gown and went all
over me with a horoscope. Their diagnosis was chronic alfalfa
and they said I must be rushed to a hospital and tattooed.

This is Henry Youngman stuff, formulaic and a bit sophomoric;
and Fitzgerald was perhaps thinking of such clowning when he
later wrote, "So one is haunted not only by a sense of personal
loss but by a conviction that Ring got less percentage of himself
on paper than any other American of the first flight." To turn
one's jokes on oneself may be kind—but it can also be demean-
ing and self-destructive. There is, in much of Lardner, a kind
of childish play, a Halloween mood of spoof and costume, an
affection for atrocious puns and bad jokes that is both charming
and disarming. But part of us must mourn, along with Fitzgerald, that Lardner didn't struggle harder to tell more of the truth.

.   .   .

Lardner did put some story collections together that read like
novellas. *You Know Me Al* (1916) is a series of "Busher" letters
satirizing the egomania of baseball players through Jack Keefe.
In *Treat 'Em Rough* (1918) and *The Real Dope* (1919), Keefe
reappears as an army recruit and then as a confused and callow
soldier overseas. But these books, though amusing, now seem
a bit dated. Of all the serial fiction Lardner wrote, *Gullible's
Travels* (1916) seems his most obvious accomplishment and the
work that best demonstrates his mastery of the vernacular style.
Here, too, Lardner found a theme: the rage and resentment

festering beneath much American joking. Gullible, the "wise boob" of suburbia, speaks for the new American middle class on the make that Lardner found so fraudulent. Alternately victim and aggressor, Gullible is a knight with thick armor but no soul; for him, there is no Holy Grail.

Gullible relates the adventures of his wife and himself after they strike out from Chicago to meet the "high polloi" of Palm Beach. He begins:

> I promised the wife that if anybody ast me what kind of a time did I have at Palm Beach I'd say I had a swell time. And if they ast me who did we meet I'd tell them everybody that was worth meetin'. And if they ast me did the trip cost a lot I'd say Yes; but it was worth the money. I promised her I wouldn't spill none o' the real details. But if you can't break a promise you made to your own wife what kind of promise can you break? Answer me that, Edgar?

This opening accomplishes a great deal. By admitting to certain lies, Gullible allays our suspicion about his veracity. Secondly, his voice—that curious amalgam of tough talk and colloquialism—catches our attention and promises to amuse. All of this might suggest that Gullible is some sort of adult Huck Finn. But nothing could be further from the truth; the more one learns about Gullible and his mate, the less one likes them.

To start with, they are snobs. "We quit attendin' pitcher shows," says Gullible, "because the rest o' the audience wasn't the kind of people you'd care to mix with." And Mrs. Gullible chimes in: "We ain't swelled on ourselves, but I know and you know that the friends we been associatin' with ain't in our class. They don't know how to dress and they can't talk about nothin' but their goldfish and their meat bills." But the Gullibles are oblivious to their foolishness, and much of the humor stems from this lack of self-knowledge. They encounter the "famous" Mrs. Potter on the fifth floor of their hotel:

> "Are you on this floor?" she says.
> The Missus shook like a leaf.
> "Yes," says she, so low you couldn't hardly hear her.
> "Please see that they's some towels put in 599," says
> the Mrs. Potter from Chicago.

So, though "The Missus" thought she had dressed "well-up," she is mistaken for the maid—a cruel comedown.

But it is difficult to pity either of them. When Gullible and his wife slink back home, no wiser, she crows:

> "Lord! Ain't it grand to be home!"
> "You said something," says I. "But wouldn't it of been grander if we hadn't never left?"
> "I don't know about that," she says. "I think we both of us learned a lesson."
> "Yes," I says; "and the tuition wasn't only a matter o' close to seven hundred bucks."

Gullible, as usual, cannot resist that one last crack.

The action of the book in many ways parallels that of *Huckleberry Finn*. Both books involve trips—Huck by raft, the Gullibles by train. But where Huck and Jim arrive at a semblance of peace, Gullible is always restless and anxious to score. Even the landscape seems reduced to an ugly monotony: "Speakin' o' the scenery, it certainly was something grand. First we'd pass a few pine trees with fuzz on 'em and then a couple o' acres o' yellow mud. After a w'ile we'd come to some pine trees with fuzz on 'em and then, it we watched close, we'd see some yellow mud." A far cry from Huck's idyllic descriptions of the river. Even Cairo, that important focal point for Huck and Jim, is now no more than a joke: "I thought we was in Venice when we woke up next mornin', but the porter says it was just Cairo, Illinois. The river'd went crazy and I bet they wasn't a room without a bath in that old burg." (Huck never needed one.) Gullible finds the inhabitants of the towns along the tracks no less shiftless than the river people of Bricksville, Arkansas:

> After their wife's attended to the chores and got the breakfast they roll out o' bed and put on their overalls and eat. Then they get on their horse or mule or cow or dog and ride down to the station and wait for the next train. When it comes they have a contest to see which can count the passengers first. The losers has to promise to work one day the followin' month. If one fella loses three times in the same month he generally always kills himself.

But there is no moral growth in *Gullible's Travels,* and the most important difference between Huck and Gullible lies in the nature of their instincts. Huck is generous to his fellow creatures even when privately aghast at their doings. He is "powerful sorry" when the Duke and the King are tarred and feathered, and protects Jim at his own peril: Huck has heart. Gullible, on the other hand, is not only uncharitable but immune to his own considerable faults. Vulgar and morally bankrupt, he measures everything in dollars and cents, spends most of his time sniffing out suspected "cons," and is full of raw ambition and unrelieved resentment.

Only Gullible's manic humor prevents the book from being an exercise in vitriol. Humor, after all, was the mask that allowed Lardner entry into so many American homes; and Gullible displays an amusing verbal felicity. He is adept at the "put-on" (though "the Missus" seems impervious to all but the most obvious of his japes) and at exposing the hard truths beneath many an American colloquialism:

> He told us we wouldn't have to write for no hotel accommodations beause the hotels had an agent right over on Madison Street that'd be glad to do everything to us.
>
> "And how much will it cost?" I ast him.
> "One dollar a suit," he says.
> "Are you on parole or haven't you ever been caught?" says I.
> "Yes, sir," he says, and smiled like it was a joke.
>
> After supper we said good-bye to the night clerk and twenty-two bucks.
>
> And when I seen 'em all grab for our baggage with one hand and hold the other out, face up, I know why they called it Palm Beach.

But there is an edginess to our laughter. We are laughing *at* Gullible as much as with him. Much of the humor depends on our recognizing his venality, and the blatant materialism of *Gullible's Travels* proved a kind of touchstone for critics. Josephine Herbst declared Lardner's theme to be the "real politik of domestic life." Marxist critic Maxwell Geismar argued for the book as a diatribe against the moral emptiness of capitalist America; Norris Yates saw it as an exposé of conspicuous consumption, the way adults have of playing king of the mountain. Surely, like Twain, Lardner was satirizing the money-grubbing excesses of democracy and the tyranny of mediocrity. Gullible's go-getter aggression is ugly and simpleminded; he is a child without youth, a man without wisdom. But as social artifact, Gullible also stands as a warning to us all. "We have met the enemy," as Walt Kelley's Pogo observed, "and he is us." We might object that Gullible is not us—he is too much a caricature. But if Gullible is absurd, he is still dangerous. By holding the Gullibles up to ridicule, Lardner hoped to stop them: *Gullible's Travels* is a chain letter he wants us all to sign.

. . .

Fitzgerald reckoned that a half-dozen Lardner stories would endure—an estimate that now seems conservative. *Round Up* (1929), a late collection of thirty-five stories, offers an impressive array; the best of these stories are very good indeed, and many entail a great deal of physical and psychological violence. We still find the hard-boiled repartee, the japes, and the wordplay, but we are not invited to laugh as easily. Rather, it is as if Lardner as prosecuting attorney wants us to act as judge and jury of his characters' "crimes." In these later stories, Lardner relies on comic burlesques to protect the innocent and to convict the guilty; and Lardner the moralist is as often in attendance as Lardner the humorist. Herbst observed, "The profoundly humorous writers, like Lardner, are humorous because they are responsive to the hopeless concatenations of life." So, in Lardner's "serious" fiction, we encounter a morally perverse world in which the good and kind are often victims of the evil and cruel.

"Champion," for instance, is a savage attack on the boxing world, a world that Lardner eventually boycotted because it embodied so much of the simpleminded violence he detested. By the mid-twenties, after such scandals as the 1919 Chicago Black Sox debacle, he had already become disillusioned with sports, and through exposing egoists like Jack Keefe and Alibi

Ike he ridiculed the public's "anile worship" of athletes. But the Midge Kelly of "Champion" is not only obtuse but cruel, and Lardner invites us to despise him.

One of Lardner's few "third-person" stories, "Champion" has a flat objectivity—as if he were dissecting a toad. The story begins coldly: "Midge Kelly scored his first knockout when he was seventeen. The knockee was his brother Connie, three years his junior and a cripple." The actual attack is described vividly:

> Doubling up his fist that held the half dollar, he landed with all his strength on his brother's mouth. Connie fell to the floor with a thud, the crutch tumbling on top of him. Midge stood before the prostrate form. "Is that enough?" he said. "Or do you want this too?"
>
> And he kicked him in the crippled leg.

Midge confronts his mother:

> "Well, then, I hit him. What of it? It ain't the first time."
>
> Her lips pressed tightly together, her face like chalk, Ellen Kelly rose from her chair and made straight for him. Midge backed against the door.
>
> "Lay off'n me, Ma. I don't want to fight no woman."
>
> Still she came on breathing heavy.
>
> "Stop where you're at, Ma," he warned.
>
> There was a brief struggle and Midge's mother lay on the floor before him.
>
> "You ain't hurt, Ma. You're lucky I didn't land good. And I told you to lay off'n me."

Like Pap Finn, Midge embodies callow violence. When one trainer says admiringly, "You certainly gave that wop a trimmin' tonight, I thought you'd kill him," Midge replies, "I would if I hadn't let up—I'll kill 'em all." Midge's fists are his Bible, his right cross his sermon. Soon he is knocking everybody out, including his wife, whom he rewards with "a crushing blow on [her] pale cheek." When one of Midge's corner men observes that he must hate himself, the other shrugs, "I never seen a good one that didn't."

Midge gets into the big money, which he proceeds to spend on loud clothes and even louder women. But success has not softened him. When he receives letters from his impoverished mother, his starving wife, and his flashy girlfriend Grace, he sends Grace two hundred dollars and throws the other letters in the trash. But when Midge finally becomes champ, the public loves him. The story ends with Midge's new manager supplying the dope to a reporter: "Just a kid; that's all he is, a regular boy. Get what I mean? Don't know the meaning o' bad habits. Never tasted liquor in his life and would prob'bly get sick if he smelled it. Clean livin' put him up where he's at. Get what I mean? And modest and unassuming as a schoolgirl." A sick inversion of the truth, still "the public don't want to see him knocked. He's champion."

I have gone to some lengths in quoting from "Champion" because it deals explicitly with physical violence, which Lardner hated but rarely treated. In his single-minded viciousness, Midge recalls Slade, the mass murderer of *Roughing It;* but Lardner's condemnation is less ambiguous than Twain's. Lardner asks us to question why such a creature as Midge should be tolerated, never mind encouraged or rewarded. In many ways, it seems almost too simple. Midge Kelly is a psychopath, his handlers caricatures of the fight game, and the story lacks the brilliant vernacular sheen of *Gullible's Travels.* But "Champion" is Lardner's most direct attack on the American public's love of violence and its champions. Americans seem to relish hero-villains—the brutish Mike Tyson in his black sneakers and shorts whose own short marital career reads like a blueprint for disaster; Dick Butkus, the ultimate "Bear," snorting and pawing the turf at linebacker; *Star Wars'* Darth Vader, etc. In America, we like our gladiators raw. Even professional wrestling, that pseudo-sport which can be viewed on television every hour of the day, owes much of its immense popularity to the fact that the crowd is part of the act and that any second the wrestlers might get away from their predetermined dives and risk actual injury by tumbling into the first few rows of spectators where elderly ladies can pummel or stick them with four-inch hat pins. So Lardner, in "Champions," also seems to be suggesting that the fight "game" is indicative of a much larger corruption encompassing, not only the leeches who directly profit, but the audience that pays them. The onlookers who applaud and envy such brute power and take vicarious pleasure from such exploits, Lardner suggests, are as despicable as Midge.

There are other acts of violence scattered throughout his stories. The narrator of "Big Town" knocks down Katie's first suitor "nine or ten times"; Mr. and Mrs. Fix-it wield axes to destroy antique furniture; "My Roomie" ends with attempted homicide. But physical violence is rare—we encounter nothing like the parade of corpses that decorate the pages of Mark Twain. Much of it is verbal violence, or "oral manslaughter" as Lardner called it, by which his narrators cut down their spouses and other ready opponents. Lardner's narrators are smart alecks, always trying to put one over on someone else. The stance may be sardonic and deadpan, but the words stab; and we laugh only because so much escapes the victims.

For what he wrote, Lardner had the perfect style, a casual vernacular that was both supple and incisive—"a whip of small cords to scourge American roughnecks," as Stuart Sherman put it. This style served Lardner as a smokescreen in that, without the verbal quips, his jeremiad would have been shrill and obvious. But he had to be careful since, as one who fought so hard to maintain his own mask, he knew that the stripping away of masks could be distinctly "unfunny." To dispel illusion often involves a kind of violence. To declare the king naked is revolutionary; to point out the nakedness of friends and neighbors, dangerous; to reveal one's own nakedness, unbearable. So Lardner walked a very narrow line—and not everyone caught on.

But often Lardner's narrators do manage to expose their venality and cruelty, not despite, but because of, themselves. The narrator of "The Golden Honeymoon" is a tiresome old boor, detailing all you don't want to know about railroad timetables and his diet. The "lovers" of "Some Like Them Cold" under their romantic claptrap, are harsh materialists. Jack Keefe cheerfully offers example after example of his own egomania. The talkative newlywed of "Who Dealt?" reveals her husband's past love for the other woman at the table—and her own

insensitivity. "The Maysville Minstrel" is a talentless fool;
"Mr. Frisbee" cheats at golf. Even "The Love Nest" turns out
to be a cage. Shoddy and pretentious, these characters allow us
to feel morally superior. After a while, the reader knows the
formula and sits back to watch the characters self-destruct.

In "Zone of Quiet" for instance, the irrepressible Miss Lyons
inflicts her trivial banter upon the laconic "man in bed" (perhaps Lardner himself on one of his frequent "ly-ins"). After
hearing her attest to a horrifying litany of patients' deaths, the
"man in bed" says simply, "It seems to me a good number of
your cases die." Miss Lyons is off:

> "Isn't it a scream!" said Miss Lyons. "But it's true; that is, it's
> been true lately. The last five cases I've been on has all died. Of
> course it's just luck, but the girls have been kidding me about it
> and calling me a jinx, and when Miss Halsey saw me here the
> evening of the day you was operated, she said, 'God help him!'
> That's the night floor nurse's name. But you're going to be mean
> and live through it and spoil my record, aren't you? I'm just
> kidding of course. I want you to get all right."

Lardner knew what this sort of "kidding" was worth. If Miss
Lyons is a fool, she is a harmful fool; ignorance, Lardner suggests, can contain its own cruelty.

Other Lardner stories detail the extremes of bad manners.
"Liberty Hall," for instance, is a painful example of how not to
treat houseguests. Songwriter Ben Drake and his wife have
come to visit the Thayers in the country. But for guests at the
Thayers' "Liberty Hall," there is neither liberty nor considera-
tion. Mrs. Thayer asks:

> "Don't you take cream, Mr. Drake?"
> "No. Never."
> "But that's because you don't get good cream in New York."
> "No, it's because I don't like cream in my coffee."
> "You would like our cream. We have our own cows and the
> cream is so rich that it's almost like butter. Won't you try just a
> little?"
> "No thanks."
> "But just a little, to see how rich it is."

   She poured about a tablespoon of cream into his coffee-cup
and for a second I was afraid he was going to pick up the cup
and throw it in her face. But he kept hold of himself, forced a
smile and declined a second cup.

Ben is forced to drink Bacardi which he doesn't like, to sit in a
"comfortable" chair when he prefers a straight-back, to listen
to Gershwin when he prefers "Oh, Miss Hannah" by The Revelers. Throughout the visit, he is polite, but his wife knows
what he is thinking. In the bedroom he says to her, "Lock the
door before she comes in to feel our feet." The story ends with
Mrs. Drake's laconic comment, "Small wonder that Ben was
credited with that month's most interesting bender."
   "Liberty Hall" is an open criticism of "well-meaning," pushy
people. In Ben Drake's mad flight we see another Lardner
theme, that of entrapment and claustrophobia. His victims
often find themselves trapped by circumstance or fate into having to listen to fools and boors. The "man in bed" is at the
mercy of the garrulous Miss Lyons. Mrs. Bartlett of "The Love
Nest," smothered by the false tinsel of her husband's public
love, becomes an at-home alcoholic. The husband in "Who
Dealt?" is trapped across the table from his wife's painful ram-
blings. Harry Barton of "Dinner" is boxed in between the intrepid Miss Rell and the infuriating Miss Coakley who cannot
finish a sentence. Shelton of "Contract" is the helpless butt of
endless "well-meant" criticism about his bridge playing. So
many of Lardner's "good" characters, trapped by bad marriages
and other bourgeois disasters, just sit there and take it.
   These characters escape (if escape is possible) through lies,
occasional rudeness, and especially drink. Harry Barton cries
out for cocktail after cocktail to drown the drone around him;
Shelton gets crocked in order to tell his "new friends" off; and
Ben Drake takes off on a memorable bender. If the reasons for
getting drunk are all too understandable, the drunk himself is
funny only on the surface. For alcohol is a last resort—containing its own destructive withdrawal symptoms, as Lardner
learned only too well. Prone himself to week-long benders, he
was a reluctant guest who abhorred cocktail parties and any
"new" friends.

Entrapment was no casual theme for Lardner; and in "Haircut," his finest story, we see this theme developed to claustrophic effect. The barber narrates, and the reader is, literally, in the barber's chair. That is, the barber has the scissors and razor, and the listener/reader is tied down, incapable, of running away from what the barber is saying. The towel is tied around the reader's neck, too, his head and face exposed—and the story inflicted on him.

The plot revolves around the cruel practical joke Jim Kendall played on Julie, humiliating her in front of a crowd of poolroom stiffs and parodying her love for Doc Stair with "Oh, Ralphie, is that you?" That is the catalyst for the shooting of Jim by Paul Dickson, the poor cuckoo, though this final irony is not comprehended by the barber. But the reader understands the ultimate justice of Jim's death, which is, like Pap's, not a death to mourn. As we learn from the barber, Jim Kendall was an adulterer and a drunk, and his hoax on Julie but one of many. He mailed anonymous postcards to merchants suggesting that their wives had been adulterous; he sent the slow-witted Paul out for a left-handed monkey wrench and the key to the pitcher's box; he tricked his own wife out of circus money for the children; he even tricked the barber into traveling to shave a "dead" man who turns up alive.

Jim Kendall is what Tom Sawyer might have become if he had grown older without growing up. He is a "good old boy" and a callow cad without any true feeling, truly a "caution." In "Haircut," Lardner exposes the cruelty at the heart of much American "cutting up," and we are advised to think twice before pulling a fast one. Even the barber admits: "I said it had been kind of a raw thing; but Jim just couldn't resist no kind of joke, no matter how raw. I said I thought he was all right at heart, but just bubblin' over with mischief. Doc turned and walked out." We might well too.

There is, then, nothing to like in Jim Kendall, though the barber, a pathetic example of a small-town mind, doesn't see that. If Jim Kendall is "like everybody else in that he wants what he can't get," then there is something terribly sick and hollow within the American soul. Whether the story works or not depends on how Lardner's readers, singly and collectively,

get up from that barber's chair. It would take someone as morally obtuse as the barber to laugh along with Jim Kendall. Lardner suggests we reserve our sympathies for decent people like
Doc and Julie who are the butts of his cruelty. A joke that hurts
terribly, Lardner insists, is just more needless violence; and he
suggests we not commit or permit such jokes. At the end, when
the barber asks, "Comb it wet or dry?" we must look him
straight in the eye and say, "Dry, thank you, and I'll get my
own hat." And never come back.

.   .   .

In his stories Lardner indicted fools and scoundrels, and his
most scathing indictments have to do with the implications of
his vision. Some critics have been put off. Clifton Fadiman
said: "The special force of Ring Lardner's work springs from a
single fact: He just doesn't like people. Except Swift, no writer
has gone further on hate alone. I believe he hates himself; more
certainly he hates his characters; and most clearly of all, his
characters hate each other. Out of this integral triune repulsion
is born his satiric power." Norris Yates sees "the implied message of his work [as] one of nihilism and despair." No nonsense
for them.

But Fadiman and Yates seem to have overlooked the function
of satire to instruct by inversion. Many of Lardner's characters
do love only themselves and revile their fellow creatures—
tricking and on occasion torturing them—and they wallow in a
slough of callousness, envy, and emotional blackmail. But
Lardner exposes them to ridicule and points out that their sel-
fishness is cruel and vicious and ultimately despicable. Lardner
created grotesques so that our disgust will revolt, remind, re-
deem us perhaps. Stripped of humor, Lardner's stories would
be unbearably bleak. But there is humor, and we should not be
surprised that Lardner tried to be funny despite what he saw.
The humorist is often a manic-depressive, and his mania helps
to fend off sorrow. Lardner's work suggests an acute awareness
of pain. "His hypersensitivity to language," as Delmore
Schwartz observed, "was a kind of hypersensitivity to human
suffering."

At the end, Lardner worried over his family's financial future and found it difficult to work, often falling asleep at the type-writer. He was in and out of various hospitals and rest homes after bouts of alcoholism and tuberculosis; and his mask failed. He fell into long silences and, on occasions, simply wept. He was dead at forty-eight.

Something strange has happened to Ring Lardner—practically no one reads him any more. Oh, one finds the occasional Lardner story in an anthology—"Haircut" or "The Love Nest," maybe even "Alibi Ike"—but often he is just lumped in with such "minor" humorists of the twenties as George Ade, Don Marquis, Frank Sullivan, and their ilk. There are reasons for this eclipse. Lardner wrote no novels, and the short story no longer attracts wide readership. Also, Lardner himself was a self-deprecating man who often refused to take himself or his work seriously. Furthermore, in a sense he hearkened back to the puns of the "phunny phellows." Just as Artemus Ward smirked about the "soshul bored" and "women's rites," so Lardner could joke about "a rye smile" and a "holycast." He employed the vernacular of his times to invoke a shrewd illiteracy, but the vernacular moulders as quickly as cheese. This, we should perhaps note, is a problem for many writers; in the age of The Tube, many readers find even Huck's dialect tough treading.

But why, then, should anyone read Lardner today? Firstly, because he is very good and had a terrific ear for "Amurrikan." As Virginia Woolf exclaimed, he wrote "the best prose that has come our way, often in a language which is not English." Secondly, because Lardner served as a seismograph for the sub-conscious tremors of his America. The best of his stories depict a society of go-getters and frauds with something empty at the core of the collective dream. Though we may laugh at the malapropisms and scathing one-liners, the moral of the Lardner story is often disturbing; and we sometimes find ourselves strangely quiet, even melancholy, at the end. Lardner's main concern was with egotism, ambition, and that implicit violence his narrators inadvertently reveal in their richly corrupt vernacular; and in his fashion he is as tough on fools and scoundrels as Bierce and Twain. The typical Lardner narrator never misses a chance to poke fun at the stupidity of his wife or friend—the real joke, however, is usually at his expense. If the portrait of human folly he limns is often slimy and detestable, Lardner himself embodied a compassion that made him perhaps the best-loved of all humorists. "He awoke a certain feeling," Sherwood Anderson said of him, "You wanted him not to be hurt, perhaps to have some feeling he did not have."

Lardner left a great deal. He "told" the world as he "heard" it with an attractive honesty. S. J. Perelman (no mean wordsmith himself) regarded Lardner at his best as "the nonpareil." Lardner's characters may do violence—not only to the English language but to those around them—and seem perhaps yahoos of a lost America. Yet his humor, finally, points us toward compassion and charity, and his message seems clear: we need better manners, better ways of not hurting each other. Cruelty must not be tolerated. Some things are just not funny.

ROUND FIVE

Kurt Vonnegut: Humorist in the Combat Zone

*"Maturity," Bokonon tells us, "is a bitter disappoint-
ment for which no remedy exists, unless laughter can
be said to remedy anything."*
　　　　　　　　　　　—Kurt Vonnegut, Cat's Cradle

Like Twain, Bierce, and Lardner, Kurt Vonnegut, Jr. (he insists
on the "Junior" to remind himself of his heritage) is a midwest-
erner, born 1922 in Indianapolis, that slab city of the heartland.
From there, the "innocent" went abroad to World War II and
the wasteland of Dresden before returning, like Odysseus, to
Ithaca, New York, Barnstable, Massachusetts, and Manhattan
Island. In the contemporary America of Dan Rather, Newspeak,
and decreasing regionalism, it is difficult to gauge what sense
of exile Vonnegut experiences as a midwestern DP. In his
work, he confesses to feeling "out of time," a cosmic outsider
like so many of his time-tripping characters; and that may be.
But Vonnegut deals volubly with his heritage, and he shares
much with earlier humorists: they are brothers under the skin.
Like Twain (after whom he named his firstborn son, Mark) and
Lardner, Vonnegut is a good court jester. Like Bierce, however,
Vonnegut is more satirist than humorist, and therein lies an
important difference. The humorist is out to please—he must
please. The satirist, on the other hand, intends to make someone—perhaps even you—uncomfortable. In order to expose
the cancerous sickness of this imperfect world, the satirist
wields his penknife to lance certain boils on the body politic.

Satire has a lengthy, if not entirely honorable, tradition. Ancient satirists were feared because of the magical efficacy of
their curses. The chiefs of Ireland, as bribes against Aithirne

the Importunate's venomous imprecations, accorded him castles of his choice, even women in childbed. Through the fury of his blasts, Archilochus of Greece caused his prospective father-in-law and two of his daughters to commit suicide. Many pre-Islamic Arab tribes and early Celts used satirists as point men to tongue-lash the enemy. "I kill with my tongue," boasted Rigoletto, jester to Francis II of France. Such "wasps" had stings that were to be avoided on pain of death. But, in our more skeptical world, most "civilized" folk no longer believe in the magical efficacy of the "hurled" word, and regard satirists with suspicion and disapproval, rather than fear. (No, names will never hurt me.)

Vonnegut himself is not interested in killing—with words or guns. As he says in *Slaughterhouse Five*, "Let the guns rust." But his attacks on such sacred cows as capitalism and Christianity have ruffled sensibilities and goaded librarians and school committees in such outposts as Drake, North Dakota, and Levittown, New York, to ban his books. For his part, he claims to be intent on writing short books with simple messages that can be read by anyone—even Richard Nixon. "The books of jokesters are short," he has observed, "which is a social disadvantage in an era when literary importance is measured by the pound. The problem is that jokes deal so efficiently with ideas that there is little more to be said after the punch line has been spoken. It is time to come up with a new idea—and another good joke." If now he has acquired a wide readership, it may only mean that his pacifism and anti-machismo have recently come to be shared by a large segment of the populace—particularly the young, who rally beneath his tattered banner perhaps because, having as yet no stake in the system, they can afford to laugh at it. In a world replete with absurdist violence, Vonnegut has continued to insist on reason and refused to abandon hope. While Vonnegut's work has been criticized as sentimental and "adolescent" by those critics who see venom (à la Swift and Philip Wylie) as the most praiseworthy ingredient of satire, it is precisely his struggle to keep from falling into misanthropy that makes his work and personality valuable and appealing.

. . .

Player Piano (1952), Vonnegut's first novel, is a takeoff on a kind of General Electric Brave New World and the dehumanization of that world. But this futuristic fantasy peers nostalgically over its shoulder, and its import is neo-Luddite. As Paul Proteus says, "a step backward, after making a wrong turn, is a step in the right direction." Proteus, fellow dropout Ed Finnerty, and the mad Dr. Lasher, become the unlikely leaders of the "reeks and recs," that unwashed refuse of industrialized society. They dub their "revolution" the "Ghost Shirt Society," after those nineteenth-century American Indians whose shamans promised invisibility to braves who wore "ghost shirts" into battle—which many did, much to their eternal sorrow.

The "player piano" of the title suggests that corporate directors "play" the workers and that behind all the glad-handing lies an Iron Fist. The heroes rebel. Ed Finnerty, for instance, refuses to see a psychiatrist for a possible "cure":

> "He'd pull me back into the center, and I want to stay as close to the edge as I can without going over. Out on the edge you see all kinds of things you can't see from the center. Big, undreamed-of things—the people on the edge see them first."

In other words, the edge is where one can see truth; and Finnerty works up a "canary-in-the-coal-mine" theory whereby artists' finely tuned nervous systems "should be treasured as alarm systems."

Like most spontaneous revolutions, however, this one fails, as the nihilistic rage of the "reeks and recs" destroys the dream. The story ends with the established order, bits in hand, closing in on the ringleaders. But, despite the revolution's failure, we are not exactly back at the beginning. The fascist underpinnings of corporate life have been exposed.

Vonnegut continued to attack Big Business and Big Government in several early short stories concerned with thought control, population control, and other oblique forms of repression. "Harrison Bergeron," another futuristic fable, satirizes the notion of forced equality. By the use of masks, intracranial buzzers and weights, (beautiful dancers, for instance, are weighed down with chains), the "Handicapper General" penalizes the strong, the beautiful, and the intelligent in order to maintain an "ideal" mediocrity. In "Welcome to the Monkey House," the government distributes antisex pills and encourages the use of elaborate Suicide Parlors in order to control the population explosion. But Billy the Poet—both sentimental anachronism and coy outlaw—in a concerted effort to bring innocent joy back into the world, seduces hostesses of Suicide Parlors with the help of that terrible drug "gin."

Jokes, to be sure. But, underneath the jokes, Vonnegut is mocking the well-intentioned impulses of enthusiastic welfare-state-ists of all stripes and alerting us to the potential violence and discrimination inherent in any "Great Society." George Orwell, the writer Vonnegut says he admires above all, obviously shares this profound skepticism about Big Brothers everywhere. In an increasingly regimented world, the "crime," Vonnegut knows only too well, is often simple individualism.

·   ·   ·

In *The Sirens of Titan* (1959), a sci-fi religio-fantastico invention, Vonnegut locked horns with the doctrines of Perpetual Progress and Divine Benevolence. The tale itself is wild and wooly, involving time travel and the oddly syncopated manifestations of "Prime Mover" Winston Niles Rumfoord. The humor is unpredictable and irreverent. Even the dedication is couched in a certain barbed whimsy: "No names have been changed to protect the innocent, since God Almighty protects the innocent as a matter of heavenly routine." Here Vonnegut depends largely on inversion for the thrust of his reductive humor. Often, to see through a Vonnegut joke is to realize something very disturbing. Rumfoord's "Church of God the Utterly Indifferent," for instance, suggests we look to ourselves for guidance and belief—devise our own commandments and strategies for survival.

Within this context, Vonnegut suggests that the dilemma of violence is something only we can solve. The "war" between Mars and Earth is a cruel farce. Rumfoord, that "chrono-syn-clastic infundibulator," whose quirky insouciance suggests a slightly batty Franklin Delano Roosevelt, has designed the war as a mass Martian suicide in hopes that Earthlings will be so sickened by the massacre that they will cease slaughtering each other. Like the Roman *naumachia,* or lake theater, in which fleets of slaves fought to the death for the amusement of the nobility, this is a kind of staged, but murderous, "happening." Rumfoord's Martian strike force is comprised of displaced Earthlings outfitted in a hodgepodge of archaic hardware: knee spikes, glossy black uniforms with an insignia of skull and crossbones, and fourteen-inch saw-toothed knives. Rumfoord disperses this hopelessly ill-equipped army in programmed spaceships to widely scattered spots across the universe where they are mercilessly cut to pieces: "Mars casualties were 149,315 killed, 446 wounded, 11 captured, and 46,643 missing. At the end of the war every Martian had been killed, wounded, captured, or been found missing." After the invasion, the skies smolder with the bitter aftertaste of the two million antiaircraft rockets fired at the Martian armada.

Vonnegut offers such cryptic moral fables to dramatize the effects of mass violence. Unk, a typically flawed Vonnegut hero, survives the war a chastened man: "Unk was at war with his environment. he had come to regard his environment as being either malevolent or cruelly mismanaged. His response was to fight it with the only weapons at hand—passive resistance and open displays of contempt." Unk's weapons, those of aggressive pacifism, we should note, are Vonnegut's own. At the end Unk asks to be left off at Indianapolis, "the first place in the United States of America where a white man was hanged for the murder of an Indian. The kind of people who'll hang a white man for murdering an Indian—that's the kind of people for me." A dark joke, indeed.

The Sirens of Titan, in many ways Vonnegut's most imaginative book, embodies a certain bleakness. Mathew Arnold's sea of faith has indeed run dry. *"Greetings!"* the message Salo has been traveling hundreds of thousands of years to bring to Earth, is sublimely farcical. As with Twain's Little Satan, revelation of a cosmic hoax tends to trivialize, though not excuse, man's own violence. Vonnegut seems to be suggesting that our sustaining myths deserve ridicule since they no longer, in fact, sustain. In its suicidal fervor, Rumfoord's war suggests the final holocaust of *A Connecticut Yankee,* the premise of which Vonnegut has described as "to wit: that the sanest, most likeable persons, employing superior technology, will enforce sanity throughout the world." *Sirens*, a similar alarm, contains the same seeds of pessimism and disgust: If things can't be patched up, they might just as well be blown up.

. . .

In *Mother Night* (1961), Vonnegut attempted to come to terms with the central event of his life—World War II. *Mother Night* is a study of deception and moral ambivalence which piles irony upon irony. Detested Nazi propagandist Howard Campbell reveals in this, his purported autobiography, how he was really an Allied counterspy beaming back valuable data. For political reasons, however, Campbell's duties could not—and still cannot—be revealed, and thus Campbell is loathed as a Nazi sympathizer and Jew-baiter. Nobody is who he or she seems to be. Arpad Kovacs, the fiercely anti-Semitic SS officer is in fact a Jew. Campbell's chess partner, abstract painter George Kraft, is a Russian spy. Even Campbell's wife Helga, who reappears after an absence of years, is really Helga's little sister Resi, also a Russian spy. Campbell himself is a master of deception—so convincing a Nazi as to have been abducted by Israelis and imprisoned with Adolf Eichmann.

Jokes abound among the confusion. Bodoskov, the Russian plagiarist of Campbell's work, is shot for "originality." The Black Fuhrer of Harlem informs Campbell:

> "The colored people gonna have hydrogen bombs all their own. They working on it right now. Pretty soon gonna be Japan's turn to drop one. The rest of the colored folks gonna give them the honor of dropping the first one."
> "Where they going to drop it?" I said.
> "China, most likely," he said.
> "On other colored people?" I said.
> He looked at my pityingly. "Who ever told you a Chinaman was a colored man?"

Paranoia contains its own blindness. Adolf Eichmann turns out to be a stupid little man concerned mostly with finding a good literary agent. He even offers Campbell a few dead Jews for his memoirs—if he needs them. Like Hanna Arendt, Vonnegut cites Eichmann to point out the banality of evil. But Eichmann's presence also reminds us that the novel is only part fiction; Nazi Germany was a reality and the destruction far from banal.

Mother Night is also concerned with revenge, the flip side of violence. In his meditation on the American response, Vonnegut blurs the edges of guilt. Revenge is the companion of victory; a fellow Am-vet assaults Campbell to avenge his dead buddies. Campbell, like most Vonnegut heroes, is a victim; and his counterassault on Bernard O'Hare, the superpatriot who comes to torment him, is unusual. But Vonnegut, through Campbell, is striking out against blind nationalism:

> "There are plenty of good reasons for fighting, but no good reason even to hate without reservations, to imagine that God Almighty Himself hates with you too. Where's the evil? It's that large part of man that wants to hate without limit, that wants to hate with God on its side . . . that part of an imbecile, that punishes and vilifies and makes war gladly."

After listening to this, O'Hare throws up.

In one of the more interesting chapters, "Hangwomen for the Hangman of Berlin," Campbell comes across an account of the hanging of Noth, his former father-in-law, in a girly magazine. But the lurid magazine cover of luscious females is deceptive: "the hangwomen on the cover had breasts like cantaloupes, hips like horse collars, and their rags were the pathetic remains of nightgowns by Schiaparelli. The women in the photograph were as pretty as catfish wrapped in mattress ticking." In fact, as the article details, the slave laborers who hang Noth have no idea who he is.

Despite the wisecracks, *Mother Night* is Vonnegut's least funny book, because the enormity of the crimes muffles our laughter. As Heinz, one of Campbell's German friends, says wearily, "All people are insane. They will do anything at any time, and God helps anybody who looks for reasons." When Heinz's wife chides him for not getting ahead in the Nazi heirarchy, Campbell observes, "The people she saw as succeeding in a brave new world were specialists in slavery, destruction, and death." By shocking the reader into fresh apprehensions of evil and the complexity of guilt, Vonnegut succeeds as a kind of literary archaeologist, scraping through the rubble of our still-smoldering past to hold up the cracked mirror of World War II. Lest we forget, he reminds us that thc Nazi nightmare occurred, not just because of the actions of a few dozen maniacs, but with the complicity of millions. But *Mother Night* also questions our right to insist on our American innocence. Revenge or self-righteous patriotism, we see, just extends the violence.

.   .   .

In *Cat's Cradle* (1963), Vonnegut returned to two pet themes, science and religion, within an equally apocalyptic framework. Dr. Felix Hoenikker, one of the "Fathers" of the atomic bomb, is a childish man who tips his wife after breakfast. When one scientist comments after the explosion of the first A-bomb, "Science has now known sin," Hoenikker asks, "What is sin?" His innocence, however, proves lethal, for his legacy, freely offered, includes "ice-nine," a crystal compound which, by freezing liquid into solid ice, becomes the instrument of the destruction of Earth. Hoenikker's inability to conceive of possible misuse of his invention is a paradigm of the naïveté of the Los Alamos World War II scientists; and Vonnegut is suggesting that, as the stakes grow painfully higher, we cannot afford such moral sloppiness. The title itself derives from the string-play which has befuddled children for thousands of years because, as Hoenikker's son points out, there is "No damn cat, and no damn cradle."

> Little Newt snorted. "Religion!"
> "Beg your pardon?" Castle said.
> "See the cat?" asked Newt. "See the cradle?"

In other words, man's theological inventions, too, are "cat's cradles," artifacts of his own invention.

Bokononism, however, the "religion" of an old Caribbean wise man, embodies skepticism and the saving grace of humility. In "The First Book of Bokonon," there is an interesting exchange between God and the "first" man:

> Man blinked. "What is the purpose of all this?" he asked politely.
> "Everything must have a purpose?" asked God.
> "Certainly," said man.
> "Then I leave it to you to think of one for all this," said God.
> And He went away.

In its implications, this too is a terrifying joke, once again suggestive of God the Utterly Indifferent.

Bokononism, for its part, is a gentle religion, maintained by the *foma* of harmless lies, ceremonialized by the *bokomaru* of mutual feet-tickling, and sustained by faith in the sacredness of man. Despite its proscription, Bokononism thrives within San Lorenzo, a tiny banana republic where poverty, disease, and violence are endemic and order is maintained by "the hook," a giant disemboweler which hangs over the public square. It is within this drab, cruel world that the gentleness of Bokononism is valuable; for, though it provides no final answer, it does offer balm. On one holiday, for instance, American ambassador Horlick Minton, a quietly honorable man, like many Vonnegut "good-guys," is invited to speak in honor of San Lorenzo's "Hundred Martyrs to Democracy"; and he does a very "unambassadorial thing," namely *says* what he really feels:

> "And I propose to you that if we are to pay our sincere respects to the children of San Lorenzo, that we might best spend the day despising what killed them; which is to say, the stupidity and viciousness of all mankind.
> "Perhaps when we remember wars, we should take off all our clothes and paint ourselves blue and go on all fours all day long and grunt like pigs. That would surely be more appropriate than noble oratory and shows of flags and well-oiled guns."

A strikingly Bokononist speech.

But Vonnegut offers no easy solutions to the problem of violence, and the jokes are far from reassuring. In his fly-ridden, overcrowded, corpse-filled hospital, Dr. Castle (who works tirelessly against the plague, à la Dr. Schweitzer) turns to his son and giggles, "Someday this will all be yours." Richard Hauck has called this an "emblematic joke, one of the keenest to be found in American literature. Mankind's inheritance is a heritage of death. The capacity to giggle is not a capacity to annihilate death; it is man's echo of death. The giggle in the jungle proves to us that the cosmic joke is our own invention after all." Whoever's invention it might be, we wince at the grief contained in such a joke.

With earth iced up solid, *Cat's Cradle* ends with Jonah, the narrator, meeting Bokonon to receive his final lesson. "If I were a younger man," says Bokonon, "I would write a history of human stupidity; and I would climb to the top of Mount McCabe and lie down on my back with my history for a pillow; and I would take from the ground some of the blue-white poison that makes statues of men; and I would make a statue of myself, lying on by back, grinning horribly, and thumbing my nose at You Know Who." Like the petrified statue of Twain's earlier hoax, one might add.

But *Cat's Cradle* is *not* just another holocaust novel. In its insistence on humanitarian values in the face of very real horrors, it argues against extinction and is an oddly optimistic book of doom.

. . .

Like *Mother Night, Slaughterhouse Five* (1969) which brought Vonnegut public acclaim at last, also deals with World War II, but it is personal history as much as fiction, a chunk of autobiography camouflaged by imagination. The narrative thread is provided by Vonnegut's experience as a prisoner of war in Dresden, and his own laconic anecdotes of horror. It is an authentic and harrowing account of the hell of war by someone who has, as they say, "been there." It is also a book dedicated to the demystification of warrior-heroes. In the spirit of Melville's defiant *No, in thunder!* Vonnegut refuses to glamorize the "heroes" of war; true to his promise to Mary O'Hare, there's no part for Frank Sinatra or John Wayne. It is also a highly polished and eloquent work of art, in which Vonnegut, through quick changes of scene and tone, orchestrates his "duty dance with death" in a macabre *pas de deux*—the rictal grin accompanied by a laconic "so it goes."

War, in *Slaughterhouse Five,* is the ultimate obscenity. Billy Pilgrim, hardly more than a boy, helps to man a 57-millimeter antitank gun that makes "a ripping sound like the opening of the fly of God Almighty." Billy cuts a preposterous figure as a soldier: "Six feet and three inches tall, with a chest and shoulders like a box of kitchen matches, he looked like a filthy flamingo." Even the Germans find Billy in abominable taste, and one growls, "I take it you find war a very comical thing." Roland Weary and Paul Lazzaro, on the other hand, are two willing and able cogs in the wheels of war—and both psychopaths with the killer instinct. Weary is an expert on the Iron Maiden, blood gutters, and other "instruments," and he lets Billy in on his own ultimate torture: "You stake a guy out on an anthill in the desert, see? He's facing upward, and you put honey all over his balls and pecker, and you cut off his eyelids so he has to stare at the sun until he dies." The ferocity of the aptly named Weary numbs. Weary's sidekick, the weaselly Paul Lazzaro, is a snarling by-product of big-city life. He recalls, with relish, feeding parts of a clock spring to a dog in order to watch him rip out his own entrails. After the war, Lazzaro vows to get everyone on his hit list, Billy included. Weary and Lazzaro are the kinds of crazies war demands—and utilizes.

Through metaphor and irony, Vonnegut suggests the dehumanization of war. Even the title is ironic, since it derives from the fact that, while more than 110,000 German civilians died, the POWs themselves were saved from the fire storm of Dresden by having been imprisoned underground in *Slaughterhouse Five.* The boxcar that transports the American POWs is itself a kind of obscene vending machine: "In went water and loaves of blackbread and sausage and cheese, and out came shit and piss and language." After a hobo keeps insisting, "I been in worse places than this. This ain't so bad," he dies during the night, a still rejoinder of self-deception. Weary, the war lover, dies of gangrene. One of the greater ironies involves Edgar Derby, a mild-mannered ex-teacher who is tried and shot for stealing a teapot. In the catalog of horror which the war encompasses, Derby's execution (a true story) is a cruel parody of justice.

But, as Vonnegut suggests, war is not an isolated phenomenon. Violence and hatred spill over into civilian life; they are
both causes and results. Dresden after the firebombing reminds
time-tripping Billy of Ilium's burned-out ghetto. Billy remembers a man back home using cripples to get magazine subscrip-
tions door-to-door. As Vonnegut sees it, even the message of
Christianity itself is suspect. In "The Gospel from Outer
Space," Kilgore Trout, Vonnegut's alter ego, suggests that the
actual moral of the Gospels is: "Before you kill somebody,
make absolutely sure he isn't well-connected." Trout's novel
"The Gutless Wonder" introduces a robot who drops napalm
on people:

> Trout's leading robot looked like a human being, and could talk
> and dance and so on, and go out with girls. And nobody held it
> against him that he dropped jellied gasoline on people. But they
> found his halitosis unforgivable. But then he cleared that up,
> and he was welcomed to the human race.

Even pluck and grit, so often praised, are seen as inadequate
and ironic. The British hold parties for new arrivals at the
camp: "They had no way of knowing it, but the candles and the
soap were made from the fat of rendered Jews and Gypsies and
fairies and communists, and other enemies of the State." So, as
Vonnegut suggests, even to function well as a prisoner is to be
guilty of some sort of complicity. The war, any war, is full of
wry absurdities. As Vonnegut has commented recently, he was
the only person he knew to have benefited by the destruction
of Dresden through the novel: "One way or another I got two
or three dollars for every person killed. Some business I'm in."
He also observed: "I mourned the destruction of Dresden because it was only temporarily a Nazi city, and had for centuries
been an art treasure belonging to earthlings everywhere. It
could have been that again. The same is true of Angkor Wat,
which military scientists have demolished more recently for
some imagined gain."
What then is the proper response to war and warriors? In
Slaughterhouse Five Vonnegut has presented us with his own
parables. He admits to having allowed his father's gun collec-

tion to rust and having advised his sons not to participate in massacres or to take joy in the massacre of national enemies. *Can* we stop war? Perhaps not. But we can certainly, Vonnegut insists, stop glorifying it.

In *Happy Birthday, Wanda June* (1970), his first Broadway play, Vonnegut continued his attack on the warrior mystique. After Harold, a white hunter, has disappeared, his wife Penelope is courted by Woodly, a pacifist. As she announces: "This is a simple-minded play about men who enjoy killing—and those who don't." When Harold returns, he says:

> "When I was a naive young recruit in Spain, I used to wonder why soldiers bayoneted oil paintings, shot the noses off of statues and defecated into grand pianos. I now understand. It was to teach civilians the deepest sort of respect for men in uniform —uncontrollable fear."
>
> "What kind of country has this become? The men wear beads and refuse to fight—and the women adore them. America's days of greatness are over."

But Woodly insists, "Gentleness must replace violence everywhere or we are doomed." And he previews the peaceful new world for Harold: "Evolution has made you a clown—with a cigar. Simple butchers like you are obsolete . . . the new hero will be a man of science and of peace—like me. He'd disarm you, of course. No more guns, no more guns." At the end, Harold goes off to commit suicide—and misses.

.   .   .

During the seventies and eighties, the emphasis in Vonnegut's work has shifted slightly and taken on a new focus, one less obsessed and tormented by the particulars of Dresden, Nazis, and World War II, and more concerned with the particular inanities and mistakes of our everyday lives—divorce and loneliness, the plethora of pill-popping, false panaceas, the cumulative mess of our oceans and cities, nuclear stockpiling, and, most obsessively, the loss of coherence in our culture. In his latest novels and essays, Vonnegut has appeared more whimsical, less hopeful—angrier.

Breakfast of Champions (1973), for example, is a furious lament. Unhappy with the deluge of advertising jingles and the melange of Burger Kings and Holiday Inns that infest the cityscape, Vonnegut pines: "I have no culture, no humane harmony in my brains. I can't live without a culture any more." In "The Big Space Fuck," a later story, he has described a futuristic rocket ship "with 800 pounds of frozen jizzum in its nose" which is to be fired at the Andromeda Galaxy two million light years away, "to make sure that human life would continue to exist somewhere in the universe, since it certainly couldn't continue much longer on Earth. Everything had turned to shit and beer cans and old automobiles and Clorox bottles." In *Champions,* Dwayne Hooper, a Pontiac dealer wandering through the Sargasso Sea of mid-American detritus, is slowly and almost unnoticeably going insane. Dwayne, we are told, is a victim of "bad chemicals" or "faulty wiring," and does finally go berserk, shoving his homosexual, piano-playing son's head through the keys of his piano.

In *Champions,* everything is quantified and measured— women's figures, penises, the composition of alcoholic drinks, bullets. When Dwayne holds a gun in his mouth, Vonnegut tells us:

> There were neat little metal packages containing charcoal, potassium nitrate and sulphur only inches from his brains. He had only to trip a lever, and the powder would turn to gas. The gas would blow a chunk of lead down a tube and through Dwayne's brains.

Vonnegut's treatment—focusing our attention on the bullet itself rather than on Dwayne—creates an odd tension.

Throughout, Vonnegut maintains a tone of weary pity and offers no easy remedy. His only suggestion, far from cheerful, seems to be that we must somehow adapt to chaos in order to prevent paranoia. But Vonnegut's reductive technique is designed to irritate as well as instruct. He has admitted, "I now make my living by being impolite," and described West Point as "a military academy which turned young men into homicidal maniacs for use in war." Elsewhere, he has summarized the Nazi menace with deceptive simplicity: "The people in a country called Germany were so full of bad chemicals that they actually built factories whose only purpose was to kill people by the millions." Isn't there something troubling, however, about this? If we make a case for Hitler and Stalin and Pol Pot as "victims" of insufficient vitamins or extra chromosomes, aren't we absolving them of responsibility and guilt? Doesn't this reduce the tragic to the trivial? If chemicals *are* the problem, then by all means let us institute a program of megavitamins and wholesome nutrition to restore health and balance and save the world. In this light, perhaps Jean Meyer, the eminent Tufts dietician, should be our head honcho and modern guru. But, but—my God, the but's.

Is Vonnegut serious?

It is hard to know for sure. "After Trout became famous," he says in *Champions*, "one of the biggest mysteries about him was whether he was kidding or not." Vonnegut certainly believes in the power of conditioning for good or evil: "I think culture is to blame for most viciousness, not human nature, and culture can be tinkered with like a Model T Ford." In "The Hocus Pocus Laundromat," he has offered an example of just such tinkering: his own rewriting of a contemporary requiem by Andrew Lloyd Weber, taken from the Latin of the "Roman Missal promulgated by Pope Pius V in 1570, by decree of the Council of Trent," because the sentiments proved worthy of Hitler and "vengeful and sadistic [and] acceptable only when put into a language almost nobody understands." So Vonnegut, as a self-styled child of the Enlightenment, *does* believe in tinkering. Like us all, he has had to sit and watch the peregrinations of the Cold War insure an atmosphere of terror in Vietnam, Afghanistan, Central America, and the Horn of Africa— among others; and he is tired of watching. *Maybe*, he seems to be muttering, *maybe* if we just took more Vitamin B, avoided dangerous food additives, did some proper tinkering—just *maybe* we could stop killing each other.

.   .   .

It is clear now that Vonnegut has also been relating his autobiography through the anecdotes and tidbits he interlaces within his books, and that he considers the lives of his friends and family as somehow miming changes and upheavals in the world at large. In his latest books there is a great deal of *Vonnegutiana* —how his mother committed suicide; how his only sister and her husband died within hours of each other (she of cancer, he of drowning); and he "inherited" their three children; how his son Mark was "cured" of schizophrenia by megavitamins; how one son became a goat farmer in Haiti and another a Hollywood joke writer; how his daughters have striven to avoid the spotlight of fame and be good, and how they and his wife took to "born-again" Christianity; and how he meanwhile divorced, battled to give up bourbon and butts, aged. It's a curious photo album he presents, compassionate but bittersweet.

Slapstick (1976) (so named, Vonnegut says, because of its "grotesque situational poetry") is just such a melange. *Slapstick*, he says, "is about what life feels like to me"; and he dedicates it to Laurel and Hardy, those "two angels of my time" whose fundamental joke "was that they did their best with every test." In some indeterminate future in Skyscraper National Park on Manhattan, "The Island of Death," twins Wilbur and Eliza attempt to solve the problem of American loneliness and the breakup of the extended family. As Eliza complains, "What civilized country could be interested in a hell-hole like America where everybody takes such lousy care of their own relatives?" In *Cat's Cradle*, Bokonon defined a true *karass* to consist of those on the same wavelength, as opposed to a *granfaloon*, which is a false *karass*—like, say, a gaggle of Hoosiers claiming kinship simply because they all hail from Indiana. Here Vonnegut proposes giving Americans new names that instantly accredit them to extended families—like Lee Razorclam-13 Zappa and Carlos Daffodil-11 Villavicencio. *Heigh-ho!*

In *Jailbird* (1979), Vonnegut returned to his old haunts—sin and guilt, mistakes and ironies. Walter F. Starbuck, despite having been a Young Communist at Harvard, is appointed President Nixon's Special Adviser on Youth Affairs and becomes embroiled in Watergate as a very minor player. Imprisoned, he is most taken by the Sermon on the Mount and says he should have sent this telegram to his boss: "YOUNG PEOPLE STILL REFUSE TO SEE THE OBVIOUS IMPOSSIBILITY OF WORLD DISARMAMENT AND ECONOMIC EQUALITY. COULD BE FAULT OF NEW TESTAMENT (QUOD VIDE)." His wife Ruth takes a rather pessimistic view: "She believed that all human beings were evil, by nature, whether tormentors or victims, or idle standers-by. They could only create meaningless tragedies, she said, since they weren't nearly intelligent enough to accomplish all the good they meant to do. We were a disease, she said, which had evolved on one tiny cinder in the universe, but could spread and spread." Ruth's toast echoes Woody Allen: "Here's to God Almighty, the laziest guy in town." Bag lady Mary Kathleen O'Looney just shrugs: "It's all such crap. I find this magazine called *People* in garbage cans, but it isn't about people. It's about crap."

Starbuck worries about what we are to do about all this "crap." After recalling Julie Nixon's reply when asked about her father, "He still has his sense of humor," Starbuck complains:

> "You know what is finally going to kill this planet?"
> "Cholesterol!" said Frank Ubriasco.
> "A total lack of seriousness," I said. "Nobody gives a damn anymore about what's really going on, what's going to happen next, or how we ever got into such a mess in the first place."

But Starbuck eventually gives in, tells another joke himself, and sits. *Jailbird* is a sad book, a reflection on how little we have learned from, or implemented, the Sermon on the Mount —or The Book of Bokonon.

In *Deadeye Dick* (1982) Vonnegut returned to the theme of violence, more specifically the gun culture promoted by the National Rifle Association. We are back once again in Midland City where Deadeye Dick is a twelve-year-old boy (*née* Rudy) whose father teaches him to shoot and says, "My boys will never have a shooting accident because their respect for weapons has become part of their nervous systems." But Deadeye/Rudy blows away a neighbor. "What, incidentally," he shrugs, "was a pregnant mother of two doing operating a vacuum cleaner on Mother's Day? She was practically asking for a bullet between the eyes, wasn't she?" As the victim's husband writes to the papers:

> My wife has been killed by a machine which should never have come into the hands of any human being. It is called a firearm.

It makes the blackest of all human wishes come true at once, at a distance: that something dies.

There is evil for you.

We can't get rid of mankind's fleetingly wicked wishes. We can get rid of the machines that make them come true.

I give you a holy word: Disarm.

At the end a "friendly" neutron bomb devastates Midland. "You want to know something," says Deadeye, "The Dark Ages —they haven't ended yet."

Galapagos (1985) is another end-of-the-world saga narrated a million years down the road by Kilgore Trout's son. After war breaks out between those perennial superpowers, Peru and Ecuador, Trout tells how a scrubby bunch on the ill-fated cruise ship *Bahia de Darwin* wash up on the Galapagos Islands and end up feeding the "vampire finches." Death here is a wry joke. Confronted with another fresh corpse, Trout shrugs, "Oh, well —she wasn't going to write Beethoven's Ninth Symphony anyway." *Galapagos*, of course, is really about today, and Trout an obvious Vonnegut stand-in. "The Era of Hopeful Monsters," Trout calls our times, because of "those great big brains capable of being cruel for cruelty's sake." He goes on: "As long as they did not use nuclear weapons, nobody was going to give the right name to all the killing that had been going on since the end of the Second World War, which was surely World War Three." Looking backward a million years later, Trout echoes Twain, "I feel like apologizing for the human race." Elsewhere, Vonnegut has spoken approvingly of radio comedians Bob and Ray: "Man is not evil, they seem to say. He is just too hilariously stupid to survive." *Galapagos*, too, details the effects of this stupidity.

In *Bluebeard* (1987), Vonnegut resurrects Abstract Expressionist Rabo Karabekian, "a minor character in *Breakfast of Champions*, whose parents survived the first attempted genocide of the century, the slaughter by Turkey of its Armenian citizens before the First World War." As Rabo observes, "The problems presented by [genocide] are purely industrial: how to kill that many big, resourceful animals cheaply and quickly, make sure that nobody gets away, and dispose of mountains of meat and bones afterward." Recounting the good old days when Americans referred to arms manufacturers as "merchants of death," he says:

> Nowadays, of course, just about our only solvent industry is the merchandising of death, bankrolled by our grandchildren, so that the message of our principal art forms, movies and television and political speeches and newspaper columns, for the sake of the economy, simply has to be this: War is hell all right, but the only way a boy can become a man is in a shoot-out of some kind, preferably, but not necessarily, on a battle-field.

Karo sighs: "Nowadays of course you can buy a machine gun with a plastic bayonet for your little kid at the nearest boutique." Even our vaunted artistic freedom is a double-edged sword. "Who is more to be pitied," Karo asks, "a writer bound and gagged by policemen or one living in perfect freedom who has nothing more to say?" Our best minds now are paid to make money, not Renaissance palaces and works of art. Like Bluebeard, Rabo forbids his wife to look in his forbidden chamber —in which lurks, not murdered ex-wives but a huge, 8' × 64' painting of the idyllic landscape of Europe when the sun came up the day the Second World War ended. The canvas is filled with thousands of concentration camp victims, soldiers, ordinary citizens. It is a colorful but gruesome Disneyland where "nobody is cute," but it is also personal and idiosyncratic: "The bombardier clinging to my leg: that's his face, as I remember it. These two Estonians in German uniforms are Laurel and Hardy. This French collaborator here is Charlie Chaplin. These two Polish slave laborers are Jackson Pollock and Terry Kitchen." A Japanese is stuck in a corner "because [they] were as responsible as the Germans for turning Americans into a bunch of bankrupt militaristic fuckups—after we'd done such a good job of being sincere war-haters after the First World War." Rabo's vision suggests Picasso's massive *Guernica,* which also reminds us of the value of art to portray our terrible mistakes and deliberate slaughters. At the end we are chilled by the echoes of Voltaire's gulled Candide, "Oh, happy Meat. Oh, happy Soul. Oh, happy Rabo Karabekian."

But we cannot be happy at what we have been reminded of.

. . .

Like Twain and Bierce, Vonnegut has also employed the popular press to lambaste contemporary idiocy; and his satirical
essays on a variety of topics, including violence and humor,
afford a revealing self-analysis. In recalling the gallows humor
of Middle Europe he has said, "Laughing or crying is what a
human being does when there's nothing else he can do. My
books are essentially mosaics made up as a whole bunch of tiny
little chips and each chip is a joke." Elsewhere, he has observed, "The only way to get a belly laugh, I've found, is to
undermine a surface joke with more unhappiness than most
mortals can bear."

This process he discovered again in Biafra during the last
days of its ill-fated independence. After meeting Odumegwu,
the Biafran chief, Vonnegut noted:

> His humor was gallows humor, since everything was falling
> apart around his charisma and air of quiet confidence. His humor
> was superb.
>
> Later, when we met his second-in-command, General Philip
> Effiong, he, too, turned out to be a gallows humorist. Vance said
> this: "Effiong should be the number-two man. He's the second
> funniest man in Biafra."
>
> Jokes. Miriam was annoyed by my conversation at one point,
> and she said scornfully, "You won't open your mouth unless you
> can make a joke." It was true. Joking was my response to misery
> I couldn't do anything about.

Vonnegut's dark jokes have caused him to be tucked neatly
beneath the Grand Umbrella of Black Humor with Joseph Heller, Terry Southern, and Philip Roth, among others. Though he
objects to this classification (just as earlier he objected to being
labeled a "sci-fi" writer), he does admit to juggling the absurd
and the pitiful, the trivial and the tragic. In "Why They Read
Hesse," he observed: "Hesse is no black humorist. Black humorists' holy wanderers find nothing but junk and lies and idiocy wherever they go. A chewing gum wrapper or a used
condom is often the best they can do for a Holy Grail." An

interesting comment, and one that suggests his wry awareness of the limited materials of contemporary America.

In laughter, critic Richard Shickel has observed, Vonnegut has found "an analgesic for the temporary relief of existential pain." Yet it seems that it is precisely the nature of the relief that troubles him the most. After the 1972 Republican Convention nominated Richard Nixon, Vonnegut sighed, "Clowning doesn't throw off the timing or slow down cruel social machinery. In fact, it usually serves as a lubricant." By diverting attention, comedy may serve to relieve frustration only too well. "I am in favor of jokes," says the fearsome Captain Concasseur of Graham Greene's *The Comedians*, "They have political value. Jokes are a release for the cowardly and impotent." Politicians often use the humorist to distract an angry electorate. As laughter consumes rage, the politician chortles. Political cartoonist Herblock said he was shocked when Nixon henchmen Erlichman and Haldeman requested the originals of his most savage caricatures of them to hang in their private offices. Jokes without teeth.

Such irony must depress a satirist devoted to laughing the rascals out of town, and Vonnegut is too much the concerned observer to take easy satisfaction in making his fellow Americans laugh—he also wants them to do something. Part of his dilemma also is that he is a satirist with heart. Even the few real Vonnegut villains seem victims; and he himself sometimes seems to view evil as a product of poor conditioning. But for all of his Pavlovian determinism, Vonnegut comes across most as an old-fashioned humanist. Like Lardner, he really does want people to act better. But if there are few real villains in Vonnegut, there is certainly violence—Ice-nine, firebombing, racism, warmongering. Above all, he has been a mordant commentator on the violence inherent in certain diseased ideas. For Vonnegut, violence includes, not only genocide, but the spirit of revenge or the subtler but still venomous code of Hemingway. In that it is allowed, planned, encouraged, and too often rewarded, he sees violence as our mutual curse; and what bothers him, in particular, is the tedious repetition. So, he argues, if man cannot be weaned, cajoled, or ridiculed away from violence, then at the very least he should be disarmed.

It has been observed, dismissively, that Vonnegut's work has

a comic-strip simplicity, in that his characters are sketched
rather than drawn and speak in quips more appropriate to cartoon balloons than to real people. But this deliberate manner-
ism is designed to maintain a fast pace and keep the reader
interested and make his ideas more palatable. For the poor, the
powerless, and the young (if that is not tautological), Vonnegut
holds a certain charm because his outrageousness (and outrage)
seems to reflect the truth of their world. Vonnegut's humor may
be a victim's humor, but it is that of an angry victim who refuses
to bow down before the lion. Much of his humor, also, is aimed
at our politicians' rather clumsy attempts to deceive through
euphemism or doublespeak; and Vonnegut's highly stylized
narrative technique is, like Orwell's, an effort to avoid rhetorical flourish and tell the unadorned truth.

Consider this "Address to Graduating Class at Bennington
College, 1970":

> What actually happened when I was twenty-one was that we
> dropped the scientific truth on Hiroshima. We killed everybody
> there.
>
> I suggest that you work for a socialist form of government.
> Free Enterprise is much too hard on the old and the sick and the
> shy and the poor and the stupid, and on people nobody likes.
> They just can't cut the mustard under Free Enterprise. They
> lack that certain something that Nelson Rockefeller, for instance,
> so abundantly has.

Or this beginning to another article:

> If I were a visitor from another planet, I would say things like
> this about the people of the United States: "These are ferocious
> creatures who imagine that they are gentle. They have experi-
> mented in very recent times with slavery and genocide."

To be sure, there is deliberate shock value in such overstated
declarations. But, in focusing on deception, Vonnegut echoes
Richard Hofstadter's concern over our historical amnesia. Like
Twain's Little Satan (another extraterrestrial visitor), he is suggesting that if we could but remove ourselves imaginatively
from our climate of violence, then we, too, would be more appropriately appalled.

Vonnegut is a hard man to pigeonhole. Like the early Twain, he can be wildly outrageous, spouting jests in sometimes questionable taste or, like the late Twain, turn to imaginative time-trips and dark fables. Like Bierce, he can be venomous, especially toward those he judges most responsible for our sorry state. His obvious concern for common decency suggests Ring Lardner, but his voice is so much more in his work than Lardner's is in his that the comparison breaks down at any further level. Reluctant to accept the depressing litany of our wars as but the inevitable outcropping of instinctual aggression, Vonnegut has taken up the problem of violence as the subject of his dark humor in order to shame the warlords. In this battle against man's basest instincts, anything goes; he may ridicule or cajole, doodle, or compose graffiti. While his humor may lack the subtlety of Lardner, the fury of Bierce, or the rich detail of character and locale we find in Twain, its intelligence makes it most valuable. In putting violence up to the light, Vonnegut is exhorting us to change—so that we will not perish.

In this light, Vonnegut exposes himself to an American audience wary of prophets, however well-meaning, and nervous about self-examination, however necessary. Whatever his serious intent, the humorist must still amuse—or he will lose his audience. Fortunately, despite his often grim subjects, Vonnegut still manages to find ways to make us laugh; and it is a mark of his success that the import of his books is felt long after the jokes are forgotten. Vonnegut seems to have grabbed hold of the many-pronged dilemma of violence with the firmest grasp. His attacks appear more consistent than Twain's; his compassion more attractive than the misanthropy of Bierce; and his openness healthier than the mask of Ring Lardner. Though the temptation to despair is always unusually powerful, the slim hope that Vonnegut holds out in the face of depressing realities does seem admirable and, in the last analysis, necessary.

· · ·

Vonnegut's popular success story is itself a writerly Horatio Alger tale fraught with irony, as if his beloved sci-fi writer Kilgore Trout were to win the National Book Award. Having Vonnegut hobnobbing with top physicists and space-people is like inviting Mata Hari to the Pentagon. His is the scuffed sneaker of American humor; for, like most great comedians, Vonnegut is a true slapstick subversive, offering the view of the steamroller from the flat of the back. Since Vonnegut is Vonnegut (and still writing), there can be no sure way of predicting the direction his work will take. Certainly, in his ridicule of our penchant for guns and violence and the plastic that masquerades as our public culture, this "old fart with his Pall Malls" has proven himself a valuable gadfly of America's most dangerous folkways.

Yet.

Yet something still troubles him. "After I'm gone," he says, "I don't want my children to have to say about me what I have to say about my father: 'He made wonderful jokes, but he was such an unhappy man.' " He is aware of the many ironies. This anti-war activist also has said he wants a military funeral with the whole shebang—"the bugler, the flag on the casket, the ceremonial firing squad, the hallowed ground [because] it will be a way of achieving something I've always wanted more than anything, the unqualified approval of my community." Beneath this, and many Vonnegut ripostes, is much unhappiness. His particular despair seems to stem from the fear that our world is veering toward Armageddon. Confronted by such bleak prospects, Vonnegut is too intelligent to profess hope and too honorable to lie—so he jokes.

But "jokes can be noble," as he told the congregation of Manhattan's St. Clement's Episcopal Church on Palm Sunday, 1980. "Laughs are exactly as honorable as tears."

As Stan Laurel would say to his tie-twiddling chum Ollie, "Right . . . *Right* you are."

ROUND SIX

Celluloid Pun(ch)sters: The Silent Clowns

In the language of screen comedians four of the main grades of laugh are the titter, the yowl, the belly laugh, and the boffo. The titter is just a titter, the yowl is a runaway titter. Anyone who has ever had the pleasure knows all about a belly laugh. The boffo is the laugh that kills. An ideally good gag, perfectly constructed and played, would bring the victim up this ladder of laughs by cruelly controlled degrees to the top rung, and would then proceed to wobble, shake, wave, and brandish the ladder until he groaned for mercy. Then after the shortest possible time out for recuperation, he would feel the first wicked tickling of the comedian's whip once more and start up a new ladder.
        —James Agee, "Comedy's Greatest Era"

Agee got it—that is, he got what every good comic already knows: that laughter is not only a release from pain but often includes pain. "You have to put in some rough stuff if you want to make them laugh," said Mack Sennett, the Kaptain of the Keystone Kops. "Only exaggeration up to the nth power gets the real shout. You have to spill soup on dignity to get a real burlesque laugh." So the boffo, "the laugh that kills," brought its victim up the "ladder of laughs" until he "groaned for mercy" before feeling again "the first wicked tickling of the comedian's whip." Comedy includes violation—and maybe it is that simple. We all know children who say as you tickle them, "Stop it—stop it, I can't stand it anymore," but if you stop they are right away poking you and begging for more. So it seems we, too, can't get enough of the laugh that kills.

Agee was not only an enthusiast, but an enthusiast with
brains and a subtle sensibility. In discovering "beauties of
comic motion hopelessly beyond the reach of words," Agee
pointed out, the silent clowns made "a poem that everybody
understands," and no account of American humor could be
complete without mention of that strange, marvelous poem.
From 1912 to 1928, the broad, raucous antics of these comics
delighted the Mob-God, filling nickelodeons and movie
houses, while genteel reviewers and social critics tsk-tsked
about their violence and vulgarity. But the comics didn't worry
"message"; they were interested in laughs, and pie-throwing
and arse-kicking did the trick there. For the title "Clown of
Clowns" there were many claimants: Sennett, the self-proclaimed "King of Comedy"; Fatty Arbuckle, "the Pagliacci of
the meringue," as theatre-owner Sid Grauman called him;
pasty-faced Harry Langdon, that helpless lump of androgynous
baby flesh; Harold Lloyd, the Perpetual Freshman; Buster Keaton, of course, "The Great Stone Face"; and "The Divine Char-
lot" himself, Charlie Chaplin. Whoever was king, there were
many Crown Princes in that golden age of comedy.

The thrust of this comedy, of course, was slapstick, whose
long roots are tangled in farce, and that is something Americans
certainly did not invent. Farce has a noble, or at least ancient,
tradition. Albert Bermel describes farce as an ancient form of
merrymaking that "deals with the worst one can dream or dread
[and] is cruel, often brutal, even murderous." The Greek pan-
tomimists, he reminds us, came on stage equipped with giant
phalluses made from inflated animal bladders dangling from
their belts. With these, they whacked each other and waved
coyly and obscenely at the audience—sex as slapstick. And if
Mel Brooks' two-thousand-year-old-man is to be believed, our
ancestors were "slapsticking" even further back. In Brooks'
History of the World, Part One, one caveman does a lame
stand-up routine in front of his yawning family—until a dino-
saur comes along and eats him, at which point they howl. So
farce, like the poor, we have always had with us. Certainly, it
sticks its grotesque head up at odd moments everywhere—
from Terence's "silly stuff" to Shakespeare's "wise-fools" and
Cervantes' Knight of the Sorrowful Countenance, from the

French "farceurs" and Italian "zannis" to English music halls and American minstrel shows, vaudeville, burlesque, and, of course, silent movies.

In medieval times, at Punch-and-Judy shows, puppets employed sticks to whack each other over the head to show anger or punctuate their jokes. When this kind of "bonking" comedy was brought to the stage, players sensibly adopted a less lethal double-paddle "slap-stick" to make the comic *whap-whap* without damaging the live goods. One account of a Grimaldi performance in 1843 described the following:

> Punch is real fighter; he beats the Negro, kicks the doctor out of doors, knocks down the Constable, whips his own dear Judy, hangs the Hangman, and is finally carried off by old Nick.

What we now refer to as "slapstick" embraces all kinds of physical comedy (with or without sticks), from the face-slapping of Abbott and Costello and the pie-throwing frenzies of Laurel and Hardy, to the bop-bop-re-bop nose-bonking of The Three Stooges and Our Gang Comedies, from the whopping of television's early puppet show, Kukla, Fran, and Ollie to the mugging of Martha Raye, Red Skelton, and Jerry Lewis, from the casual cartoon violence of Tom and Jerry and the Roadrunner's pancaking of poor Wile E. Coyote to the Samurai excesses of the late John Belushi and his fellow Saturday Night Live muggers. At circuses, we still find clowns booting each other around and slipping on banana peels; and even if we know that they don't really get "hurt," we must recognize that slapstick is violent comedy and that, whatever its roots, it still works: we laugh.

But the American roots of slapstick are more obscure. We know something of the Maypole doings of Merrymount (which took place *despite* the Puritans) because Thomas Morton, that disreputable friend of the redman, wrote it down. We know something of the the rough-and-tumble saloon shows of the Wild West, not only from the notices and posters that appeared in the local press, but also from comtemporary accounts, memoirs, and scenes in novels like *Huckleberry Finn*. We know something of the nineteenth-century minstrel shows in which

Mister Bones, Tambo, and the Interlocutor "played the dozens," (that is, insulted each other in humorous ways); and we
know something of the "revues" and "burlesque" acts that became so popular with immigrants. But there is little on paper
(how could there be?) of the actual routines. What we do know
is that there was a tradition of broad physical comedy—in
music halls, makeshift theatres, and outdoor tents (P. T.
Barnum was in on that). We know that the tradition started
before the Civil War, flourished through the turn of the century,
and carried on, nostalgically, right up through the 1920s. And
we know it because so many early film comics, such as Arbuckle, Keaton, and W. C. Fields, were schooled in that tradition,
and we can see the fruits of those slapstick techniques in their
films.

Yes, *see*, which is very important. Because of movie prints,
we can see just what it was our grandparents were laughing at
and laugh ourselves. There was a secret—and a glory. "When a
silent comedian got hit on the head," Agee pointed out, "it was
his business to be as funny as possible physically, without the
help or the hindrance of words. So he gave us a figure of
speech, or rather a vision, for loss of consciousness." And when
we think of slapstick today, we think of artists like Chaplin and
Keaton, or those great comedy teams who managed to be funny
despite having to talk—Laurel and Hardy of course, the Marx
Brothers, and that other great comic duo, W. C. Fields and his
gin bottle.

.   .   .

Right off the bat, there was something funny/peculiar as well
as funny/ha-ha about film—something very special. First of all,
like photography, film caught something and provided a record
—a precarious one perhaps, but still a record. Secondly, it was
a supremely democratic art. All you needed was to put another
nickel in the nickelodeon. Soon, improved projection techniques allowed expansion from postcard-size flickerings to
giant screens on which film actors loomed truly larger than life.
Stars were born who seemed to shine more brightly than super-
novas. (Even Al Capone was said to have wept at Fatty Arbuc-

kle's Chicago comeback.) Also, and perhaps most importantly, the cinema had an advantage over "litter-cha," in that its audience no longer had to be literate to follow the thread of a joke —they merely had to keep their eyes open. So cinema became our most popular art. Almost overnight it seemed, movies and moviemakers insinuated themselves (and their values) into ghettoes and backyards, bayous and backwoods cabins, in a way the written word (except for the Bible, and perhaps Twain and Dickens) never had. Whereas thousands had chuckled over the doings of a Tom Sawyer or Huck Finn, millions now guffawed at the antics of Lloyd and Ben Turpin, sighed at the dilemmas of Chaplin's Little Tramp and the resourceful Mabel Normand, and hissed villains such as Matt Swain and Chester Conklin.

Because the first films were silent, the comedy was slapstick, *had* to be slapstick, and many of the comics—Turpin, Chaplin, and Stan Laurel (Chaplin's understudy with *Fred Karno's London Comedians*)—were imports from English music halls where they had mastered the stable of arse-kicks, cane-trips, and pratfalls. But, despite the influx of "limey" comics (and "immigrant" producers like Adolph Zukor and Joe Schenk), the product remained geared to the American market and the game was played according to the rules by which American comedy has always operated, namely glorification of the underdog and ridicule of pomp and circumstance. Sennett's Keystone Kops are fools rather than authority figures, fat fools at that (all the easier for the Little Tramp to scurry between their legs), and his women, unfeeling, pompous snobs who deserve to have their parties ruined.

In the production of these early comedies, writers (novelists, scriptwriters, what-have-you) huddled far down the totem pole of respect. The dictatorial Sennett even forbade his writers to use the studio cafeteria because he thought food would make their minds soggy. Sennett ignored writers anyway and depended on improvisation, often just suggesting a situation (a day at the beach, for instance, or a night in jail) and expecting the comics themselves to "milk" the running gag with appropriate thrills, chills, and spills. It was a dangerous business. All in day's work, Fatty Arbuckle fell down stairs, banged his head on open bureau drawers, slammed doors on his fingers, and

cracked heads with other comics. Some actors (Lloyd, Arbuckle, and of course, Chaplin and Keaton), graduated to "auteur-
ship" and even to their own studios. But as long as they kept to
two-reelers with running times of approximately twenty-five
minutes, these actor-directors were content just to dip into their
reservoir of gags. It was only in the twenties, when the public
began to crave feature films, that writers were finally needed—
and used. So, in dealing with these early films, one finds oneself describing performances rather than scripts.

There are other problems as well. A film, of course, is only a
series of celluloid strips that project images; the early celluloid
was particularly fragile and many have been burnt, discarded,
turned to dust or otherwise lost. Furthermore, while it seems
every video store in America carries several copies of *Rambo,
Part Twelve* and the various installments of *Dirty Harry* (speaking of the humor of violence), to find a Buster Keaton film or,
God help us, a Fatty Arbuckle is a harder chore. In writing
about these old classics, then, I find myself unsure what to
gloss. I offer a sampling—and how I hope the reader will be
angry at me for omitting favorites! What I have tried to emphasize is how much of the method and substance of our literary
comedians carried over into American film comedy. In these
early films we meet up with that same odd amalgam of violence
and humor—the pie-in-the-face and the exploding cigar, of
course—but also the violence of farce in which, to borrow Eric
Bentley's apt phrase, "hostility enjoys and feeds on itself."
Many of these films revel in hostility of one sort or another—
the rich toward the poor, one sex toward the other, the powerless toward the powerful—masked by much funny business, to
be sure. Comedy, as Chaplin and Keaton were fond of saying,
is serious business; and we enjoy, perhaps even need, to see a
big fat waiter kicked in the seat of the pants.

.   .   .

It was Mack Sennett who started the ball rolling. From 1913 to
1916 Sennett ran about the only comedy game in town. He
attracted (or seduced) many of the great comics to his crude
studio in Edendale, California—Arbuckle, Chaplin, Laurel,

Langdon, Lloyd, Swain, Conklin, etc. Sennett's style was pure
slapstick: the madcap chase, the arbitrary destruction of property, and an all-out assault on notions of dignity and exclusivity.
To Sennett, speed was not of the essence—it *was* the essence.
He slowed the cranking of the hand-held camera to create a fast
pace and, in Agee's memorable phrase, "made the screen dance
like a witches' Sabbath." Sennett's two-reelers were usually
completed in a less than a week; on one memorable day he took
Chaplin and Arbuckle out to a dance hall and canned "Tango
Tangles" in two hours. At Edendale, if some one had a funny
idea, the camera rolled—and kept rolling. Many actors worked
in over fifty films a year. Arbuckle—the greatest pie-slinger of
all time, the supreme grand lama of the meringue, as Gene
Fowler dubbed him for his dead-eyed, ambidextrous pie-
throwing—was Sennett's star, even more popular than Chaplin.

Sennett made scores of fast-paced shorts; but perhaps the
most important of his films was that 1914 six-reeler, *Tillie's
Punctured Romance*, featuring Chaplin as "The City Slicker"
with the versatile Mabel Normand as his girlfriend and the
formidable Marie Dressler as a ridiculously coy farmer's daughter. The story line hinges on that second-oldest of all evils—
money: Dressler's father has it, and Charlie courts the ugly
daughter to get it, a simple enough plot. But the film is propelled by a frantic pace, and we find ourselves careening back
and forth from farmhouse to city, from jail house to ballroom.
As Charlie courts Dressler, Sennett, in true slapstick style, exploits the disparity between Dressler, this vast Brunhilde, and
the diminutive Charlie. She knocks him "daintily" over a
fence, dangles him in her arms on the dance floor, and rolls him
about like a rag doll in amorous clinches. Charlie, of course,
steals Dressler's money to elope with Sweet Mabel, only to
renege when he learns Dressler is about to inherit a fortune.
The burlesque continues when Dressler (who is wearing what
must be the most comical hat in all of filmdom—a Viking-like
furry concoction with Mouseketeer ears) gives a "high-society"
ball, where Mabel appears as a maid, and soon jealous Charlie
is involved in a fight in the kitchen, punching, tripping, arse-
kicking and jumping on his hapless adversary—a fight funny
because so unmerciful and clever. Eggs are thrown, guns dis-

charged, Rich Uncle resurrected—*oops*, there goes the inheritance—but by now Mabel wants no part of Charlie, either. So the Keystone Kops appear (who knows why—this is Sennett, remember?), flying around corners, skidding off with Dressler into the drink, and piling up on one another like circus clowns. THE END . . . lights, please . . . open the exits.

Now there's a lot of interesting things about *Tillie*, not the least being Charlie's acrobatics and Dressler's mugging. But Chaplin shows little of the charm he was later to develop as his own "Little Tramp," the funny bits seem isolated and unconnected, beads without a string, so there is little sense of wholeness or building, and the end is pure chaos. Sennett may have been the first; but he was certainly not the best; Sennett slapstick was often slapdash. (Perhaps we shouldn't be surprised. A plaque over his desk said: "The extent of the intelligence of the average public mind is eleven years old. Moving pictures should be made accordingly.") It would be left to others, most notably Keaton and Chaplin, to alchemize such slapstick into art.

                    .   .   .

Charlie Chaplin was not an immediate star—nor was he particularly appealing. In the early Sennett productions he proved himself a very good physical comic working tried-and-true slapstick routines, but critics complained about his malice and cruelty. After viewing *The Rink* (1916), Heywood Broun wrote: "Gone is the comedy of submission, and in its place has grown up a comedy of aggression." Certainly, there is a lot of violence in Chaplin's early films. In *Work* (1915), for instance, Charlie and his boss, as interior decorators, set about a delirium of destruction. In *The Pawnshop* (1916), Charlie opens a customer's watch and peers in like a surgeon, only to mangle and crush it with a mallet before returning it with a shrug. Some critics viewed such destruction as a satire on the bourgeois class. But this seems dubious—all Sennett films were brouhahas. Whatever Chaplin's thoughts on their content (and he *always* thought) their slapdash nature rankled him, as did Sennett's insistence on just getting it "in the can."

With Chaplin's own films at Essanay and Mutual and after, we see an artist developing—*thinking* and attempting not just to make people laugh but to make a coherent statement about the evils he felt and saw. The Little Tramp, for instance, is just that—little and a tramp—at odds with the world, or rather with the world that refuses to appreciate him; and it is a hardscrabble existence he leads. Chaplin kept refining the Tramp's image to play off against the injustice around him. Note all the eating in Chaplin films; he and his various gamins always seem hungry and desperate to know where their next meal is coming from. There is a double edge to the best of Chaplin's films, a sorrow and pity mixed in with the slapstick, even in such relatively early films as *The Vagabond* (1916) in which he portrays a poverty-stricken violinist and *Easy Street* (1917) in which he plays a reluctant policeman surrounded by voracious slum dwellers.

In real life, Chaplin was never comfortable with fame. Even in Hollywood he preferred eating at automats because "he couldn't bear masses of knives and forks on the table, and the magnificence of headwaiters gave him a feeling of inferiority." Once, after being mobbed by admirers, he lamented to a friend:

> But Tommy, isn't it pathetic that these people should hang around me and shout "God bless you Charlie!" and want to touch my overcoat, and laugh and even shed tears. Why? Simply because I've cheered 'em up. God, Tommy, what kind of filthy world is this that makes people lead such wretched lives that if anybody makes 'em laugh they want to kneel down and touch his overcoat as though he were Jesus Christ raising 'em from the dead.

Chaplin insisted on not losing the common touch; and what is wonderful about Charlie's Tramp, with his baggy pants, dented bowler, oversized shoes and clever cane, is that he remains undaunted throughout and acts as if he expects to be loved and rewarded. The world *is* Charlie's oyster—even if there is no pearl. What we admire, what we love, is his courage; and we applaud his cheerful and ingenious resourcefulness. The world may be hard, even perverse, but Charlie will find a way to deflect its cruelty and set things right. Charlie refuses to believe it his fault that he has no money to buy food or that he is threatened by a huge cannibalistic prospector or has not been invited to the party. If the world will not appreciate or reward him, he can (and will) make a meal of a pea, slip through the arms and legs of a giant, or escape the clutches of a *klatch* of bouncers by elegantly roller-skating away. Caught out, in the right or no, Charlie's response is to slap his accuser's face. By its absurdity, the blow does not so much hurt (the Tramp is too small for that) as it ridicules the very notion of force. Yet it seems so much the appropriate response, we laugh.

Chaplin had as well a great physical talent. "The bastard was a ballet dancer," growled W. C. Fields. The demanding routines of the *Commedia dell'arte* had great influence on English music-hall performers. A good player was a rare, angelic creature who

> should possess and cultivate a variety of qualities. He had to be light on his feet and a skillful acrobat, for a good effect could be secured by tripping over something, by tumbling head over heels on receiving a blow, by suddenly leaping down beside, at the back of, in front of, or on top of someone who was passing beneath a window.

In the Sennett films, Chaplin utilized many *commedia dell'arte* tricks—swinging his leg coyly across a girl's lap or vaulting into the arms of a man about to hit him (tricks Harpo Marx would also later employ), sitting on a hot stove in *The Vagabond*, impaling himself on a helmet's pike in *Behind the Scenes*, sticking a fork into Chester Conklin's rump in *Those Love Pangs*, and thrusting a sword into Henry Bergman's capacious derriere in *His New Job*. When critics complained of the violence and vulgarity, Chaplin blamed it on his down-and-out Cockney upbringing: "The Elizabethan style of humor, this crude form of farce and slapstick comedy that I employed in my work was due entirely to my early environment and I am now trying to steer clear from this sort of humor and adopt myself to a more subtle and finer shade of acting."

But Chaplin utilized his physical gifts to create comedy of

character, and on screen he remained the busiest of all comedians. Where other comics might manage to squeeze a laugh or
two a minute out of a gag, Chaplin's resourceful genius could
milk five or six. Contemporary comics still speak in awe of his
timing and constant toppers. In *Shoulder Arms* (1918), for instance, Charlie's trench kit includes a mousetrap and a combi-
nation cheese-grater/back-scratcher for lice; he lights his
cigarettes with passing bullets and chalks up hits like a school-
boy. Even his titles were especially funny; asked how he had
captured thirteen Germans, Charlie shrugs, "I surrounded
them." But Chaplin never forgot the "low" roots of his comedy.
He seemed to recognize instinctually that it was a mongrel art;
for *A Dog's Life,* he spent days searching for the suitable mongrel. "What I want," he said, "is a dog that can appreciate a
bone and is hungry enough to be funny for his feed." The dog,
and the film, are wonderful. "Chaplin is vulgar . . . a buffoon,"
said Minnie Fiske, a critic for *Harper's Weekly,* pointing out
the obvious, "[but] vulgarity and distinguished art can exist
together."

What is clear, however, is that Chaplin was never comfortable with just slapstick. He wanted something more; and in his
own films he made more, wedding slapstick with melodrama to
bittersweet effect. In *The Immigrant* (1917), one of Chaplin's
finest Mutual releases, the tragic impinges on the comic. As the
film opens, aboard ship in steerage, we see the passengers eating at long tables while the ship's rolling keeps tipping their
food away—and we laugh nervously. When Charlie wins
money gambling, he gives it to a woman and her daughter
whose money has been stolen. In New York harbor, the "huddled masses" stare somberly at the Statue of Liberty while the
authorities throw ropes around them as if they are so many
herded cattle. Once ashore, Charlie finds a coin and enters a
restaurant where he finds the girl from the boat (she is wearing
a black handkerchief because her mother has died) and invites
her to dine with him. But the coin has slipped out through a
hole in his pocket; and when Charlie realizes he has no money,
he can only wince as he watches the huge waiter manhandle
another patron who cannot pay. When fortuitously, they are
joined by an artist who offers to hire them and pay for their

dinner, Charlie foolishly wrestles him for the check—and loses. But their savior gives the lovebirds an advance on their salary and they pay up and rush off to get married. *Immigrants* is not only a funny film, but a funny film with heart.

If *Immigrants* wedded Chaplin's two major themes, money (or food) and love, *The Gold Rush* (1925), a full-length feature inspired by the 1846 tragedy of the Donner Pass (where pioneers were reduced to cannibalism) melded those themes into an even more profound work of art, with an even more ominous subsurface. In *Gold Rush* Chaplin transfers the setting to Alaska (all that white snow and ice) where desperate men seek to make a killing out of the frozen earth. As Chaplin wrote in his *Autobiography*, "It is paradoxical that tragedy stimulates the spirit of ridicule [which] I suppose, is an attitude of defiance. We must laugh in the face of our helplessness against the forces of nature—or go insane." We see this tragedy—and this defiance—clearly in *Gold Rush*. In one of the more memorable scenes, Charlie and Big Jim have been driven by a snowstorm into the cabin of outlaw Black Larson. Since there is no food, so Larson sets out, but dies in an avalanche. To fend off starvation, Charlie cooks his shoes, imagining the laces as spaghetti, the nails as meat-bones, and shares his meal with Big Jim. But Charlie is not alone in fantasy; Big Jim dreams Charlie is a plump hen and pursues him around the cabin. The glorious thing that Charlie now does, on the screen, is to actually become a real chicken, ripe and plump as a Perdue roaster. We laugh the killer-laugh at what we are witnessing. When later, the cabin teeters on the edge of a precipice, this comic struggle of life and death truly becomes a comedy of the abyss.

Later, Charlie falls in love with a dance hall girl, for whom he prepares an elaborate dinner. She fails to show up, and he sneaks back to town, only to see her at another party. When the girl finally remembers, she visits and is touched by his elaborate preparations. But it is as if Charlie and the girl are sliding by each other on ice, and once again that odd but powerful coupling of food and love serves to wrench our hearts. In one memorable sequence, Charlie makes two bread-rolls dance like a can-can girl's legs; what begins as a trick soon becomes totally engrossing, and we are enchanted by this "Dance of the Buns."

Despite the "happy" ending (Charlie strikes it rich and bumps into the girl on board the ship home), the thrust of the film ("the funniest and saddest of all comedies," as Mildred Spain, reviewer for the *New York Daily News* called it), reminds us of the grim reality of money; and we think of that long after we have stopped laughing. To Chaplin's credit, his own poverty-stricken London childhood never left his mind or soul. *The Gold Rush*, at heart, is a poor boy's poignant version of happiness.

After the financial success of *The Gold Rush*, Chaplin was free to make quality films at his own pace. He wrestled for two years with *City Lights* (1931), which he called "A Comedy Romance in Pantomime." It is indeed something special (in much the same way as a "Blue-Period" Picasso), the greatest of Chaplin's socially-conscious films. "One of the things most quickly learned in theatrical work," Chaplin once observed, "is that people as a whole get satisfaction from seeing the rich get the worst of things. The reason for this, of course, is that nine-tenths of the people in the world are poor, and secretly resent the wealth of the other tenth." Chaplin certainly knew how to play upon this resentment—and tug at the heartstrings.

City Lights opens in a Manhattan park where politicians and society matrons are talking in *blah-blah* blurs (Chaplin's sly rejoinder to "talkies"). In this first marvelous satiric image, a bigwig draws the curtain to expose a Statue of Peace and Prosperity with the Tramp asleep in her arms. Charlie awakens and bows, flirts with the nude statue, salutes the flag (impaled on the sword of Peace), and leans against her face, seeming to thumb her (and his) nose at the onlookers. Soon after, Charlie escapes the wrath of the law and comes upon a girl who pins a flower on him and drenches him with a pan of water. We watch as Charlie, his face a pallette of emotion, slowly comprehends the girl is blind. The Poor Flower Girl is one thread.

The other thread is the Drunken Millionaire (played broadly by that old Sennett clown, Harry Myers) whom Charlie encounters trying to do away with himself by a pier. When Charlie tries to save Harry, he becomes entangled in the rope and stone with the noose around his own neck. He tumbles in the water only to be saved (sort of) by the drunk who slobbers over him and gives him money and a car, which Charlie uses to buy all the girl's flowers and give her a ride home. But the universe refuses to cooperate. Charlie is conked by a flower pot, and the millionaire sobers up only to reject his "best friend." To make money for an eye operation for the girl, Charlie agrees to substitute for a sick boxer. After his tough opponent rejects Charlie's bribe, he is forced into the ring, where he puts on a hilarious ring ballet—tying his gloves on backward, using the ropes as a trampoline, and hiding behind the huge referee before being knocked out—all for love, kindness, and $22.

Soon after, Charlie manages to get $100 from his drunk-again "friend" whom he kisses (in *City Lights* Charlie displays his most androgynous charms); but when thieves steal from the drunk, Charlie is accused, and he barely manages to get the money to the girl before the police (à la Keystone Kops) catch up to him. After his release, Charlie goes to her flower shop. Now the girl *sees;* and what she sees is a tramp tormented by boys with bean shooters, so she giggles. But when she notices him stoop to retrieve a flower from the gutter, she softens and rushes out to offer him a fresh flower. Their hands touch, ("It is you!" she says), and Charlie drops his head and offers a wistful smile. "It is enough to shrivel the heart to see," Agee has said, "it is the greatest piece of acting and the highest moment in movies."

It was no accident. Chaplin worked months at the ending, retake after retake, to get the effect he wanted. Unlike Sennett, Chaplin believed in the rhythm of an entire film, and he worked from his own script. Though it contains much physical comedy (the boxing scene alone is a *tour de farce*), *City Lights* has a poignancy that goes beyond slapstick. It was in fact a new type of film—a comedic romance, yes, but also a comedy with soul. "Comedy," Chaplin once mused, "is life viewed from a distance; tragedy, life in close-up." But he was not afraid to take *us* up close—to use comedy to highlight and emphasize hidden tragedies. So *City Lights* remains also a critique of the vagaries of capitalism. After the laughter is over, the thing we think about, again, is money. The drunk (who never works) has more money than he needs, and the flower girl has none. Charlie the Tramp, one of society's great unwashed, does all he can to rectify this injustice. As he observed in his autobiography, "The saddest thing I can imagine is to get used to luxury." Perhaps, as certain detractors have suggested, Chaplin was a simpleminded Communist; he was certainly, as *City Lights* clearly demonstrates, a simple-minded Christian.

Throughout his career, Chaplin continued to be socially conscious and skeptical of patriotism, which he considered "the greatest insanity the world has ever suffered." But he might have been thinking of Winston Churchill's wry dictum ("Had capitalism a heart, there would be no need for socialism.") when he made *Modern Times* (1935). In his script, Chaplin describes the film as "a story of industry, of individual enterprise—humanity crusading in the pursuit of happiness," and it is certainly all of that; but it is also a satire on the violence that modern industrialism inflicts on the masses. It is also a deliberately silent film. Despite the talkie era, Chaplin remained skeptical of words. "Dialogue, to my way of thinking," he said, "always slows action because action must wait upon words." In *Modern Times* he set out to show critics and the public just how eloquent a silent film still could be. As Gerald Mast has observed, "The soul of comedy is the brain," and no one, except perhaps for Keaton, had a better brain for it than Chaplin.

Modern Times, for instance, begins with a brilliant montage (clock to sheep to workers to giant gears grinding—an image which suggests the workers are but cogs in some vast machine) before cutting to the Electro Steel Corporation's president piecing together a jigsaw puzzle in his glass-walled office while watching the assembly lines beneath him. An efficiency expert appears with an automated feeder for workers; and Charlie is plucked from the line to be strapped in as a guinea pig. At first the feeder works well, offering Charlie a sip of soup, a nibble of corn. But it soon goes haywire—the ear of corn thumps Charlie, soup cascades over his face, etc. Afterward, Charlie is caught on the assembly line and swallowed up by the machine. Spit out at last, he attacks the machine, only to be carted off to the loony bin.

On his release, Charlie finds himself swept up in a parade of angry unemployed men and women, so he swipes a red flag from a manhole (in a marvelous piece of invention) and ends up leading a "Red" march. When police attack, Charlie runs away, only to notice The Gamin (Paulette Goddard) apprehended for stealing a loaf of bread. He attempts to take the rap for her; then they both flee. Later, when Charlie becomes a night watchman, he and The Gamin spend a night in the toy department where Charlie roller-skates—at the edge of a precipice. Thieves come ("We aint burglars—we're hungry," they say), and the managers arrive to find Charlie asleep and arrest him. Free once again, Charlie joins The Gamin in a shack ("It's paradise!"), and goes back to work repairing machinery. But things get mucked up again when Charlie's fireman becomes enmeshed in the cogs of the machine. Nothing works in *Modern Times* —that is, nothing mechanical (and nobody powerful) works.

But what does work, and works excellently, is the simple human heart. At the end Charlie and The Gamin skip off together "the only two live spirits in a world of automatons," as Chaplin described them in his script notes, "playmates, comrades, two joyous spirits living by their wits. Both have an eternal spirit of youth and are absolutely unmoral [*sic*]." To be sure, the film is pastiche—both a romantic comedy and a satire of the "machine world" and of its Lord High Executioner, King Capitalism—but pastiche of a very high order. The violence that Chaplin is satirizing here (and in *City Lights*) is that of a heartless capitalism, which does not take pity on, or take care of, those who slip through the cracks (to employ Ronald Reagan's own slippery phrase). It *is* a cruel world without a safety net. It was no doubt films like *Modern Times* he was thinking of when Jean Cocteau observed that pity was the secret of Chaplin's art, "pity for himself, the tramp, for us, pity for the poor waif whom he drags after him to make her eat because she is hungry."

Chaplin's career did not end with *Modern Times*. He went on to parody Hitler in *The Great Dictator* (the greatest comic genius taking on the greatest evil genius of this century); to portray a bitter Bluebeard in *Monsieur Verdoux* (a comedy of murder!); and to offer a penultimate bow as an aging clown (with Buster Keaton) in *Limelight*. But the cruel realities of twentieth-century politics often struck too close to home. "Had

I known of the actual horrors of the concentration camps," he admitted, "I could not have made *The Great Dictator*; I could not have made fun of the homicidal insanity of the Nazi." Also, after World War II, the Cold War seemed to freeze America's collective heart. Such a climate offered little place for pity, or social conscience, and moviegoers opted for escapist fare. Chaplin, and his politics, fell out of favor. In his last years, "this hard, bright, ice creature," as his friend Tom Burke called him, retreated to a mountaintop chalet in Switzerland and brooded over the wayward ways of the world.

Chaplin's driving force, of course, was anger—*Chaplin's*, not Charlie's. Much has been made of the Little Tramp's charm and generosity of spirit and the pathos of his comic business. But as Chaplin became an incresasingly angry man and finally spoke out (on screen and in public), the American public came to resent and ultimately to reject his scolding social conscience. Charlie the sad clown with a heart of gold was just fine, but Chaplin the satirist who insisted on the evils of capitalism was a dangerous Communist. Yet it is precisely the anger that raises his films above those of Sennet, Lloyd, and others. When Charlie sabotages the machine in *Modern Times*, he is acting for all "machine-slaves"; and, as victims of the machine-culture ourselves, we sympathize. Like Twain, Chaplin utilized victim's humor rather than a spectator's humor so that we are asked not just to witness a violent act but to *feel* and condemn it. In *Monsieur Verdoux*, Chaplin has Verdoux say to the judge: "You wallow in murder. You legalize it. You adorn it with gold braid. You celebrate and parade it. Killing is the enterprise by which your system prospers—upon which your enterprise thrives." Chaplin despised violence. "More than machinery we need humanity," he insisted, "More than cleverness we need kindness and gentleness. Without these qualities, life will be violent and all will be lost." Asked what he would have said if called before the House Unamerican Activities Committee, Chaplin replied: "I'd have turned up in my tramp outfit— baggy pants, bowler hat and cane—and when I was questioned I'd have used all sorts of comic business to make a laughing stock of the inquisitors."

But can a comic also be an effective social thinker? Perhaps

Chaplin, in *Limelight,* was thinking of this dilemma when he has Buster Keaton say to Calvero-Chaplin, "The more you think, the less funny you become." Certainly, Calvero's leap into the drum skin marked Chaplin's farewell to farce. Keaton felt Chaplin took himself too seriously. "Sometimes," he wrote in *My Wonderful World of Slapstick,* "I suspect that much of the trouble he's been in started the first time he read he was a 'sublime satirist' and a first-rate artist." But, to the end and despite detractors, Chaplin refused to shut up. "All of my life I have always loathed and abhorred violence," he said, echoing Faulkner's Nobel Prize speech, simply if less eloquently. "Now I think the atom bomb is the most horrible invention of mankind. I think it is creating so much horror and fear that we are going to grow up a bunch of neurotics." But, like Twain, Chaplin will be known less for the bitterness of his last years than for his invention of that courageous Little Tramp, as tough as Huck, who survived the immigrant experience, World War I, the Roaring Twenties, and the hangover of the Thirties and still lives—twiddling his cane and waddling off in search of a fresh flower to give, a new wrong to right.

.   .   .

Unlike Chaplin, Buster Keaton, the other *so-*silent genius, had no real politics. He changed historical sides for *The General,* for instance, because the South had lost and he thought simply "[y]ou can't make a villain out of the South—you can always make villains out of Northerners." But, as pantomimist Marcel Marceau has pointed out, "Chaplin and Keaton were alike in that one was at odds with the police and Victorian society, the other was at odds with props, women or the absurdity of life itself. The first a Shakespearean fool, and the other a Greek or Roman mime philosopher or moralist." Such high praise always made Keaton squirm; Sir Charles and others could hobnob with royalty—he was content to stay plain old "Buster," just a clown. Oh, but Keaton was good—so very, very good; and in playing off the absurdity of life itself he did often seem as much stoic philosopher as clown. In Keaton films, the violence and outrage is total—both in the human and the natural worlds—from nasty gun-toting brothers and gangsters to torrents, earthquakes, and deadly waterfalls. And Keaton "faced" it all with that Great Stone Face. And what a face it is, all deadpan except for the eyes—those bruised, unblinking eyes staring out at the indignities the strange world keeps heaping on poor Buster. Indeed, the conspiracies that bedevil him seem so universal that we can only conclude that if there is a villain it must be God.

It was no accident that Samuel Beckett, that determined minimalist whose own decrepit old men and women in ashcans respond to the woes of their world with tragicomic quips, chose Keaton to act in his *Film* (1965). Both artists seem to accept an inheritance of the burdens of the doomed Sisyphus condemned to push a boulder up a mountain, only to have it roll back down —again and again, forever. Indeed, in *Seven Chances* (1924), Keaton carried the Sisyphus story to a new absurdity. He had his crew construct 1500 rocks, ranging from grapefruit-size to four-hundred-pounders measuring eight feet in diameter, and then had these runaway rocks pursue him down a mountainside. Indeed, in all his finest comic routines (aboard *The General*, for instance, or in *Steamboat Bill, Jr.*), Keaton overcomes one obstacle only to be confronted with another—and another. In this, Keaton seemed to understand instinctively that repetition is the soul of cinematic wit (heightened expectation that ends in a pratfall). In the actions and "re-actions" of his films, he "hearsed" and re-hearsed life's own frustrations. Maybe it seems rather "swell" to link Keaton with the likes of Beckett. Certainly, there have been plenty of other clowns—Milton Berle, Mel Brooks, Chaplin himself—who adored Buster for other reasons, and one can see why. For if Keaton is in one sense the greatest of our "existential comedians" (*well, excuse me!*), he is also one of the floppiest and funniest slapstickers of all time. Maybe the pie-in-the-face is the existential dilemma.

Chaplin's childhood, as we know, was hardly a piece of cake; his father was an alcoholic tenor who abandoned his family and died of cirrhosis at thirty-seven, his mother a manic-depressive often carted away to mental hospitals. Only by going on stage did Charlie manage to extricate himself from the morass of broken homes and depressing workhouses. But, for its oddity and sheer cruelty, Keaton's childhood was one of a kind. After literally crawling onstage as a baby, Buster joined his vaudevillian family in an act unrivalled in sheer violence even during those wild times. As one 1905 poster proclaimed: "Maybe you think you were handled roughly when you were a kid—Watch the way they handle Buster!" The act had something to do with training a child. Buster would hit his father Joe over the head with a broom handle (Joe wore a metal plate under his hat), and Joe would respond by throwing Buster about the stage like a bean bag and end by throwing him into the wings or orchestra pit, or even (on one notable occasion in New Haven) onto the laps of some rowdy Yale youths.

Buster soon earned for himself such doubtful sobriquets as "The Human Mop" and "Mister Black-and-Blue." One of his most successful gags was a long-delayed "Ouch!," which he would later utilize in his films. It was at this time, too, that Buster began to get laughs with his famous deadpan, and Joe would kick him even harder if he so much as smiled. "Face, face!" Joe would shout to get Buster to "Freeze the puss!" Joe was occasionally dragged before a judge and fined for breaking the child-labor laws, but he was never convicted of cruelty; no one could find any bruises on Buster. Nor did Buster ever speak of his father with bitterness but later gave Joe parts in his films —when Joe could manage to stay sober. "I was unique," Keaton later bragged, "the only hell-raising Huck Finn type in vaudeville."

Keaton emerged from this bizarre childhood with an amazing acrobatic agility coupled with fearlessness. Nobody, it was said, took a fall better than Buster Keaton. In 1917, at twenty-one, Buster left the act to work in vaudeville but was enticed by Fatty Arbuckle to join his New York-based Comique Film Corp. With characteristic curiosity, the first thing Keaton did was to take apart a film camera to learn how it worked—he wanted to *know* what lenses did, what kinds of trick shots you could do. Keaton was always intrigued with mechanics and machines; his films are full of Tin Lizzies, steamships, ocean liners, and (his favorites) locomotives.

Keaton learned much from Arbuckle; but his true genius was revealed in the marvelous films he imagined and devised for himself. As a farceur, Keaton soon proved to be an orchestra unto himself. His timing, in particular, was excellent; not only could he milk a gag for all it was worth, he became expert at building the audience's expectation of disaster before cleverly foiling it. In one especially dangerous stunt in *Steamboat Bill, Jr.*, the facade of a house falls on top of Buster, while he remains unscathed (deadpan, of course) with an open window surrounding him. In *Sherlock, Jr.* (1924), he plays pool with two gangsters who have juiced up a "13" ball with a high-explosive. After calmly putting away the other balls (without ever touching the "13"), Buster finally takes aim while the gangsters (and the audience) hold their breath—and the "13" slips quietly into a corner pocket. Buster, we learn, has substituted the regular "13" ball while pocketing the "hot" one, so that later, when the gangsters chase him, he can toss the explosive "13" to wreck their car. Thus the First Law of Slapstick is obeyed: *Nothing wasted, no prop before its time.* In all his best films there is a satisfying sense of closure.

Violence was not only a method but a subject for Keaton. In *Our Hospitality* (1923), for instance, Keaton parodies blood feuds as Twain did in *Huckleberry Finn.* Buster, as the last of the McKays, is coming home to claim his Southern estate via a rickety, amusing, toylike train that bounces over (and off) a very strange track. (How Keaton loved all forms of "loco"-motion! "The moment you give me a locomotive and things like that to play with," he said once, "as a rule I find something to get laughs out of it.") On the train he meets and falls in love with a young woman (played by his wife Natalie) of the dreaded Canfield clan; and the rest of the movie involves the attempts of the Canfields, *père* and *deux fils*, to do away with Buster without arousing the ire of the lovely Canfield *fille.*

Our Hospitality is replete with sight gags. Settlers throw rocks at the train in order to collect the wood the firemen throw back. When they can't move a mule from the tracks, the trainmen move the tracks instead. When Buster reaches the McKay "estate," the front door falls off and beams topple on him. While Buster is fishing, the dam blows, so he puts up an umbrella against the water cascading over him, thereby masking him from his assassins, just before a fish he has caught pulls him in—a typical series of connected visual puns creating the multipart gag of which he was such a master.

But it is love and death, that ironic odd couple, which dominate the film. The Canfields welcome Buster to "God's country" with pistols; a sign in their home proclaims "Love thy neighbor as thyself," while they are intent on making a sieve of him. Since their "code of honor" protects guests, Buster decides never to leave. But when Natalie plays "We'll Miss You When You're Gone," Buster can only offer his "stoneface" to her—and to us. In one of his better gags, Buster escapes disguised as a woman, then dresses up a horse in the same clothes to foil the Canfields. He jumps in the river and churns downstream until Natalie tries to haul him in and almost goes over the falls herself, only to be rescued by Buster in a brilliant stunt involving tricky logs, cascading falls, and slippery cliff walls. (Catch the many *only to's* which link the gags and stunts of these early films.) The young lovers beat it back to the house to be married by a kindly parson who scolds the Canfields as they storm in with guns drawn. Mutual disarmament ensues; but, in one last gag (and Keaton knows how to hit all the right stops—*one, two, three, four*—splat), Buster shakes out gun after gun, even from his stockings.

Our Hospitality contains the same kind of uneasy jokiness as Twain's treatment of the Grangerfords and Shepherdsons. The effect—and the affect—is the same; Keaton, like Twain, is ridiculing "the Southern code." In this, perhaps his most open attack on senseless violence, he is satirizing the moronic stupidity of the blood feud and his message is clear: Tread lightly but carry a big stick. A big slap-stick, that is.

Terrible things are always happening in Keaton's films: so why do we laugh? Maybe it has something to do with our expectations. If, as Bergson suggests, we find it funny when machines act like people (even "eating" people as in Chaplin's *Modern Times,* or seemingly operating with a mind of their own, as in Keaton's films), then we may also find it funny when humans behave mechanically. Certainly, the mechanical Keaton makes us laugh. With his supple body, he could pull off the most breathtaking stunts so as to appear but another version of those machines—trains, cars, and planes—that were always threatening him. At times there seemed something almost inhuman about Keaton. "Everything that he was and did bore out his rigid face and played laughs against it," Agee observed.

"When he moved his eyes, it was like seeing them move in a statue. His short-legged body was all sudden, machinelike angles, governed by a daft aplomb." In Keaton films, it often seems we are witnessing, not just man against machine, but mechanical man against automated machine, which suggests a truly farcical universe.

Keaton's cinematic technique encouraged this view. To be "honest," he refused to make cuts (sometimes at great expense), so we see a whole stunt with no "cheating." He also made frequent use of long shots to outline the gags he was performing, so that often the background resembles nothing so much as the stark, lunar landscape of George Herrimann's Coconimo County where Krazy Kat is eternally bopped by the bricks of her love object, Ignatz Mouse, who is in turn eternally threatened by the officious Offiser Pupp. It is as if the whole stage is on the moon. Keaton also employed huge props for his running gags. In *One Week* (1920), he assembles a prefab house using the wrong plans, only to learn it is (of course) on the wrong site. So then he drags the surrealist house across railroad tracks, where it gets stuck. When a train comes, Buster and his wife cover their faces and wince. But the train, running on a parallel track, misses the house. Buster and his wife hug—whereupon *another* train from the *opposite* direction crashes into the house. In *Cops* (1922), Buster rides his horsecart into the middle of the Policemen's Day Parade, only to catch an anarchist's bomb, which he uses to light his cigarette before casually throwing it over his shoulder and blowing up the reviewing stand. After a series of minor disasters in *The Boat* (1921), Buster finally hops onto and launches his boat—which slips quietly down into (and under) the water, so that our last sight is of Buster, also descending, until just his porkpie hat is left floating in the water. *Boffo!*

What these scenes have in common is the dark Keaton touch, which piles disaster on top of disaster. The effect is hilarious, but strange. Perhaps we laugh because we remember how we, too, have often tried hard and failed; and our laughter is wry acknowledgment that disaster is part of our birthright as well. Keaton's logic may be the logic of the absurd, but it is still a rigid logic. In *Sherlock, Jr.*, for instance, Buster falls asleep and enters his "dream picture," only to be kicked out; when he does manage to get in, the door of a house is firmly locked. Finally, on-screen as a splendidly-tuxedoed Sherlock Holmes, Jr., he becomes part and parcel of the dream logic of film itself with all its cuts and dissolves. He flees a desert to find himself suddenly in a jungle, dives off a rock in the ocean and lands in a snowdrift. Similarly, in *The Navigator* (1924), when Buster and Kathryn McGuire are drowning, a trapdoor in the ocean opens to save them—but it is the conning tower of a submarine! In Keaton films, things rarely are what they seem.

Keaton's struggles often seem a parable of life's larger struggles, with the difficulties disguised (or highlighted) by the gags: tragicomedy presented by the greatest stuntman of all time. In *Hard Luck* (1924), Buster tries to commit suicide, only to be thwarted, hilariously, at every turn. Agee described Keaton's works as "a transcendent juggling act in which it seems that the whole universe is in exquisite flying motion [with] the one point of repose the juggler's effortless, uninterested face": and Agee sensed, in Keaton's comedy, "a freezing whisper not of pathos but of melancholia." It is true that in film after film we see Buster forced to fight man or nature against overwhelming odds. When we see him, in one of those patented long shots, bobbing out of the horizon, legs churning and arms pumping ("His physique," as Bermel says, "more than articulate: it is eloquent."), we are struck by how far he must come, how fast he must run—and we know how little difference it will probably make. Perhaps Joe ("Freeze that Puss!") Keaton was right; maybe Buster's greatest asset was his "Great Stone Face." Certainly, it makes us laugh when he confronts runaway locomotives, exploding cannons, and pistol-whipping varmints with that noble impassivity. But if we find his actions in the face of disaster screamingly funny, Buster sees nothing to laugh about. That mug, the ultimate deadpan, seems justified by the hard life in which Buster staves off one disaster only to encounter a host of fresh ones. At the end of a Keaton film, Buster has survived; but he is not smiling. The face is still as ice; but the eyes, those luminous coals, are alert and suspicious, scoping the field even when staring straight ahead, ready for a new threat from around the corner, a fresh trap beneath his feet.

Keaton's genius seems to have sprung, not so much from anger as from bafflement. In Keaton films, the cards are stacked so absolutely, in that flat, linear *loony*-scape, that simple anger, even rage, seems inadequate; the problem is beyond social repair. "[His] physical universe is violent," Walter Kerr observed, "no question about that. It may do a man in. Then again, just as violently, it may do him a favor. What Keaton understands is the essential neutrality of its behavior. . . . He is at heart and at his best, a man waiting for a favorable hurricane." Rather than focusing on politics or the injustice of the moment, Keaton's films seem to question the gods themselves. Every day presents a new dilemma, every encounter a new threat, every opening a trap. He is screamingly funny—but so sad, *so* sad.

Keaton's own career eventually contained greater hardship than Chaplin's—alcoholism, money troubles, neglect; but through it all there emerges a sense of hard-earned consistency, even triumph. In a touching comeback, he became a clown-hit in European circuses during the fifties. The French called him *Malec*, "the hole in the donut" and the Spanish dubbed him *Pamplinas*, "a little piece of nothing" suggesting that, like all great comics he, too, could make a joke out of *nothing, sir,* like the fool in Shakespeare's darkest tragedy, King Lear. Keaton's films present such a tragic universe; they suggest that Keaton, despite his disclaimers, knew what he was doing. Spanish playwright Frederico Garcia Lorca wrote a short farce called "Buster Keaton Takes a Walk," in which Buster enters with four sons, hand in hand, to exclaim, "My poor little boys!" before drawing a wooden sword and killing them. Wooden sword, nice touch. Lorca might have been onto something, some recognition of that quality D. H. Lawrence saw in the American soul: the cold killer, hard, isolate, and stoic. Buster is certainly no killer, but the society we see around him is certainly violent, peopled by anarchists and homicidal maniacs, and propelled by machines dangerously out of control.

Unlike Chaplin, however, Keaton was never one to complain. "When the knocks came," he shrugged, "it was no surprise. I had always known that life was like that, full of uppercuts for the deserving and undeserving alike." To the end, Keaton re-

mained optimistic. "As long as I can remember I have considered myself a fabulously lucky man," he insisted, "and my
greatest pleasure was to have been with a happy crowd."

.   .   .

Of all the silent comics, Chaplin and Keaton seem to strike the
most universal chord in their responses to life's frustrations—
Keaton in his stoic fight regardless of the odds, Chaplin in his
blithe refusal even to admit the possibility of defeat. Their
comedy *was* violent—slapstick and disaster—and yet, in its
most profound roots, it pleaded for sanity and sweetness. Also,
although Keaton and Chaplin recognized that the violent forces
that plague and threaten us are indeed powerful, Buster and
Charlie on-screen fought the unjust society around them with a
pluck we can all applaud. The laughter they invoke is one that
Agee described eloquently: "We laugh till it hurts. We laugh
because it hurts. We laugh after it hurts because we know they
have touched something profound and painful in us. Sure, the
world hurts like that, my God it hurts, isn't that something that
it can hurt like that and we can still live!" So comedy responds
to tragedy, relieves it perhaps.

Great laughter, like great pain, is, perhaps, ultimately inarticulate. When asked to work in sound films, Keaton pleaded
only, "Don't give me puns. Don't give me jokes. No wisecracks." Words, he knew, were never enough, and Keaton remained the most silent of the silent clowns. Like Chaplin, he
knew that his best comedy, when all was said and done, was
beyond words. Of all the great clowns, if Chaplin was king,
Keaton was the sublime court jester, and they ruled the perverse comic universe as one, tiptoeing through the tulips and
mine-fields together.

ROUND SEVEN

The Sound and the Fury:
The Talking Clowns

*The first thing which disappears when men are turn-
ing a country into a totalitarian state is comedy and
comics. Because we are laughed at, I don't think people really understand how essential we are to their
sanity.* —Groucho Marx

*The American comic tradition and American movies
were made for each other . . . they were both black
sheep, outcasts, and embarassments to respectable
American society. Alone, each was pressed to conform
to upright, moral, four-square, genteel American
standards and was for long periods confused as to
how properly to behave. But when they found each
other, they found support for their freest and wildest
natures, for the crudity and the bawdiness which the
middle-class social code tried so persistently to sup-
press. Together they gave expression to the underside
of American values and behavior, the opposite pole
from order and decorum. Together they projected
their grotesque exaggeration, violence, and sexual li-
cense, on a screen as large as the world.*
—Ronald Sklar, *Movie-Made America*

With Al Jolson's 1928 *Jazz Singer,* in itself a strange "talkie"
harkening back to the minstrel show, the death knell sounded
for the silent clowns. Most of the clowns died hard and sudden.
Langdon and Lloyd were finished, and Arbuckle drummed out
as much by his 1921 murder trial as by anything else, "the day
the laughter stopped," as Keaton put it. Keaton's own gravelly
voice grated on the public's collective ear, and he ended up

working as a gagman for Harpo Marx, as a patsy for the frantic Jimmy Durante, and as a foil for Phil Silvers and Zero Mostel in the Richard Lester farce *A Funny Thing Happened on the Way to the Forum*. Chaplin kept working, but revealed a much darker vision—even for him, the simple joy of "tramping" was gone.

Some critics have argued that film comedy never reached such heights again, that sound could never substitute for Keaton's brilliant stunts or Chaplin's magnificent invention. As producer Joe Schenk is said to have quipped, "There will be silent films when talking pictures are forgotten. The trouble with the whole industry is that it talked before it thought." But many fine comedians—most notably Laurel and Hardy, and W. C. Fields (who created himself)—not only managed the crossover from the physical comedy of the silent era to the verbal barrage of the 1930s, but went on to do their best work. As patter and repartee drowned out the silent poem, comedy teams replaced individuals. With the advent of sound, it seemed a single comic was no longer enough, and the public lost patience with the extended gag. So you had duos and trios who could play against one another (duels and triangles), and jokes and jousting, gradually nudged out slapstick.

One of the best teams was certainly that of Laurel and Hardy, whose providential pairing was almost accidental. Though they appeared together in films as early as 1916 (Hardy was usually a heavy), they never really worked *as a team* until Hal Roach encouraged Laurel to take Hardy on in 1926. Even in their early silents they function more as two very funny men on stage rather than as an actual comic partnership. But when they finally did team up, they concocted a heady brew of "Stan-and-Ollie"—true foils sleeping (not only in metaphor but often in fact) in the same bed of comic ineptitude. Hardy played, he said, "the dumbest kind of guy there is: the guy who thinks he's smart. There's nothing funnier than a guy being dignified and dumb at the same time." Unless it's a guy who's really a baby like Stanley, who exaggerated his childishness with extra-white pancake make-up.

Kurt Vonnegut, in dedicating *Slapstick* to Laurel and Hardy, wrote: "The fundamental joke with Laurel and Hardy it seems to me was that they did their best with every test." Certainly, they tried—and failed brilliantly. "The Boys" (as Roach dubbed them) delighted us with their bumbling antics, indomitable spirit, resilience, and charm. "Fools of God," Marcel Marceau, the great French pantomimist, has called them, praising "the beautiful lightness of Ollie, the slow-motion grace of Stan." Ollie is the whimsical and ineffective flimflam man attached by invisible (and sometimes visible) ropes of love to Stanley, his hapless companion and frequent victim. Ollie may whack Stanley regularly, but Stanley will exact revenge—often by accident. If Stanley enters a room, Ollie is inevitably propelled into a trap-bed or closet or out a window; when he leaves, something falls on Ollie's head—a gallon of paint, a lamp, a bed, a ceiling. Through it all, Ollie howls and Stanley whines; and if it adds up to "nothing" in the end, then maybe, just maybe, there is "nothing" to add up to.

Laurel and Hardy humor was much more than situational comedy. In many ways, they are the oddest of odd couples, funny just to look at—fat, pushy Ollie and thin, timorous Stanley. Where Ollie slicks his hair forward, Stan's sticks up, all the better for him to dip his fingers into like flour batter. Ollie is forever hatching plans, fluttering his fat fingers and tie-twiddling, while Stanley stands by, openmouthed, almost incapable of speech, constantly brow-furrowing and scratching that empty head. And what of those absurd derbies which seem such essential parts of their being and which they are always knocking off and mixing up? Often words seem just more props, uncomfortable in their mouths. Their best films are still filled with slapstick; they were terrific with pies and banana peels and pratfalls. But, unlike the slapstick of Abbott and Costello, say, or The Three Stooges, theirs had magic and bite.

Many of their best films were two-reelers they did for Hal Roach. In *Berth Marks* (1929), Roach's "Boys" play musicians who have to get, *well*, somewhere. At the station they flutter past each other repeatedly just missing contact, can't understand the "caller" (neither can we) and, of course, almost miss the train. Once aboard, Stanley promptly sits down right on top of a short guy, begs pardon, doffs his hat, and proceeds to sit on a straw boater. Soon the whole car erupts in a paroxysm of coat-ripping—they can make others crazy, too. Of course they have only one berth, so they have to keep trying to stuff each other in until they get entangled in each other's pajamas, and the exhausted white-whale face of Ollie looks out at us, appealing for sympathy for having hooked up with such a noodlehead as Stanley. At the end they hop off in long johns (with neither cello nor shoes), Ollie picks up a rock to conk Stanley, and Stanley runs off, waddling like the Little Tramp.

Like Keaton, the Boys were master builders of disaster comedy; and if their elaborately detailed best-laid plans inevitably go awry, their skewed logic remains not only hilarious but poignant. As Ronald Durgnat so neatly puts it: "The ungentle art of self-destructive escalation was worked out by Stan and Ollie long before Herman Kahn applied its logic to nuclear war." *Beau Hunks* (1931), for instance, works out of this crazy rhythm. Ollie, crushed by a "Dear Ollie" letter from his beloved Jeannie Weenie, has convinced Stanley to join him in the French Foreign Legion. Searching for their post in a sandstorm, they stumble across a sentry, whereupon Ollie inquires (as if asking for directions on 48th Street and Madison), "Excuse me, please, is this Fort Arid?" Like Billy Pilgrim, the "Boys" are ludicrous soldiers, always getting lost or turning the wrong way. Stanley catches his rifle in his pantaloons, and Ollie sighs at Stanley's haplessness. Of course the joke is that Ollie is every bit as hapless as Stanley; both are unsuited to any "real" world and can function only in the "reel" world of farce. When other recruits produce photos of Jeannie Weenie (Jean Harlow), Ollie gushes, "She's traveled all over the world, and she's loved by everyone—and she's mine, *all* mine!" But we're not through with Jeannie yet. (Slapstick Rule #1: *If something is funny, do it again.*) So when the captured Arab leader pulls out a photo at the end, it's Jeannie Weenie of course. So much for romance.

The farcical serviceman was a staple of their comedy. They played sappy on-shore sailors in *Two Tars* and *Men O' War* and *Our Relations*, doughty doughboys in *Pack Up Your Troubles*, hapless, skirted Highlanders in *Bonnie Scotland*, French legionnaires in *The Flying Deuces*. But these films are takeoffs and pastiches on the arbitrariness of military logic. The real war for the Boys was always the battle of the sexes, and it was a battle they never won. In *Chicken, Come Home* (1931), another movie demonstrating how not to keep the ladies in line, Stan and Ollie deal in high-grade fertilizer (chicken shit, that is), and "Big Executive" Ollie's mayoral campaign is threatened by a "bimbo" who produces an incriminating photo. (Ollie's wife, we soon learn, is a dead ringer for the "bimbo"—a sly reprise on the dubious thrill of adultery.) When Ollie's wife says she would love to meet his wife, Stanley blurts out, "I'd love to neither too." Once again, the right rhythm, just the wrong sense. Later, when Stanley's wife calls to say she'll break his arm if he isn't home for dinner, "See," crows Ollie, "everything's fine." There is much Feydeau farce. Stanley, commandeered to hide the bimbo, rushes her in and out of rooms and closets. Catching Ollie in a lie, Ollie's wife slugs him; meanwhile the bimbo is throwing things at Stanley who is still bravely blocking the door, and Stanley's wife takes an ax to Ollie's shoes. (Could the women be in league with one another?) "Somebody's coming to my house," sings Ollie sweetly at the end. Oh my, yes!

The Boys are not good marriage material, as Dr. Ruth might say; it is certainly a hilariously jaundiced version of marriage they offer us. "Mister Hardy was married," announces the opening title of *Their First Mistake,* "—Mister Laurel was also unhappy." *Soitinly,* as Ollie would say, they try to please their harridan wives. But they would prefer to flee—and they do in *Should Married Men Go Home, Oliver the Eighth,* and their classic *Sons of the Desert.* But the Boys can't always flee; sometimes, like Ring Lardner's victims, they are trapped. *Helpmates* (1932) opens with Ollie surveying the debris from a wild night of carouse at his own house. With his wife due back, he calls Stanley, who does his bumbling best to clean up the mess. Ollie announces they will have a nice breakfast and then "we'll put our shoulder to the wheel, grab the bull by the horns, and put our best foot forward," whereupon he steps on a carpet sweeper and hurtles onto Stan's stacked dishes. After Ollie manages to ruin his only two suits with soot, flour, and water, he is forced to don his lodge uniform (complete with sword and plumed hat) to pick up the wife, only to return (with a black eye and his ceremonial sword bent) to see Stanley hosing down the ruins of his smouldering house. With Stanley blubbering, Ollie surveys the scene and says calmly, "Would you mind closing the door—I'd like to be left alone." Stanley closes the door (of course there are no walls), it begins to rain, and our last view is of Ollie sitting in the only chair left in the devastated house and with great dignity removing a piece of lint from his pants. Ah, we've all had days like that.

The Boys were also fond of parodies. They were themselves parodies of course—of servicemen, husbands, and especially gentlemen. Whatever happened, they were *always* unfailingly courteous. Ollie would twiddle his tie before announcing, "I'm Mr. Hardy, and this is my good friend Mr. Laurel," and Stanley would dip his head in a parody of a bow. Their 1934 parody of gangster movies, *Going Bye-Bye,* opens with Stanley testifying against a tough hoodlum. After the judge praises him for telling the truth, Stanley applauds himself and asks, "Aren't you going to hang him?" When the hoodlum threatens revenge, the Boys make plans to get out of town. But nothing comes easy to the Boys. Stanley mixes the telephone up with a milk bottle, so Ollie purrs into the receiver, "Er, excuse me please, my ear is full of milk." He shreds Ollie's coat with a razor hidden in the brush he is using, then shorts a buzzer causing an alarm bell to fall on Ollie's head.

When they go to visit a potential traveling companion (with flowers of course), she turns out to be the "moll" of the hoodlum trapped in a trunk. Divinely innocent, the Boys work to free him—blowtorching, flooding, boring holes—managing, through all of this, to keep the bunches of flowers in their busy, busy hands. When Butch finally emerges, only the arrival of the police prevents mayhem. At the end Ollie and Stan embrace on the couch, shivering in fear; and Ollie complains, "Well, here's another nice mess you've got me into!" and Stanley whines, "Well, I—", never quite managing to finish that explanation which once seemed so clear but which now escapes him.

The Boys played policemen (*The Midnight Patrol*) and detectives (*Do Detectives Think* and *The Laurel and Hardy Murder Case*), yet seemed most in their element behind bars (*The Second Hundred Years, Liberty,* and *Pardon Us*). Certainly, they deserved to be locked up. But they were at their best as

PUNCHLINES   157

simple tradesmen (and how simple!) who had to build an addi-
tion, paint a house, or (as in *The Music Box*) deliver a player
piano. Like Keaton's *The General* and Chaplin's *Gold Rush*,
The Music Box (1932) is a great comic film, which makes up in
sidesplitting comedy what it lacks in heroism or pathos. It is,
again, another of those films in which the Boys take on very
superable tasks only to make them insuperable. Asked to deliver a piano, the Boys make it to the top of a long stoop only to
lose the piano and watch it bump noisily back down; manage
to drop it twice into a pond; and finally hack it open with a saw
and crowbars. Along the way they also get into jousts with a
nanny, a cop, and a professor. When the observant nanny giggles, "Of all the dumb things!" Stanley boots her, so she breaks
a bottle over (of course) Ollie's head, and complains about
being kicked "in the middle of my daily duties," so the cop
kicks Ollie once again and punches Stanley in the stomach for
good measure. Very inspiring, indeed.

The Music Box contains some wonderful touches. A sign on
the boys' horse-drawn truck proclaims the company was
Foundered in 1927 and reminds us, *Tall oaks from little acorns
grow*. Over their work overalls, the Boys are decked out in
white gloves, ties, and derbies. Ollie stops Stanley periodically
to ponder, like a true mover: "Just a moment—*this* requires a
little thought." Even clichés are a bit beyond poor Stanley, who
protests to the cop, "Don't you think you're bounding over your
steps." When they finally hook up the piano (miraculously, it
works!), the Boys dance a knee-slapping, fast-stepping minuet
to the patriotic tunes it emits. The Boys would often stop to
dance or sing; since their world is surrealistic, nothing has to
follow anything. Besides, Hardy had a wonderful tenor voice,
and both could really dance, ergo. . . . When the furious professor protests the destruction of his house, his assault is mo-
mentarily halted by the national anthem which brings them all
to attention. *The Music Box* is a masterpiece of bumbling destruction in which the Boys win out by revenging themselves
on everything that is thwarting them.

Their parody of "oaters," *Way Out West* (1937), begins in a
saloon where Lola (a Mae West clone played by Sharon Lynne)
is doing a burlesque number ("Will you be my lov-ee dov-ee?")

for a rough sourdough audience. When we cut to the Boys, Stanley is walking alongside a mule pulling Ollie along on an Indian sledge—until they ford a river and Ollie sinks. (So much for the lap of luxury.) Stanley tries to hitch into Brushwood Gulch but has trouble getting his thumb to work, and nobody stops until he shows a bit of leg and the stage screeches to a halt. Bouncing along, Ollie tries to butter up a pretty girl: "A lot of weather we've been having lately—and it's only *four* months to Xmas." (Quite the masher!) A barbershop quartet is playing in front of the town saloon, so Stan and Ollie stop to perform another wonderful dance of synchronized nonsense *apropos* of nothing. They have been sent on a secret errand to find the rightful heir to a "goldmine" map, so Stanley straight off reveals their secret to the bartender, the villainous Mickey Finn, who schemes to have his wife Lola pretend to be the heir.

There is some marvelous slapstick—Stan stuffing tough-as-shoe-leather meat in the hole of his sole, only to be hounded by dogs; Stan smoking a pipe with the stem detached, then lighting a match with his thumb to ignite Ollie's cigar until Ollie imitates him and finally succeeds, only to howl in pain; Stan's eating Ollie's hat, which he salts and seems to like, until once again Ollie's curiosity gets the better of him and he nibbles the brim and spits it out in disgust. Attempting to retrieve the map, Ollie insists on getting on Finn's roof ahead of Stanley —and of course falls through. When the Boys try a block and tackle, Ollie falls down rudely, then yanks the rope to dump Stanley, who yanks the rope to dump Ollie, who yanks again— but Stanley has let go, so again Ollie falls. Once inside, Ollie falls through the floor and gets his head stuck, so Stanley covers it with a pail—which Finn kicks. The Boys hide in the piano, but Finn suspects they are there and hits the keys so that they are tattoed in the face—and the piano collapses.

Unwittingly perhaps, but nonetheless absolutely, the Boys sow total destruction. By the end of one of their films, nothing is left intact. "It is remarkable what a tremendous amount of violence there was in the Laurel and Hardy films," observes Steve Allen, "and, for that matter, in hundreds of other early comedies." But no one ever bled. Or *did* they? As in Keaton, the world around the Boys is unfailingly hostile; other folks are always threatening—and often delivering—violence. In the 1930s, when so much actual misery was hovering over the dust bowls of America and former businessmen could be seen hawking apples on street corners, such comedy must have come as a relief, an acting out of so much pent-up frustration. And, of course, the secret of Laurel and Hardy is that they never seemed to intend to do what they did. In their films, things die, not people. Undoubtedly, part of their charm—and genius—has to do with their unflagging optimism (especially in the face of facts!) which has them marching off to ruin, smiling and waving briskly, like boys on their way to summer camp. Disasters might happen (disasters *did* happen). But in their refusal ever to give up, the message the Boys give us is that we can survive. Yes, even if the world falls on our heads, as it so often fell on theirs, we, too, can survive.

A sweet afterword: in homage to the Boys, Orson Bean has rallied a semiserious fan club called *The Sons of the Desert*, which has many watery chapters in cities and towns across America. Article Eight of the Constitution reads:

The Annual Meeting shall be conducted in the following sequence:

 a. Cocktails

 b. Business meeting and cocktails

 c. Dinner (with cocktails)

 d. After-dinner speeches and cocktails

 e. Cocktails

 f. Coffee and cocktails

 g. Showing of Laurel and Hardy films

 h. After-film critique and cocktails

 i. After-after-film critique and cocktails.

 j. Stan has suggested this period. In his words: "All members are requested to park their camels and hire a taxi; then return for "One more for the desert.""

Yippee!

W. C. Fields came to movies late. After punching out his father at the age of twelve and running away from home, he worked as a roustabout in circuses before working up a juggling act (at that time he stuttered) to get him onstage rather than work cleaning up in the wings. Eschewing drink (ah, the ironies of life!), he soon earned a reputation as one of the best, introducing comedy into the act (pretending to miss, etc.) and working an almost-dumb act in blackface as *The Eccentric Tramp Juggler.* During World War I, when Sennett and Chaplin were breaking fresh ground in Hollywood, Fields was developing a series of successful vaudeville routines in which he played a much-put-upon husband traveling in a Pullman sleeper or driving to the country, surrounded by a shrewish wife and a parcel of impossible and violent children. In the music halls, he learned how to use his hat and cane skillfully and hilariously. In vaudeville and on Broadway he learned how to wed his physical legerdemain with verbal prestidigitation—made himself over into a kind of oral magician, so to speak, with a riveting mutter, so you had to listen closely to get the best snarls and mumbles. By the time he came to Hollywood after the stock market crash, Fields had mastered the traditions of broad comedy and had a great deal of material to work into his films.

But if, in 1929, you had predicted that such an aging, puff-nosed, alcoholic ex-juggler could become one of the giant laugh-getters of all time, you would have been laughed out of Hollywood. But that is precisely what Fields managed, seemingly without effort, on often cheesey sets with second-rate performers and third-rate scripts; and he managed it because of his own protean skills and a simple formula: he portrayed a man at war with the world. When you see Fields on screen you can't take your eyes off him. He is eternally vigilant—ever alert to a new threat and looking for an edge to make a buck or slip away for a drink. All life, Fields insists, is a con; and his absolute misanthropy, misogyny or mis-*what-have-you* makes us laugh, once again, at the nasty reality behind the pretense. We have certainly had comics with more range and more invention, but none so pure, so indelible, so frightening. It is a dog-eat-dog world Fields gives us; and to the victor goes the biggest bone—even if he has to snatch it from Baby LeRoy.

Fields delighted not only in the non sequitur but in the impossible: "There's an Ethiopian in the fuel supply," or "I think I'll go out and milk the elk." On-screen, Fields is never at a loss for words. After falling ten thousand feet to retrieve a flask of whiskey dropped from an airplane, Fields might land in the lap of a beautiful blonde only to smile grimly, "Suffering sciatica, the last time it was pink elephants." In a greasy spoon he sputters over his cup of "mocha java" and mutters, "I don't know why I ever come in here. The flies get the best of everything." Keeping the thread, he later scolds a soda jerk about to swat a fly, "Don't hurt that fly. That's Old Tom—they named a gin after him." Scowling at the soda jerk and the dead fly, he sighs, "It's killers like you that give the West a bad name." Fields' misanthropy and counterpunching quickly became a trademark. In many of his early shorts, he played dentists and barbers whose "customers" are trapped (as in Lardner's "Haircut") and at his mercy. In "The Barber," he shaves off a man's wart while ogling a girl's legs; and, after moving a giant safety pin out of a baby's reach only to have the baby clout him with a full milk bottle, Fields edges the pin back. In "The Dentist," Fields reaches new heights of cruelty—wrestling with recalcitrant molars, wrenching breaking jaws, yanking a patient out of the chair—so that he may rush to the golf course and bean an old man with his tee shot. As the old man is dragged away, Fields just points to his dentures, "Get those things out of here. They're in my line."

Fields drew on his vaudeville sketches to portray that hoariest of all hoary stock characters, the harried husband, replete with harridan wife and hellish children. We see him operating in a world stacked against him, where marriage is not longer, "it just seems longer." Long before Rodney Dangerfield, Fields got a lot of laughs out of getting no respect. In *The Bank Dick*, as Egbert Sousè, Fields is as much sinned against as sinning. His wife harps on his smoking and drinking; his bratty daughter, Elsie Mae Adele Brunch Sousè, pelts him with rocks; another daughter is lovestruck and suicidal; and his own mother sneers every time he appears. Whenever he can, Fields sneaks off to the Black Pussy Cat Saloon; and he maintains his marvelous, synthetic patter, his defense and his revenge. "Don't be a fuddie-duddie," he pooh-poohs his son-in-law about embezzle-ment, *"don't* be a mooncalf, *don't* be a jabbernowl—you don't want to be any of *those,* do you?"

In *My Little Chickadee* (1940), Fields hammed it up with that other fine put-on artist, Mae West. With West as Her Tart-ness, Flower Belle Lee, Fields played His Biliousness, con man Cuthbert J. Twillie. *Chickadee,* like *Way Out West,* is a Western parody, set in a Greasewood City replete with crooked politicians, political crooks, and drunken Indians ("Is he a full-blooded Indian?"—"Quite the antithesis, he's very anemic."). West and Fields meet on a train (she has been run out of town), and Fields initiates their first wry exchange:

> "Nice day."
> "Is it?" deadpans Flower Belle.
> Twillie shrugs. "Of course it's only one man's opinion."

Twillie is soon moving in on The Flower. "What symmetrical digits!" he exults, kissing her fingers, "May I avail myself of a second helping?" The Flower, noticing his cash, lets him nib-ble away; and when Twillie offers to marry her forthwith, she consents, since she can return to Greasewood only as a married woman.

Twillie hustles about town. When one rube asks if a card game is a game of chance, "Not the way I play it," he mutters. But Flower manages to out-con Twillie—even refusing him entrance to her suite. Flower is taken up with a Cisco Kid-like masked bandit who "comes" many times a night. When she sings and wiggles to "Willy the Miner" ("Gold was hissun/ and that's where I come in"), West seems herself a kind of female impersonator wangling charms for gold. Sex is West's bargain-ing tool—and she is always dropping her eyes, inspecting a man from the thighs up as if sizing up his "tool" (Remember "Is that a gun you're wearing or are you just happy to see me?"); and when her masked lover takes off, Flower shrugs wistfully, "Adios, my fastest one." Twillie's assault on Flower's "virtue" is comical because she doesn't have any. When Twil-lie finally does manage to talk himself into Flower's boudoir, he is foiled again when she sticks a goat in her bed, which he embraces tenderly: "Don't recoil from me, my sweet. Take off your coat." The goat nah-nahs. "Beelzebub," roars Twillie, "I have been hoodwinked." Twillie later mutters to his wooden Indian, "Sleep, the most beautiful experience in life—except drink." In *Chickadee,* there *is* no high road—only the low.

The Fields-West pairing works well (in *life,* they hated each other, but no matter) because we know them and expect the "con." Parody, Hamlin Hill has observed, "exaggerates ... without trying to reform." True to form, *My Little Chickadee* parodies the con games of the West without criticizing. But, by the end, nothing has changed; we have just had a few laughs— at pretense and goodness which (according to these two clowns) are essentially the same.

But the violence in Fields's films is simple, complete, and irredeemable. Life is confrontation and daily battle; at best there is only revenge. When Baby LeRoy "kills" Fields's watch, Fields purrs, "How can you possibly *hurt* a watch by dipping it into molasses? It just makes me love the little nipper all the more." Alone at last with "the little nipper," Fields offers his backside a good quick boot. When a daughter bawls, "You don't love me any more," Fields takes a swing at her, shouting, "*Certainly* I love you." Asked about burying his wife, "Yes, I had to," he growls, "she died." He argues with a barman over who knocked Chicago Nellie down first, before reluctantly ceding, "All right—but I began *kicking* her." Fields's films are not just "about" violence—they *are* violent.

Fields's humor, like much American humor, was also racist and sexist. He could tell an anecdote about a dentist treating a man for yellow jaundice for eleven years before finding out he was a Jap, or stroll into a group of blacks to ask for "the chief Ubangi around here" or call Topsy "Stove Polish" or "Charcoal" without the slightest tinge of self-consciousness. By all accounts, his real life mirrored his on-screen persona. He could be as cantankerous, prejudiced, and paranoid off-screen as on: writing scorching rebukes to his wife-in-name-only, embarassing paramours, attacking stagehands, reviling children and dogs. Groucho Marx recalls Fields showing him a stash of $50,000 worth of booze which he kept in his attic on the off chance that prohibition might return. Fields would go to almost any length for a practical joke—even to bribing an undertaker to borrow John Barrymore's corpse to prop against a tree in order to scare the wits out of their drinking buddy Errol Flynn. If he did not exactly invent himself, Fields certainly invented those parts of his public persona which happened to coincide with his private vices (he claimed no virtues). Fields the performer coincided so precisely with his off-screen personality that it is hard to tell where, or if, a dividing line existed. In fact, he was extremely skillful at creating precisely the movie self he could be most comfortable with.

So, with Fields, what you saw was what you got; he denied even the possibility of more. His humor could be—often was—cruel, and Fields was the first to admit it. But he insisted on cruelty and pain as the primary wellspring of humor, "I never saw anything funny that wasn't terrible," he said. "If it causes pain, it's funny; if it doesn't, it isn't."

· · ·

W. C. Fields was not the only crazy man of the 1930s. There were also the Marx Brothers, those masters of what Robert Benchley called the *dementia praecox* school of humor, who managed somehow to bring their raucous, vaudeville act to Broadway and translate it onto the sound stage. And even here we must keep in mind that their act wasn't all words; Harpo never talked—not even when offered $50,000 by an aspiring producer who wanted to run up HARPO TALKS AT LAST on the marquee. But Groucho and Chico more than made up for Harpo's silence—Groucho with wisecracking ad libs ("I'd horse-whip you if I had a horse.") and Chico ("the Italian embezzler" as Morrie Ryskind called him) speaking his *not-a quite-a* right immigrantese. And they not only talked, they ripped into language as if punishing it, with atrocious puns, double entendres, and colorful insults.

Like all great comedy teams, each developed his personal signature. Groucho was the Perelmanesque put-down artist who could be counted on to outwit and outbluster any attempt by so-called "real" people to bring sanity to bear. Sublime Harpo floated through the films like a child satyr with a motley paraphernalia of destructive devices (scissors of course, but also blowtorch, butcher knife, sledgehammer, axe, and even a live turkey), snipping ties, goosing blondes, grabbing legs, and sleeping anywhere, anytime. And there was Chico, hawking peanuts and swamps, working boardrooms or street corners to hustle a buck, "shooting the piano keys" as Groucho called it, and aping the American immigrant with his absurd hat and even absurder accent.

No Marx Brother was ever as good alone as they were together. The whole was always greater than the sum of its parts, and the success of their comedy depended on excess. Excess, *always* excess. Even in their early vaudeville act, they would just pile on stage (sometimes as many as nineteen people— relatives, aunts, cousins, chorus girls) and proceed to rip things up, kicking, slapping, fighting, shouting, singing, and moving —always moving. If one piece of stolen silverware could get a laugh, then two would be even funnier; and Harpo worked out a bit in which he dropped enough cutlery to stock a beanery. Perhaps Marxist comedy became so popular in the Depression Thirties because "excess" had become such a dirty word. For a great percentage of the population, the American dream had become a nightmare; and many were feeling a sense of having somehow been cheated out of their "natural-born" superiority. So along came the Marx Brothers. And, if their comedy conveyed anything, it proclaimed to the public (particularly to The Great Unwashed), that it was all a mug's game. The "hoity-toities" were just fat fools floating around in a thick moat of unearned moolah (oh, that excess!) and therefore you should just grab all you could get. Maybe that is to oversimplify; but, for whatever reason, the outrageousness of the Marx Brothers struck a sympathetic chord in the public's shrinking heart.

The Marx Brothers were sons of immigrants (Daddy Marx an East Side tailor, Mommy Marx the backstage mother) and shared an early poverty. But, characteristically, they never looked back; it was America they always cared about and wanted to "beat," in more ways than one. The new wave of immigrants, particularly the Jewish comics, according to film critic Ron Durgnat, introduced to vaudeville a "New Humor" —a humor that was "sharp, rapid, cynical, and often cruel."

Certainly, "Marxist humor" was not only wild and wooly, but rough, and provides another link in that particularly American chain of violent comedy. The joke that got the most laughs, Groucho told Richard Anobile, was their "garbage" joke; when Zeppo said, "Dad, the garbageman is here," Groucho would shoot back, "Tell him we don't want any."

Even in their films, which they began in their thirties, they have only one plan and one mode of discourse, and that is *ATTACK!* Groucho's mouth is a machine-gun. Caught out with the wife of an angry gangster in *Horse Feathers*, Groucho acts as if *he* is the injured party; rather than apologize to the opposing defense minister in *Duck Soup*, he slaps him. No truce ever works with Harpo; he still cuts your tie with a smile, jumps in your arms. And Chico, well, Chico is always ready to steal whatever he can. Though their humor is always edgy, that of *Animal Crackers* is particularly barbed. When Groucho arrives at a "swell" party, carried in on a litter, he protests the charge of $1.85, "*What?*—from Africa to here? It's an outrage." Soon he is singing, "Hello, I must be going." Then he criticizes Margaret Dumont for her wallpaper, tries to sell her insurance, asks if she minds if he doesn't smoke. (*Non sequitur* is part of the attack.) Professor Harpo enters playing oom-pa-pa music, a gate opens, and a fig newton appears—shades of Ring Lardner's surrealism. Harpo blows chocolate smoke rings, then begins firing as if in a shooting gallery. In a card game he leads all aces and steals one of the lady's shoes from under the table. Asked if he loves anyone, he nods happily and shows a girl a photo of a horse. Chico, Señor Manuel Reveli, continues the non sequiturs, "Couldn't I-ya come yesterday?"

Charlie Chaplin confessed he found the Marx Brothers frightening. After seeing *Animal Crackers*, French playwright Antonin Artaud, self-proclaimed prophet of the Theatre of Cruelty, hailed their comedy as "an essential liberation of boiling anarchy." Certainly, its essence *was* anarchy; and the films that have weathered best—*Animal Crackers, Horse Feathers, Duck Soup*—are those in which the Bros were least fettered by production numbers or romantic subplots and were allowed room to operate and demolish. Everyone has a favorite Marx Brothers routine: the mirror scene in *Duck Soup*, the stuffed stateroom of *A Night at the Opera,* Harpo's leg-shakes and snipperies, Groucho's verbal assaults on the hapless Dumont. Was there a method to their madness? Often the method and the madness seem clear, but sometimes unrelated. In *Animal Crackers* and *Horse Feathers,* for instance, the doyens of upper-class society, with their butlers, evening gowns, and expensive artworks, are satirized, but the mayhem is so general that we never really know why. Perhaps the public knew or felt enough to supply their own resentments.

But this can scarcely be said of *Duck Soup* (1933), which focuses *its* satire on war. Groucho considered *Duck Soup* their best film, and a strong argument can be made that it is. Under the able direction of Leo McCarey, and with a good supporting cast, including Margaret Dumont and Edgar Kennedy, *Duck Soup* provides typical Marx Brothers fare, but here there is a coherent thread parodying (parody again, *hmm?*) simple-minded nationalism and patriotism. The film opens with dignitaries and Swiss guards awaiting the arrival of Rufus T. Firefly to save Fredonia, and there is a long sennet (of trumpets, not Maxes) but no Firefly until Groucho wakes and shimmies down a pole in his dressing-gown to join his own receiving line. Pinky (Harpo) whirls up in a sidecycle to whisk Groucho away, only to leave him sitting in the "side" (sans cycle), chomping on his cigar. Pinky proceeds to work his subversive magic with his scissors, cutting cigars and tails off formal coats (those symbols of pomp and circumstance). At the senate, Firefly, bouncing a rubber ball, offers Ciccolini (Chico) a job as Public Nuisance and Secretary of War after a Groucho-grilling (Sample: "What'll you do?"—"Have a standing army to save-a money on chairs.") After slapping the rival ambassador, Groucho sings, "This means war," whereupon a baton-twirling Harpo appears, leading soldiers stopping only to cut the plumes off their helmets as they parade past.

Soon we are at war, but what a war it is, preposterous and zany, mostly World War I, with touches of the Civil War thrown in for relish. The Bros set up a minstrel line to sing "All God's Chillun Got Guns." Harpo rides his horse to alert the citizenry *à la* Paul Revere. Spotting a blonde readying for a shower, he whoahs and sneaks up to join her. She turns out to be the wife of Edgar Kennedy, a Harpo nemesis; and when Kennedy steps into the tub, Harpo emerges from the depths, all smiles. Meanwhile (in Marx Brothers films there is always a *meanwhile*), Groucho in Union blues is at GHQ negotiating to buy trenches. A bomb whistles through. Groucho mistakenly machine-guns his own men, then offers an aide $5 to keep it under his hat. Chico announces he is going to defect because "the food is a-better over there." Groucho reappears (in Confederate uniform this time), and Harpo puts out a HELP-WANTED sign. Groucho says to Harpo, "When *you're* out there risking life and limb, *we'll* be in here thinking what a sucker you are." Another sign announces HELP IS ON ITS WAY—followed by a host of firemen, swimmers, marathoners, and monkeys . . . and Groucho surrenders because everyone is throwing fruit at him.

As a spoof of war—and war-making—*Duck Soup* is extremely effective. It is, of course, farce, but suggests the tragicomedy of World War I, which was precipitated by the assassination of Archduke Ferdinand and his consort (Groucho and Harpo assassinated by Chico?). Was it heroism or farce when twenty thousand British soldiers raced out of their trenches at the Somme only to be mowed down by German machine-guns? In its satirizing of petty rivalries and entangling treaties, *Duck Soup* seems on the mark. It is a pity that, unlike Chaplin and Mel Brooks, the Bros never got around to satirizing Hitler.

The Marx Brothers (Groucho anyway) spanned at least three generations of entertainment—vaudeville, film, and television —and they combined the best of the silent and sound traditions: Harpo with his sight gags and slapstick, all sensation, no sense; Groucho and Chico with their insults, verbal humor, and general mangling of language. Like Fields, they lived as they played, and played as they lived. "There are three things that my brother Chico is always on," Groucho remarked, "a phone, a horse, or a broad." Harpo became the toast of artists and musicians; Salvadore Dali made him a harp out of piano wire. Groucho wisecracked for a living ("It was a beautiful night— all the stars were out, including Cary Grant.") and hosted a mock quiz show on TV. When one contestant with thirteen children proclaimed her love for her husband, "I like my cigar too," quipped Groucho, "but I take it out once in a while." They never changed.

The Marx Brothers were unique, not as lovable perhaps as Laurel and Hardy (though Harpo was loved by many), nor as consistently clever as Fields at his best, but special, still. How alive they seemed, and how stiff and formal and foolish, how "dead," seemed those other people on stage with them, those emissaries from the "real world" who we know only too well can hurt us. When Groucho reviled them, Chico chiseled them, and Harpo cut them, literally, down to size, we rejoiced. As Ronald Durgnat observed, "Aggressiveness is the catalyst of humor rather than its content. . . . Laughter is not simply derisive toward other human beings [but] also a gurgle of relief, of triumph, at breaking a taboo." We desired, we reveled in, the revenge the Marx Brothers exacted. In many ways, they, too, seem fit precursors of today's "attack" comics. After watching their stage routine on stage, W. C. Fields said, "Nobody follows the Marx Brothers." He refused. So, here, do I.

ROUND EIGHT

The Comics: Or Sick Sick Sick (sic)

*I can't live any more in a world given its meaning and
dimension by some vulgar nightclub clown. By some
—some black humorist!*
                    —Philip Roth to Doctor Spielvogel,
                              Portnoy's Complaint [1]

*Freedom of speech is one thing, but these gents are
overdoing it. And when I say "gents," this is where
most of them should be doing their act.*
                    —Groucho Marx, in a letter to Robert Ruark,
                              June 26, 1963

*One trembles to think of that mysterious thing in the
soul, which seems to acknowledge no human jurisdiction, but in spite of the individual's self, will still
dream horrid dreams and mutter unmentionable
thoughts.*   —Herman Melville, *Pierre*

Americans did not invent stand-up comedy—God did. But in
the last thirty years American comics have taken stand-up and
muttered unmentionable thoughts at a level of ferocity that
might make even "De Lawd" shudder. The minstrel shows had
Tambo and Bones; vaudeville and burlesque saw slapstick
comics like Weber and Fields, Abbott and Costello; and radio
listeners heard dialecticians like Amos 'n' Andy, Fred Allen,
and Jack Benny spinning out groaning puns and hoary chestnuts right through the 1940s. But the coming to life of the stand-
up comic (that Frankenstein monster of our unsaid thoughts)
had to wait till the 1950s and 1960s, and what started essentially as a hip San Francisco/New York occasional light, has

flashed into an open circuit of three hundred comedy clubs pulsing from coast to coast.

When comics speak of "knocking 'em dead," it is barely a metaphor. Comics rate their success on how much they devastate their audience. "I made a woman laugh so hard she started hyperventilating," Joe Bolster exults. "She was kind of panting, so I thought she was kidding. She was right in front, and I started making faces right in her face . . . and she's gasping, but I still thought she was joking. Finally her boyfriend said, 'My God, stop! You've got to stop! You're *killing* her!' Then I realized it was serious and I didn't know what to do—so a waitress came with a paper bag and the woman blew into it. It was the ultimate in comedy—literally killing."

The mechanics of stand-up are as confrontational and rigid as those of boxing. A comic enters, takes the mike, and tries to "destroy" his audience with some feints, a few well-placed jabs, a haymaker or two. His job is to deliver the payoff, the punch line—"the precious cargo," in Betsy Borns's apt metaphor—"that must be guided gently through a crowded room, insinuated into every corner table, nurtured to maturation, then delivered at the right instant, of which there is only one." But if jokes are bombs set to explode at an exact time, that means they can also fizzle. The "suckers," the customers, have paid to see the comic and *want* to laugh. But they will not laugh automatically; they want a comic to earn his laughs. Every audience has its share of hecklers, drunks, melancholics, and nasties; and a few lame jokes can set them off in a feeding frenzy aimed at a comic's jugular. A comic, too, can "bomb," can "die." The stand-up comic is the most vulnerable artist in the business because he *needs* laughs. "A clown is a warrior who fights gloom," says comic Red Skelton, "[and] when deafening silence greets his gestures, he stands there and bleeds."

And there's a whole lot of bleeding going on. Today's audiences, sated by the overexposure of stand-up comedy on late-night talk shows and cable TV, are heckling more than ever, and comics are responding in kind—by attacking. The comics themselves are hip to the adversarial relationship between themselves and their audience. "To laugh is to be dominated," insists Jerry Seinfeld, buying into not only Hobbes's superiority theory but suggesting a dose of sadomasochism to boot. "Bobcat" Goldthwait sees the laugh process as a kind of transference: "I think part of my appeal is that a lot of people would like to scream, tell everybody to get fucked—so they pay money to watch me say it instead." Stand-up, for George Carlin, is a socially acceptable form of aggression: "You get to name the targets, you get to fire the bullets, and what you're doing is putting people in an impossible situation where they're forced to like it. There's a great deal of hostility involved—and the wonderful part is, after you're finished, you say, 'Hey, can't you take a joke? This is humor, sir! What's the matter with you?' You shame them into agreeing, nobody wants to be accused of not taking a joke, so it's a double bind for them."

With such a scary formula at work, who would *want* to be a comic anyhow? Richard Fields claims his own choice was simple: "I was either going to be a comic or I was going to kill people." Rita Rudner shrugs, "The only reason you want to be a comedian is because you're profoundly unhappy." Phyllis Diller suggests comedy is but tragedy revisited. Which Mel Brooks twists into his own dizzy formula: "Tragedy is if *I* cut my finger. Comedy is if *you* walk into an open sewer and die." After drying out, Goldthwait tells of his fear of coming back: "When I first got sober I was so happy, but all of a sudden I thought, How can I do comedy? I'm too happy. And then a friend of mine said, 'Don't worry, God will put enough pain in your life—you'll still be able to do it'; and lo and behold, he was right." But comedy does not always camouflage pain. Former class clowns David Letterman and Robert Klein insist they just enjoy performing. "Being onstage is coming," claims Mitzi Shore, "it's having an orgasm." On a more mercenary note, there is also a lot of gold in them thar comic hills—as Eddie "Big Dick" Murphy or Steve "Cruel Shoes" Martin can attest. Perhaps the simplest explanation is that comics not only think funny but enjoy showing off their funniness for others. "Comics are cerebral strippers," suggests Borns, "seducing us, ever so slowly, as they peel off layer upon layer of our collective repression." until finally we too, like "johns," are naked before the truth.

. . .

This has not always been so. Older comedians just told jokes, the cornier the better. Milton Berle opened with his "Good evening, Ladies and Germs," Henny Youngman pleaded "Take my wife—please"—and the predictability was part of the joke. Slapstick, yes; Miltie in drag, yes; but no real challenge to the audience to grapple with anything more serious than a rubber banana. It was Lenny Bruce ("the first modern comedian," as Steve Allen calls him) who broke the mold. "The big thing Lenny did wasn't to change the language but the style," Seinfeld points out. "He talked about the comedy of the life we're all really leading—about how people really felt when they had sex, which is a tremendous jump from 'My wife is so fat—'" *Time* may have called him "sick" and network television boycotted him as "too hot," but today's comics look upon Lenny (not Bruce, not Schneider, just Lenny, thanks) as a kind of Messiah, (flanked by those two blessed thieves Richard Pryor and George Carlin) who "stood-up" and was crucified on the Calvary of Profane Comedy.

"I'm not a comedian," Lenny insisted, "I'm Lenny Bruce." Even as a young comic filling in between strippers in "toilets," he was outrageous—sometimes (*what the hell, right?*) shlepping, Groucho-style, naked across the stage. Some guys didn't like that; naked chicks were one thing, but a naked shmuck reminding them of their own ball-hanging, flaccid maleness was quite another. The "suckers" might have been outraged, but it was pure Lenny. He was never one to dress up the truth —or himself. Before declaring any king, Kennedy, or pope naked, Lenny insisted on his own nakedness. *Always.* You had to start with that.

Hip, hep, hype—it was all part of his act. Lenny was *hip*, which meant not only New York cool, but also (in the jargon of the jazz musicians whose lingo he adopted) *in* on the truth, the real truth, beneath all the square bullshit. *Hep* was Doris Day, Beach Party Bingo, Pat Boone's white bucks, Lawrence Welk's champagne bubbles, Bob Hope. *Hype* was Hollywood and Las Vegas, Oscars and Tonys, making the world "safe for democracy," the Legion of Decency and Norman Vincent Peale.

Oh, yes, Lenny was hip; and, like Finnerty in Vonnegut's *Player Piano*, he enjoyed operating on the edge, just rapping about "the shit coming through my head." And if it cost him

jobs, hassles with the law, his life eventually, so be it, so be it.
He was even hip offstage. Once, down on his luck, he imper-
sonated a priest and canvassed a wealthy Florida neighborhood
for donations to a leper colony. "My permit?" he bubbled,
when finally confronted by police, "Gracious, let's see, didn't
Brother Leon take care of that matter? I know I spoke to the
Cardinal about it after Mass." Lenny considered himself a satirist rather than a comedian, and he had nothing but raised eye-
brows for the Bob Hopes and Henny Youngmans who
rehearsed with stopwatches and performed from cue cards. For
Lenny, satire, "tragedy plus time," that was where it was at;
and he even made up "bits" about Christ and Hitler, though he
thought Hitler, like cheese, needed a little aging to become
really funny. Oh, yes, Lenny was hip, and hip was death on hep
and hype.

One of Lenny's targets was violence, particularly the violence Hollywood and other image-makers exploited and
cloaked in stereotypes and mindless slogans. In one routine,
Father Flotsky's Triumph, he does a complex takeoff of a su-
perhackneyed prison movie called *Brute Force* which might
have been created by Warner Brothers on acid:

"Okay, *Prison Break*, cut one, a riot is in progress and guards
are being held hostage in the yard below. . . .
PRISON WARDEN (*harsh, heavy voice over loudspeaker*): Alright,
Dutch! This the warden! You've got eighteen men down there,
prison guards who've served me faithfully. Give up, Dutch, and
we will meet any reasonable demands you've got—except the
vibrators. Forget it, you're not getting the vibrators. Can you
hear me?
DUTCH: Yahdeyah! Yahdudeyahdudeyah!
WARDEN: Never mind those Louis Armstrong impressions. Give
up! You're a rotten, vicious criminal! You never were any good
to your family—you're your own worst enemy, Dutch, believe
me. *Hab mir gesucht.* Give it up.
DUTCH: Yahdeyah!
WARDEN: Shut up! You goddam nut you! "Yahdeyahda" . . .
putzo. I'm sorry I gave him the library card, that moron. I dunno
what we're gonna do with these guys. Maybe if we just killed
four or five for an example. (*Picks up telephone*) Tower C! Kill

about twelve down there! The bullets? Ask my wife . . . look in
the back of my brown slacks, you'll find them, come on! What?
Don't put me on. You know which ones to kill—the ones in the
grey shirts, turkeys.
FATHER FLOTSKY (*with a thick brogue*): Just a moment! Before
there's killing, I'll go down there.
WARDEN: Will you come off the Pat O'Brien bits now? Father,
you don't understand—these guys are monsters. They got
knives and guns—
FLOTSKY: Son, you seem to forget that I've got something
stronger than knives and guns—
WARDEN: You mean, ah—
FLOTSKY: That's right—jujitsu.

Okay, cut to Death Row, the worst part of the last mile—real
Uncle Tom scene—the first cell.

NEGRO PRISONER (*singing*): Wadduh—boy, wadduh—boy. Soon
ahm gwine up to hebben on de big riber boat. Deen, when I
gets up dere, I gwine gets me a lotta fried chicken and waddy-
melone . . . (*singing*) Fried chicken and waddy-melone . . .
chicken and waddy-melone. Yassuh, you don' mine dyin, boss,
if ya got a nach'ral sense of rhythm, yuck, yuck, yuck. Yessuh.
There's one thing that's fun to be colored folk—that's all you do
is get up in de mo'nnin and gwine ta hebben. (Sings)

> Ahm gwine ta hebbin, Lawd
> Yes, gwine ta hebbin, Lawd
> Ahm gwine to hebbin,
> Lawd

Now a white guy is going to the chair—the last mile.

WHITE PRISONER (*weeping*): I don't wanna die, I don't wanna
die.
NEGRO: Don worry, boss, it aint so bad.
WHITE: Whaddayou care, you niggers are used to gettin
lynched!
NEGRO: Don't worry. We gwine ta hebbin. Fust thing ahm gwine
ta do when ahve gwine ta hebbin is find out jus what a "gwine"
is.

Alright, Flotsky's down in the yard now . . .

> FLOTSKY: Hello, Dutch. You remember Father Flotsky now,
> don't ya, son? You'd never hurt Father Flotsky. You're not a bad
> boy now, Dutchie, are you now? Killing six children doesn't
> make a person all bad. Give me the gun now.
> DUTCH: Yahdeyah! Yahdeyahdedah!
> FLOTSKY: Oh, he's disgusting! He's a goddam nut! They're no
> good, the lot of them—"Yahdeyahda"—they're animals! Pour it
> on—kill them all! They're no good. I'll give them mass
> confessions—but first I've gotta bless the motorcycles.
> WARDEN (*over loudspeaker*): You men—the prison guards! Look,
> I dunno what the hell it is, but Dutch don wanna give up, and I
> don't wanna screw up my pension and, ah, it's dog eat dog, you
> know what I mean. You guards knew what the gig was when
> you took the job. Only hope that your old ladies swung with
> Mutual of Omaha. Dutch, ya got three seconds, three big ones.
> Ya gonna listen?
> DUTCH: Imma lissenna nobody—nobody in this whole stinking
> prison! Nobody!!! Nobody!
> KINKY (*high effeminate voice over loudspeaker*):
> DUTCH: lithen to me, bubby—
> DUTCH: Who is that?
> KINKY:Who *ith* it!!! Ith Kinky, the hothpital attendant! The one
> who gave you the bed baths, bubby, don't screw up your good
> time.
> DUTCH: Kinky, sweetheart! Kinky, baby! I'll give it all up faw
> you!
> KINKY: Did you hear that? OO-oo! He's giving it all up for me?
> Did you hear that, all you bitcheth in thell-block eleven. Did
> you hear him, warden?
> WARDEN: I heard him, ya fruit!
> KINKY: Watch it, warden, hmmmmm? Don't overthtep your
> boundth. Are we gonna get all our demanth?
> WARDEN: Whaddaya want, ya fag bastard you?
> KINKY: A gay bar in the west wing.
> WARDEN: (*with Yiddish inflection*): Awrighty—you'll get, you'll
> get. What else?
> KINKY: I wanna be the Avon representative for the prithon.

Cut.

Well. Among other things, what this routine does is to satirize
the Hollywood stereotypes of the hard-ass warden, the

wronged killer, the priest with the heart-of-gold. In Lenny's "movie," the warden himself is a con, Dutch a hopeless psychopath, the priest a bumbling fool, and Kinky the *coup de gras*, who reminds us that sadomasochistic homosexuality is one of the staples of prison life. The language is a creative mix of Hollywood clichés and raunchy multilevel dialects from Yiddish to ghetto-black to "pink." The thrust of the bit is sobering in what it implies about what people *think* happens in prisons and what *really* does. The piece has the complexities of a jazz fugue, as music critic Orrin Keepnews has observed, with Lenny going further and further out until he passes mockery and hits a raw and shocking bit of twisted reality. We see the grinning skull exposed beneath the prettified ideal: *the truth.*

Lenny had that one rule for himself—to tell the truth. As he said, "People should be taught what is, not what should be. All my humor is based on destruction and despair. If the whole world were tranquil, without disease and violence, I'd be standing in the breadline—right back of J. Edgar Hoover." He hit at the hidden prejudices of his audience:

> [*Outraged whisper*] What did he say? 'Are there any niggers here tonight?' Jesus Christ! Is that cruel. Does he have to get that low for laughs? *Wow!* Have I ever talked about the *schwartzes* when they've gone home? Or placated some Southerner by absence of voice when he ranted and raved about *nigger nigger nigger?*

Lenny kept on going to stab home his point. "Are there any niggers here tonight? I know that one nigger works here, I see him back there. Oh, there's two nigger customers, and, ah, *aha!* Between those two niggers sits one kike—man, thank God for the kike." That last touch puts the joke back on himself. A "kike" himself, Lenny is throwing out the old double-whammy boomerang. What he's *really* doing is trying to "get the shit out into the open" and strip racial epithets of their venom. If the bullshit *was* out in the open, then maybe we might get somewhere.

Lenny *noodged* liberals as well—defending Lyndon Johnson by pointing out that Northerners assume that "people who tawk lahk thayat" must be redneck "shitkickuhs." But when all was said and done, "the South, whew!" was Lenny's reaction, and if there was a problem, well—well?

> We got to stop pissing away all the money on Radio Free Europe. Mississippi is like the Amazon with those missionaries down there. Let's face it—you'd be afraid to go to Mississippi— you'd be afraid to walk the street alone. It doesn't say on your visa—"stamp O" for Old Miss. We never give one nickel to Radio Free South—ever.
>
> And I haven't seen one newspaper that understood anything about those people, it's just *rank rank rank rank rank*.

Lenny kept going South, asking us to try this on for size: "Tell you what a bad guy Castro is. Since Castro came, you can get no narcotics, no abortions, and there's no prostitutes there. He's really screwed it up for vacationers. That's right. He's really an asshole, this guy."

Lenny didn't always hit. "Greyliners," his term for tourist-bus folks, often regarded him as just some foulmouthed Jew spoofing their cherished way of life and huffed out of his performances. Lenny also got into trouble by *saying* things you were not supposed even to *think*. He was hopped on for referring to Bobby Franks, the victim of joy-killers Leopold and Loeb, as "a snotty kid." And when he mentioned that film footage of the Kennedy assassination made it look as if Jackie was trying to flee a bad scene by crawling out of the limo, some critics considered that the ultimate in bad taste. Whatever, Lenny would shrug, you win some and you lose some.

But Lenny did not insult his audience, just their prejudices. He never considered himself an "insult" comedian in the mold of a Jack E. Leonard or Don Rickles, who take on the audience as part of their act and then bless them at the end. To Lenny, insulting was no big deal; everybody had an Uncle Morty who could do that. Lenny was after bigger game. He wanted his audience to think—*insisted* on it—as he shpritzed about such things as "The Bomb," "Religions, Inc." and "How to Entertain a Colored Guy at Home." It didn't always work, nor was he always funny. Sometimes (particularly when obsessed about his busts) he would just, *well*, go on and on and on about the legal system. Even his true fans sometimes gave up on him then, and he'd be left reading trial transcripts to empty tables.

But, despite addictions, compulsions, and occasional wipe-outs, Lenny *was* special. Young people today, exposed to the latest scatologists of the nightclub circuit and "gross-out" movies like *Animal House* and Cheech and Chong's *Smoke,* might find it hard to understand just what all the fuss was about Lenny. But to anyone who grew up in the sanitized fifties of Ed Sullivan and Elvis-from-the-waist-up, there is no mystery about his special niche. We knew what the truth was—we just had not heard it. As Jules Feiffer says, "The blatant, mischievous disinformation practiced on us from birth seemed like such a norm that you didn't know you had a right to expect anything different. [We felt abnormal] just as Huck Finn felt foolish and self-conscious for feeling loyal to Jim when he should have turned him in. The rules of society were so corrupt and cynical . . . that anybody pointing out the obvious was considered the cynic instead. In a time of blandness and conformity, Lenny was the ultimate hipster who took it all—literature, politics, religion, sex, race—and ran with it. Lenny spoke the unspeakable—or something so close to it that sacred cows became raging bulls under his withering sarcasm.

Lenny was valuable in other ways too. He showed audiences as well as other comedians what a "performance" could be. If it was a far cry from the lectures of Mark Twain and Artemus Ward on the Chautauqua circuit, he utilized many of the same techniques—impersonation, broad references to the world at large, and a mocking, self-deprecating manner. Lenny had no "act" as such, just bits or pieces of material he kept changing so they were never quite the same. He would just come on shpritzing about some "shit," changing voices, creating characters, sliding from one bit into another—even stepping out of character to comment on the bit; and he deliberately left off some of the polish to keep the feeling raw, so that no two shows were ever the same. Rather than performing, he treated his audience like fellow human beings who would care to hear his thoughts. In short, he welcomed us into his head. For Lenny, the ultimate insult was "dumb." He wanted his listeners to be hip and he wanted the world to be hip because hip meant aware of the truth beneath the surface. "The what-should-be never did exist," he said, "but people keep trying to live up to it. There is only what is." But this quest for some sort of truth night after night extracted a toll. Lenny not only needled the uptight world of Lima, Ohio, out there in what he called Eisenhower-Land, he also "needled" himself until finally (that last heroin-filled needle stuck in his thigh) he was gone.

There were many contradictions in Lenny. Take his attitude toward women. Lenny liked women—but he was confused about what he liked them *for*. He said he wanted a down-to-earth woman. "I don't want some sharpee that can quote Kerouac and walk with poise," he said, "I jus wanna hear my old lady say, 'Get up and fix the toilet, it's still making noise.' But sometimes, he confessed, he just wanted "to squirt the poison and run." He married Honey Harlow, a bright stripper who could cut "feminity" to bone truth as quickly as Lenny could reduce a man to a "shlong" or a "putz." But they were both raunchy romantics, and their on-again, off-again marriage didn't last. He knew that guys were different than women when it came to sex, but he found that comical not shameful, just the way it was: "Guys will it do to their fist, to mud, to barrels," he would begin; and then he was off, fantasizing about a poor woman coming home to find her husband making it with a chicken. But he carried the riff further, citing an obscure New York law which forbade intercourse with a chicken. Himself doing it to a chicken? *No way.* They're too short—how could you kiss a chicken? Ah, but the wife, back to the wife. "Where's your chicken? How come you're alone tonight—your chicken left town? Don't *touch* me. You want dinner, let your chicken get it, you asshole, you!" Ah yes, women, chickens, sex!—it was all a mess. But never, Lenny warned, never admit you've cheated, just roll: "I'm telling ya, this chick came downstairs with a sign around her neck LAY ON TOP OF ME OR I'LL DIE. What was I to do?"

But though he made fun of differences, he made no claim for male supremacy or macho ways and defended woman's vulnerability as well. "We're *all* whores," he insisted. And he railed against the hypocrisy of casinos: "Since all the moralists and purists support Las Vegas as the entertainment capital of the world, one would assume that the attraction at the Star Dust is a Passion Play or a Monet exhibit or the New York City Ballet with Eugene Ormandy conducting. But, no, what is the big attraction? Tits and Ass. *I beg your pardon?*" After his divorce he asked plaintively: "How can I get married again? I'd have to say the same things to another woman that I said to Honey. And I couldn't say the same things to another woman because somehow that would be corrupt to me."

To Lenny, if sex was not corrupt, religion often was:

> Why don't religious institutions use their influence to relieve human suffering instead of sponsoring such things as the Legion of Decency, which dares to say it's indecent that men should watch some heavy-titted Italian starlet because to them breasts are dirty.
>
> Beautiful, sweet, tender, womanly breasts that I love to kiss; pink nipples that I love to feel against my clean-shaven face. They're clean.
>
> I say to you, Legion of Decency—you with your dings scrubbed with holy water and soap—*you're* dirty!

The self-righteousness of conservative Christianity bugged him in particular "And since they condone capital punishment," Lenny japed, "I want them to stop bitching about Jesus getting nailed up." And he wasn't afraid to take on the Jew-Christian thing, front-and-center. Often, early in his act, he would nod and shrug, "Yeah, we did it—my family. I found a note in my basement: "We killed him—signed Morty."

> "Why did you kill Christ, Jew?"
> "We killed him because he didn't want to become a doctor, that's why."

Unlike many Jewish comics, Lenny emphasized his Jewishness, talked about being an outsider in "Christian" America; and he shpritzed Yiddishisms with the casual aplomb of a Catskills comic. But he also appropriated that ironic idiom of the jazz hipster, in which inflection is all. He did an airplane bit that was the height of "cool."

PILOT: What was that?
CO-PILOT: The back end of the plane just blew off. Hey, man, seventeen people just fell out.
PILOT: Cool it.
CO-PILOT: Is this weird? There go twenty more. Are we ever gonna get yelled at!

Lenny did not so much write his material as "discover" it. "I'll ad lib things on the floor, and then they become bits, right? It'll be funny. Then the next night I'll do another line, or I'll be thinking about it, like in a cab, and it'll get some form, and I'll work it into a bit." If he was going good, he'd work up maybe fifteen fresh minutes a night, but on the average he figured on four or five. Ad lib, he said, gave him the feeling of "free form." But this "pissing on the velvet" as he called it didn't come easy:

The truth. When I'm interested in truth, it's really a truth truth, one hundred per cent. And that's a terrible kind of truth to be interested in.
    Dig. The only honest art form is laughter, comedy. You can't fake it, Jim. Try to fake three laughs in an hour—ha ha ha ha ha —they'll take you away, man. You can't.

Lenny denied that his comedy was "sick." "Take Zsa Zsa who gets 50K a week in Las Vegas and school teachers' top salary is 6K a year. That is really sick to me." Comics before did harelip jokes and moron jokes and performed as Rastus in blackface and fright wigs. Now *that* was cruel, Jack.
    Lenny was far out, no bones about it, operating in his own constellation of hip hucksters and rube hayseeds, prison wardens and wheeler-dealer popes. Lenny intrigued the young, perhaps because he seemed so All Alone—too weird and testy for the old folks, who preferred Red Skelton, Uncle Miltie, Jackie Gleason's *Honeymooners*, or Bob Hope, that Lawrence Welk of the one-liner with his and-a-one-and-a-two, laugh-laugh. For Hope, delivery was (and still is) all; his jokes are as topical and disposable as the years, and he gives people their money's worth as we move from war to war. But for Lenny, the performance was all (Spaulding Grey and Laurie Anderson take note), and it was *live*, oh, yes, was it live! For Lenny, words were nothing without accents, without context, and the worst

"drag" of all was war. And when Lenny did his riffs on the hypocrisy of religion, the stupidity of racism, the muddle of sex, "dirty words," the Bomb, he was, we could see, "out there" —and he spent enough days in court and nights in jail to prove that *something* was on the line.

Before George Carlin, Lenny was trying to take the bite out of words. Although on stage you could say "nigger," you couldn't say "fuck"; so Lenny said, "I want the Supreme Court to stand up and tell me that fucking is dirty and no good," and waited for the cops to bust him. In order for something to be obscene, it had to appeal to prurient interest; "Now if I get you horny listening to me," he smiled at his audiences, "—well that's cool, but also weird." Lenny even used his own name to drive home the absurdity of censorship:

> "Mommy, look, there's a man sitting over there with his bruce hanging out."
> "Beverly Schmidlap is a real bruce-teaser, y'know?"
> "Kiss my bruce, baby."

He pointed out how this hypocrisy applied to the everyday:

> If I'm at your house, I can never say to you, "Excuse me, where's the toilet?" I have to get hung up with that corrupt facade of "Excuse me, where's the little boy's room?"
> "Oh, you mean the tinkle-dinkle ha-ha room, where they have sachets and cough drops and pastels?"
> "That's right, I wanna shit in the cough drop box."

Today the "dirty word" war continues with The Moral Majority taking up the campaign of the Legion of Decency. Yet, in the Age of Permission, few comics are attacked any more (the gay community's attack on Eddie Murphy being one notable exception). But as resistance has lessened, many comics seem to be making just more and more outrageous (yet harmless) gross-outs. But it wasn't that way in the fifties. Lenny's fight mattered, and the burden is lighter because of him. Lenny's quirky but honest intelligence was his personal signature, and his dedication of *How to Talk Dirty and Influence Friends* reminds one of Vonnegut: "I dedicate this book to all the followers of Christ and his teachings; in particular to a true Christian—Jimmy Hoffa—because he hired ex-convicts as, I assume, Christ would have."

Lenny tried to point out proper priorities; war, for example, he argued was the real obscenity:

> You can't do anything with anybody's body to make it dirty to me. Six people, eight people, one person—you can do only one thing to make it dirty: kill it. Hiroshima was dirty. Chessman was dirty. Remember, THOU SHALT NOT KILL—means just that.

Lenny always lampooned, and preached against, violence. Violence was the true evil. Kenneth Tynan sees Lenny as "a pearl miscast before swine." "[C]onstant, abrasive irritation produces the pearl; it is a disease of the oyster . . . and Lenny Bruce was a disease of America." Jack Parr called him "a junky Mark Twain." Nat Hentoff wrote, "It is in Lenny Bruce—and only in him—that there has emerged a cohesively 'new' comedy of nakedly honest moral rage in the deceptions all down the line in our society." To Arthur Gelb, Lenny's humor was "biting, sardonic, certainly stimulating and often quite funny— but never in a jovial way. His mocking diatribe rarely elicits a comfortable belly laugh. It requires concentration." Richard Pryor says simply, "Well, there was Lenny."

Certain images haunt. In his autobiography, Lenny confessed that his parents' divorce was traumatic for him. He imagines himself on the Boardwalk in Atlantic City, watching his parents kiss and hearing them say, "It's all over, Lenny, it was just a joke." One wishes Lenny could be called back from the dead with the same one-liner.

·   ·   ·

Besides Lenny, there have been many Jewish comics who have distinguished themselves on the American stage and screen— the Marx Brothers, Weber and Fields, Fanny Brice, Milton Berle, Jack Benny, the antic Sid Caesar, Jackie Mason, Mel Brooks, David Brenner, Shecky Greene, Myron Cohen. The list could go on and on. Certainly, Jewish-Americans have occupied a place on the comic stage far out of proportion to their 3 percent share of the population. Steve Allen has estimated that during the sixties, 80 percent of working comedians were Jewish. If Hitler had applied his anti-Semitic paranoia to comedy instead of banking, he might have had something. But *why* is this? Perhaps comedy does indeed spring from pain, from having to scrap to survive, and the Lower East Side immigrant backgrounds of so many of these comics might account for a great deal. Certainly, they shared the same poverty and acquired the same hard edge; they all went to the same school—the College of Hard Knocks.

This environmental theory might also account for the prominence of so many black comedians today. Of course, there were always black comics. From the first minute the slaves set foot in America, some among them no doubt tried to joke away their pain. One slave story features a slave paying homage to his master in this deathbed scene: "Farewell massa! Pleasant journey. You soon be dere, massa—[it's] all the way down hill!" Blacks put on the mask to slip past white scrutiny.

> I fooled old Master seven years,
> Fooled the overseer three.
> Hand me down my banjo,
> And I'll tickle your bel-lee.

We have little of that humor on paper, but we know slavery was no joke.

In the nineteenth century, white minstrel shows picked up on the "darky" jokes that had been invented and exchanged in the slave barns. In other words, they joked about the joke. But until recently, whites insisted on their black entertainers appearing almost without words—smiling and tap dancing, Stepan Fetchitting along. It was the Civil Rights revolution of the late fifties and sixties that brought black comedians into white clubs and white living rooms and allowed them to expresss their own thoughts and tell their real jokes. Not surprisingly, some of these thoughts (and many of these jokes), were as bitter as Billy Holiday's "Strange Fruit." A clutch of bright, talented black comics emerged—Redd Foxx, Nipsey Russell, Flip Wilson, Slapsy White (even the names betray the old minstrel show flavor). Of that early group, Dick Gregory was perhaps the best and the brightest; and *Nigger*, his autobiography, is the most moving document of black comedy, which of course is based on the legacy of slavery—and how *funny* is that? Recollecting one of his trips to the movies as a kid, Gregory recalls a certain rage:

> Used to sit there and laugh at all those dumb Hollywood Africans grunting and jumping around and trying to fight the white men, spears against high-powered rifles. Once we had a riot in the movies when Tarzan jumped down from a tree and grabbed about a hundred Africans. We didn't mind when Tarzan beat up five or ten, but this was just too many, a whole tribe, and we took that movie house apart, ran up on the stage and kicked the screen and fought the guys who still dug Tarzan.

In his nightclub, act, Gregory was alternately abrasive and consolatory. He was particularly good at deflecting and turning back racial slurs. He silenced one drunken white heckler by saying, "I'd rather be your slave than your liver." If someone shouted out the magic word "Nigger!," Gregory just smiled, "You hear what that guy just called me? Roy Roger's horse. He called me Trigger." Or even better: "You know my contract reads that every time I hear *that* word, I get fifty dollars more a night. I'm only making ten dollars a night, and I'd like to put the owner out of business. Will everybody in the room please stand up and yell nigger?"

Gregory even worked his Civil Rights marches into his act:

> Last time I was down South I walked into this restaurant, and this waitress came up to me and said: "We don't serve colored people here."
>
> I said: "That's all right. I don't eat colored people. Bring me a whole fried chicken."

But Gregory has long since given up stand-up comedy to fight campaigns against racism and obesity. Godfrey Cambridge, another black comic of that generation, was good ("Down South the black pool and the white pool are the same except there's no water in the black pool—and the diving board's higher."), but he died young. Today we have Bill Cosby and Eddie Murphy of course—all over. But as Cosby has broken through barrier after barrier, his brand of humor has become notably blander. He threatens to become a black Bob Hope or a white Bill Cosby (which may not be such a bad thing for America). Murphy seems to have settled in as a macho smart aleck par excellence (Sample Murphy: "Man, gonorrhea—your dick hurt, you took a shot. Herpes, you keep that shit forever like luggage. Then AIDS kills people. What's next—You put your dick in and it *explodes?*" Even trailblazer Redd Foxx seems now actually to have *become* Fred Sanford and settled into a bath of dyspepsic grumbling.

But we do have Richard Pryor who is "out there," still winging it and proving to be something special. Pryor is probably loved (and hated) with more intensity than any comic in America—and for good reasons. Like Dick Gregory, the young Richard Pryor came on during the sixties as an "angry nigger," denouncing the hypocrisies of white America. In his race material, Pryor got much mileage out of his considerable skills as a mimic, demonstrating—colorfully, sometimes cruelly—differences between whites and blacks talking, walking, eating, fucking. RACE, my, yes, he did talk about RACE—nigger, honky, whatever. He hardly talked about anything else, slashing away at the difference between official truth (the *de jure* equality of the law) and unofficial truth (the *de facto* inequality in the streets) and trying to describe what it feels like to be black—and what it feels like, he told us, is that you're perpetually getting screwed. Outrageous antiwhite slurs were part of Pryor's act; yet he developed and kept a hard-core white following because of his intelligence and versatility—and because much of what he implied, inferred, and said was true. Now Pryor shies away from "race" material and even offers solemn anti-drug warnings. But if he has toned down his self-destructive "crazy nigger" wingings, Pryor still showcases his manic energy and street smarts to hone in on the same melange of hypocricies that Gregory and Cambridge attacked. Pryor is also a great "linguist"—that is, he can do a crackerjack "cracker" or an excellent uptight yuppy; and his myriad black voices range from Motown to Tupelo, Mississippi, to Beverly Hills. He employs an offbeat, off-color jive that is outrageous, constantly inventive, *and* funny.

In many respects, Pryor's is a crossover act; along with his corrosive tongue, he is a genius of mime. Had Chaplin found his right voice, says Pauline Kael, he might have become something like Pryor, whom she calls "a master of lyrical obscenity" and "the only great poet satirist among our comics." High praise indeed. Pryor has been often dubbed "the black ghost of Lenny Bruce"—a dark moniker to hang on anyone, particularly a self-destructive hyperdude like Pryor. But we can see that Pryor, along with George Carlin, has updated Lenny's drug, sex, and social raps, smoothing over the roughness, the hardness, the Jewishness. Pryor, however, carries his own hardness —and his own suitcase of moral outrage. In the early 1960s, tired of "safe" humor and his cornball audience. Pryor, like Lenny, walked off the stage of a Las Vegas club, determined to "rap" and tell the truth. Pryor has some reservations about Lenny's example, however: "Lenny was alone, way ahead of his time. But it really doesn't make much sense to make another martyr." But on June 9, 1980, Pryor almost became, if not another martyr, certainly a victim—barely surviving "the great burn-up" in which he immolated himself free-basing cocaine. Now he claims to have changed his life-style—he has certainly changed his act. "There's been a whole lie that comics can't be funny unless they're unhappy," he says now. "It's a shame to think you have to be miserable to be successful. You don't have to take drugs and drink yourself to death or act irrational or be different on purpose to be anything." Hokay, right on, Richard —we be watching, brother.

Pryor's concerns, and his methods, recall Lenny's. Like Lenny, his concern is with truth—with the difference, for instance, between what men and women *think* they want from each other and what they really *get*; with what being black really means in the white-dominated society; with what virtue can exist in a hypocritical society. Pryor recalls, as a boy, peeking over a transom in the whorehouse in which he lived to see the same white officials who wouldn't give blacks the time of day humping black women. It is such hypocrisy that stirs up Pryor's comic mind. For instance, even married life, for Pryor, retains some flavor of the marketplace. A man (or rather his "dick" which has a life of its own) not only wants, but is willing to pay for, "pussy," so a woman might well think that her "pussy" is made of gold and therefore negotiates for the highest bid. In the Pryor scenario, men are driven, and women, like toreadors, parry and deflect these bulls until they get what they want—which might be a new washing machine. So sex is really "pussy-power," because the "dick" is just this helpless, foolish animal that drives a man to destruction. Sex as slapstick once again. Pryor didn't invent this view (as I have previously mentioned—the clowns of ancient Greece with their enormous phalluses were there long before him), but he has so refined it that in his fast-moving hands it continues to be a not-so-subtle metaphor for the joking of the gods.

Pryor has starred in a series of highly-financed and mostly mediocre films, but his best can be caught in videotapes of his chameleon act, most notably *Richard Pryor Live* and *Richard Pryor—Live on Sunset Strip*. Here he can be a tiger in Africa, a snake in the woods, "Mudbone," the old Mississippi Delta black philosopher, or just Richard Pryor, a multidivorced man speculating about the nature of women and the mystery of marriage and wondering about his own alternatingly homicidal and tender feelings. Though Pryor's blackness is certainly part and parcel of his special appeal, he manages to transcend race and tell us something about those parts of life that somehow oft go wrong. As he shrugs, "You gotta get through the day, Jack."

Pre-burn-up, in *Richard Pryor Live*, at Long Beach in 1979, Pryor starts off with some "wise-ass nigger" stuff.

> Know what I like? White people come back after intermission and find niggers done steal their seats. (*"Bad-ass Black voice*): "Sit yer ass *down! (Pause)* Sit yer *ugly* ass down!"
>   White people be funky (*imitates up-tight white person walking*), but niggers run *over* people. Eight white people dead in the parking lot.

He then segues to having been arrested for "killing his car" with a .357 Magnum: "The cops, dey don't kill *cahs*, dey kill *Nig*-gahs!" But then (and this is part of his charm) he is suddenly "doing" animals—a mean Doberman, a sex-crazed pet squirrel-monkey named Fran who humps him in the ear, a Ger-

WILLIAM KEOUGH

man Shepherd who leaps over the fence when Fran dies to sympathize with "Rich," only to add, "I be back chasing your ass t'morrow."

Soon Pryor is down on the floor, restaging his heart attack, calling Heaven to speak to God, only to get "some bitch angel" who says, "I'm sorry but we'll have to put you on hold." Writhing on the stage floor, acting out his pleading, wondering about the wisdom of mouth-to-mouth resuscitation. What if (always *what if,* right?) what if it made Death back up and crawl down into the healthy person: "Death don't care where it go. He go down your lung, he get two-for-one, that a *good* day for him." At the hospital now, trying to piss in a bottle, Pryor is moving, always moving, and using those wide eyes and mobile body to act it all out—stopping suddenly to look out, as if he just understood something: "A hospital ain't no place to get *well.*" Smiling: "John Wayne kicked death's ass. *(Wayne's voice)*: Get the fuck out of here, Death."

When Pryor goes on to talk of his family, it is an irreverent and poignant mixture: "My father died fucking. He was fifty-seven and the woman was eighteen. My father came and went at the same time." Then he is doing blacks and whites at funerals, the whites teary-eyed and restrained, the blacks letting it all hang out—*take-me, take-me, Lawd, Lawd Lawdy-Lawd.* And then he's suddenly a little boy, being switched by his grandmother (something both blacks and whites can remember), and afraid of his father: "I piss on myself sometimes he call my name. *(Deep black voice)* Rich———ard. He hit me so hard my chest caved in and wrapped around his fist."

Then he's back to animals again and Nature . . . soft creaking of twigs in the woods (Pryor is an expert at using the mike as a prop). But nature is weird, and he is weird *in* nature, still urban and anxious. He does a bit about going out hunting and confronting a frightened deer (also played by Pryor) cautiously drinking water. "Beautiful, ain't it?" "Give me the rifle," says the other dude. Then he is "Macho Man," toughest dude on the block, crippled by a kick to the "nuts" trying to fight fair. So much for Macho Man! Then he is one of his own children "explaining" how something got broken, and Pryor can be a wonderful child, open-eyed, cute, shrewd. But afterward he shrugs: "I can't bring myself to beat my kids up, y'know, standard parent stuff. I don't wan't to fuck them up like I'm fucked up. So I just say, 'Shut the fuck up and get out of my face.' "

What are we to make of that sort of brutal admission? What is interesting about a Pryor performance is how often he moves from the brutal to the vulnerable and back again. This mix of violence and sensitivity is not Pryor's unique property, but he is perhaps the best at it. Pryor is not just an "attack" comic; he is too human for that, we see. With painful honesty, Pryor tells stories about himself and his own shortcomings; he is as much perpetrator as victim. Pryor's violence is random and real—*awful;* and we wince as well as laugh.

In *Live on the Sunset Strip,* Pryor comes on with that same hip swagger, sharp red suit, black shirt, a glad-to-be-back smirk. And just to show he hasn't gone soft, he starts in hard, joking about fucking. But soon he is talking about some post-burn-up changes as he questions his capacity for rage. He shrugs, "Maybe I don't have it in me any more—maybe I'm not angry at anything any more." He admits that for the last six years his wife thought her name was "white honky bitch." Of himself he shrugs, "I'm no day at the beach," and goes on, "Feelings are some *hard* fucking things to deal with. When you feel heartache you want to kill somebody—everybody in the *whole* world." He offers a parable. While making a movie at the Arizona State Penitentiary, he asked a "brother" why he had killed everybody in the house only to get the reply, *They was home.* Pryor sighs: "Thank God for penitentiaries." But he admits to fear when he hears white people going "Yeehah!" at night because they might be about to rope themselves a "black ma'-fuggah." And he says things that make the audience applaud as well as laugh: "Racism is a bitch—it's hard enough being a human being. But if you're black, it's enough to make you crazy."

Recalling his tour through Africa where he saw "all these black people, one hundred million strong, but no niggers," Pryor says, "I ain't never gonna call another black man a nigger, the word's dead. We use it to perpetuate our own wretchedness." After this seriousness, he moves on, like quicksilver, to the animals he freaks out on—the gazelles and lions—the lion with that look of "Get yer ass outta the car." And he does a wonderful imitation of a speedy cheetah trying to chase down a crafty antelope. In perhaps his funniest bit, he offers an eerily lifelike impression of a mafioso who just laughs when nineteen-year-old Richard tries to hold him up for his pay. The man then tells Richard the (to him) hilarious story of how they killed this guy *(unh-unh-unh)* with an ice pick *(unh-unh-unh)* but the ice pick broke *(unh-unh-unh, unh-unh-unh.)* Pryor shudders. This, he suggests, is violence which is too far out even to bear comment. *Whoah,* just whoah. He is quiet a moment.

When some one calls for Mudbone, his old Mississippi "Ni-grah," Pryor agrees, somewhat reluctantly, and announces it is his last Mudbone. But even Mudbone now talks about the real Richard, "Fire got on his ass—fried what brains he had left." And then Pryor is doing the story of his burn-up, of how as an addict he was hounded by Jim Brown who kept asking, "Whatcha gonna do now?" and how the insidious cocaine pipe would whisper, "Stay here, Rich. I'll take care of you." Pryor mimes how much a simple wash can hurt, for instance, when your whole body is burnt and the skin peels off. At the end of the concert he holds up a match, suggesting that as master of the humor of pain, he is on to our own dark jokes, "What's *that?* Richard Pryor running down the street." Pryor looks out, his face splitting into a grin; and the audience stomps and claps—as if he is a national treasure.

.   .   .

That other "their" who sits on the left hand of Bruce is George Carlin. In the sixties, when Lenny saw Carlin working in Haight-Ashbury, he liked what he saw and gave him his blessing to work up some of his bits. Irish-Catholic George owes something to Pryor and other black comics as well. "I was attracted by the freedom blacks had," he says, "they were free with their bodies, their attitudes, and their street personalities. It was a silent revolution going on within me. . . . I picked up the Dozens from the blacks." Scuffling about as a semifreak, Carlin carried on the fight for freedom of speech with his classic *Seven Dirty Words* routine. Fired in Las Vegas ("for saying shit where the big game is crap," he now jokes), Carlin took his act to college campuses where his audience didn't care if he went "too far."

For Carlin, language is a live grenade to be inspected. In his concert film, *Playing With Your Head,* he throws some. *Battered housewives?* Carlin suggests we form a Battered Plants Club. "Hanging plants, hmm, no wonder they're frightened, no wonder ivy clings." He makes fresh wrinkles out of tired clichés. He asks for a moment of silence for forty-seven mentally retarded Bolivian senior citizens who stood up together on the same corner of the roller coaster, then shouts, "What's all this favoritism toward the dead? Fuck the dead—what about the injured?" And he's a master of the nasty retort, particularly to stupidity. "Are they keeping you busy?—Your wife is keeping me busy." When he wore an earring, he says, guys asked, "Are you gay?" so he would just smile and say, "Well, let's see, bend over and let's find out."

Carlin's hip, fertile imagination keeps him, and his audience, on the edge. As the Hippy-Dippy Weatherman, he offers an ominous nightly forecast: "Dark." Even more than Lenny and Pryor, Carlin has lambasted the American love affair with violence. In one spiel, he combines his "peace" and "free speech" rhetoric to suggest we substitute "fuck" for "kill" in old movies. So it goes, "Mad fucker still on the loose. . . . Stop me before I fuck again. . . . Fuck the ump." Carlin shrugs, "I'm an American. Give me a little violence and I'm happy." He goes on to recommend a few changes in sports to liven things up— like leaving the injured on the football field or placing random land mines in the outfield to spice up a baseball game. Boxing? "When police brutality becomes an Olympic sport, then boxing is a sport." Hunting? "You think hunting is a sport?—ask the deer."

Carlin uses the topical to point out hypocrisy:

> Muhammad Ali had an unusual job—beating people up. The government wanted him to change jobs. They wanted him to kill people. He said, Noooo, that's where I draw the line. I'll beat 'em up, but I don't want to kill'em. And the government said, If you won't kill'em, we won't let ya beat'em up.

Carlin consults his "hostility scoreboard" to find out how we're treating each other round the world: "According to our scoreboard we've got four civil wars going on right now, two brush-fire wars, four vest-pocket wars, four wars of liberation, two police actions, sixteen revolutions, ninety-five commando operations, fifty-two border clashes, 400 guerrilla operations, 237 cease-fire violations, forty-four surprise attacks, six outside aggressions," and so on through a depressing litany.

Like Lenny, Carlin does not so much insult people as diseased ideas. He wants his audience to see things in a new way or, rather, as things really are without the frosting. His insults are not free-form so much as directed—against censorship, stupidity, and, of course, violence. Carlin is interesting because his ideas are interesting; his humor is angry, but angry in specific and healthy directions.

                                    .   .   .

Carlin, Pryor, and Bruce are certainly no wimps. But something has happened lately to make even them shudder—namely the emergence of an "attack comedy" that has taken the freedom these older comics earned and used it to club everything and everybody, especially the unsuspecting and unfortunate.

There have always been comics who specialized in this sort of strip act. Insult comedian Jack E. Leonard, a huge fat man, said he discovered his own technique almost by accident in dealing with hecklers ("Errh . . . I just want to say . . . if you had lived . . . you would have been a very sick man"). Jonathan Winters admits he "remembers assholes" and does them on stage, "the hip rube, the Babbitts, the pseudo-intellectuals, the little politicians." Robin Williams, Rodney Dangerfield, Robert Klein—they all can hit. And insult humor is by no means an exclusively male property. Phyllis Diller dinged Fang; Joan Rivers propelled herself into a late-night talk show with nasty jokes about Liz Taylor ("The woman has more chins than a Chinese phonebook") and Bo Derek ("She's so stupid she saw a sign saying WET FLOOR so she did").

But Don Rickles, a/k/a "Mr. Warmth" and "The Kamikaze Kid," has taken this kind of assault to new heights—or fresh depths. On his first Carson show, Rickles stepped out, squinted at Johnny—and attacked. "Hi, dum-dum," he said, cutting off Johnny's comeback, "Where's it say you butt in, dummy? That's it, laugh it up. You're making fifty million a year, and your parents are home in Nebraska eating locusts for dinner." Another night, he invited a gaggle of Japanese tourists on stage and regaled his studio audience with a steady stream of ripostes about Pearl Harbor and Dr. Fu Manchu while his uncomprehending "guests" smiled and bowed. Rickles's act is simple; he comes on, this roly-poly bald guy with the street-smart smirk, and points. "Look—the Jew's laughing and the black guy next to him just picked his pocket." He spots an elderly woman: "Hiya, Mom, I spoke to the home, you go in Friday." Zing-zing-zing, all the way through. *Watch it, you hockey puck*, he seems to be saying, *you could be next*. And then Rickles smiles, tells us how wonderful we are, *really, God bless*, blows a kiss and exits.

Rickles takes some zingers too, and he is a frequent invitee to "roasts" where someone is made fun of to show, not only that he can take a joke, but that we all love him because he can take a joke. The roast itself may not be an exclusively American phenomenon, but we certainly celebrate it with Dionysian glee. At one such roast, comic Pat McCormick rose to announce, "Rickles will be a little late—he's out walking his pet rat." But such roasting is harmless, nonsubversive. Unlike Lenny, Rickles doesn't demand of his audience that they change one iota; as a matter of fact, he's a bit squirmy about any suggestion that there's any real anger in his act. "My style is to rib people I like," he says, "if there's anger in it, it isn't funny." Rickles admits there is a thin line between insult comedy and outright cruelty, but he claims he is merely satirizing our prejudices and insists "most people understand that I'm not speaking with venom."

But Sam Kinison, "the Master of Fang" and other proponents of "attack comedy" such as Eddie Murphy, Bobcat Goldthwait, Andrew Dice Clay, and Jay Charboneau, make no such claim. Goldthwaite sighs, "When will Bob Hope die?" He asks his audience what's the difference between a hamster and a gerbil. "I'm pretty sure there's more dark meat on a gerbil." And he shrieks, "I can *legally* kill anybody I want." Charboneau's idea of a message is that "We oughtta get a big middle finger bobbing on the roof of the car." Murphy has made a specialty out of antigay comedy. Dice Clay insults women, foreigners, and anyone who isn't white or male. Sam Kinison attacks any notion of compassion. Attack comedy borrows some of its style from Leonard and Rickles but, as critic Jim Sullivan points out, it is akin to the "gonzo" journalism of Hunter Thompson and "the comedic equivalent of heavy metal or punk rock," with the same rabid audience. Whatever its roots, attack comedy is the latest rage in comedy clubs, where such comics as Kinison give their audience kicks by letting it all hang out and catapulting into the stratosphere of screaming anger.

A short, fat, long-haired toad of a man, Kinison bounces around the stage in a beret and a long overcoat, ranting and raving about the injustices done to him and looking for targets. For instance, Lenny once asked a couple in his audience for their number and then called their baby-sitter to tell her they had just died in a car crash—but he *did* say he was just kidding. Kinison, on the other hand, is not kidding. He gets the name of a recently divorced guy and calls and "rags" on him while the audience listens. He has even had radio stations give prizes for the "saddest love story" so he can call the guy's "ex" to harangue her in person. An ex-minister himself, Kinison performs like a mad preacher, setting about to revenge himself on his congregation for all the lies he has had to tell in the pulpit. "Ethiopia, *hmm*," he chuckles, "of *course* those silly motherfuckers are dying. Whoever told them to live in a desert? *Human Beings Are Not Supposed to Live in the Fucking Desert!*" So much for OX-FAM. To gays: "Thanks, guys—thanks for giving us the Black Plague of the eighties." Even his own family is just more fodder for his act. Kinison tells of being at the wake of his younger brother, who committed suicide, and having to listen to his mother crying, "He was the best . . . he was the best," until he got fed up and asked, "What are you trying to *say*, Mom?"

What are *you* trying to say, Sam?

Kinison's deliberately tasteless style seems designed to make us squirm, and suggests a world so crazy that rage is the only sane response. In many ways, Sam Kinison seems proof positive of A. M. Ludovici's claim that "the audible aspect of laughter is a spiritualized snarl."But Kinison's humor seems more akin to the world of Texas chain-saw massacres than to the spirit of Lenny Bruce. Instead of truth, Kinison calls for "lies, more lies, and better lies." Women are vile, the world is vile, he says, so the only recourse is to be vile first. There is no bottom to the vileness. There is no bottom to Sam Kinison. Perhaps the audience for Kinison comes right out of that host of disenchanted Baby Boomers who grew up on The Roadrunner and The Three Stooges and were nurtured by the cut-and-slash humor of "Saturday Night Live."

But Kinison's should not, perhaps, be the last word. There are several other comedians flourishing in America whose work is more subtle and far-ranging, if harder to categorize or to encapsulate, than the explosions of attack comedians. There is, of course, Lily Tomlin, whose offbeat five-year-old Edith Ann could tell Kinison a thing or two about rage: "You know what happens when you get angry? First your hand gets just like a fist, and then your heart gets like a bunch of bees and flies up and stings your brain, and then your two eyes are like dark clouds looking for trouble and your blood is like a tornado and then you have bad weather inside your body." Yup. Is it like *that*, Sam?

Before discussing Tomlin as a healthy foil to Kinison, something must be said about sex and humor in America. Often, and perhaps not surprisingly, women have served as foils or butts for male humorists. Just consider the sex-starved widows who amuse Sut Lovingood; the stern, moralistic biddies who bedevil Huck; the "femininnies" Ambrose Bierce lampooned; the surrealistic sex objects (like Montana Wildhack) that Kurt Vonnegut invented; the pompous Margaret Dumont of the Marx Brothers' films; the female smotherers in the Chaplin and Keaton films; the She Who Must Be Obeyed (or at least *thwarted*) of James Thurber. Not surprisingly, also, women have resented these portrayals of themselves as bimbos, bumpkins, Brunhildes, or female Brownshirts. The roots of much anti-female humor seem to lie in simple ignorance (Harris, Twain, Vonnegut), fear (Lardner, Chaplin, Keaton), and misogyny (Bierce, Fields, et al.) Whatever the roots, women have rejected these portraits and have mounted some subtle and not so subtle counterattacks.

But it was only in the 1920s that women writers of sufficient bite and savvy—most particularly Anita Loos and Dorothy Parker—emerged to take on the men and stand up in their own right. Often, of course, their subject was the cabalistic battle between the sexes. Lorelei Lee, the heroine of Loos's *Gentlemen Prefer Blonds* (1925), though seemingly an empty-headed floozy, is actually a shrewd capitalist who understands that diamonds, not flowers, *are* a girl's best friend. For Parker, too, sex was a two-sided deception; and her icy skepticism threw a wet blanket over fuzzy notions of romantic love in such poems as "The Perfect Rose," which ends with her bemoaning the fact that no none ever sends *her* "a perfect limousine." But Parker, like many female humorists before and after, also turned her acid wit upon herself, so that there is more than an occasional note of masochism and self-mockery. Take "Resume," for instance:

> Razors pain you;
> Rivers are damp;
> Acids stain you;
> And drugs cause cramp.
> Guns aren't lawful;
> Nooses give;
> Gas smells awful;
> You might as well live.

Other women followed, though humor was not always their major weapon—Mary McCarthy in *The Group* and *The Company She Keeps;* the incomparable Flannery O'Connor with her gallery of Southern grotesques searching hysterically and movingly for God; Mae West in such parodies as *She Done Him Wrong* and *I'm No Angel;* "housewife" humorists such as Jean Kerr, Phyllis McKinley, and Erma Bombeck, who made fun of "supermoms" and jerky husbands. Much of this humor, however, served to strengthen the female stereotypes of *bitch*, *bimbo*, and *bubblehead*. As Martin and Seagrave point out in their *Women in Comedy*, "Comedy is aggressive and hard. Women are not supposed to be hard. They are supposed to be nice to men, children, and animals." But in the seventies an-

other sort of humor began to emerge, a kind of "closet" femin-
ism in the case of Judith Viorst, a clearly feminist humor in
such anthologies as Gloria Kaufman and Mary Kay Blakeley's
Pulling Our Own Strings and Deanne Stillman and Ann
Beatts's *Titters*, collections of humor by women that attacked
male chauvinism and demonstrated that women could be every
bit as caustic, nihilistic, and irreverent as men.

So what? one may well ask. Is that a real accomplishment? *Is*
there, really, a sexist difference in the humor game? Certainly,
women comics have felt a difference. As the late Gilda Radner
observed, "There are men who just don't think chicks can be
funny." Also, women have been constantly warned not to draw
attention to themselves as women. Comics like Phyllis Diller
and Joan Rivers had to downplay, even disguise, their sexuality
under loose-fitting clothes and fright wigs, offering self-deprecating parodies such as Heidi Ambramovitz, Rivers's tramp ex-
traordinaire. Diller played up the battle between the sexes as
farce, using her husband "Fang" as a caricature of "the Beast,"
and parodying herself as "the Beauty." Despite this, Diller was
told "You smile too much. Be hostile." Diller now shrugs off
the criticism and says she accepts the bitch role. "Comedy is
tragedy revisited. See, if everything was good, you've got Grace
Kelly and that's not funny." Perhaps the most outrageous self-
parodist has been Bette Midler, whose rock 'n' roll act combined tongue-in-cheek raunch and men's steambath humor. "If
Dick Nixon," she once japed, "would only do to Pat what he's
done to the rest of the country."

But, as anthropologist Mahadev Apte points out, "Men's
capacity for humor is not superior to women's" rather "the
prevalent cultural values emphasize male superiority and dom-
inance together with female passivity." Women, therefore, are
not *supposed* to be funny. Deanne Stillman has speculated that
male resentment against female comics stems also from a fear
that they are the ones being laughed at. Radner agreed: "I see
that being funny—and being open about it—frightens some
men, some women, too." Quite often, being a female comic has
meant feeling a special responsibility; writer Rosie Shuster
speaks of exercising self-censorship if her pieces denigrate
women. While Joan Rivers denies the very existence of *wom-*

en's humor ("If something is funny, it's funny"), her own film, *The Girl Most Likely To,* was itself a variation on the Cinderella story, with a distinctly female revenge-fantasy (based on her own story) of an ugly fat girl transformed by plastic surgery and dieting into a knockout who then snubs the man who once snubbed her. And her humor plays up to the revenge fantasies of the women in her audience who want beautiful women to be taken down a step or two. It is reductionist humor ad absurdem: "Bo Derek is so dumb she studied for her pap test."

Recent television shows such as "Laugh-In" and "Saturday Night Live" have served to showcase such female comics as Judy Carne, Goldie Hawn, Gilda Radner, the irrepressible Whoopi Goldberg, and of course Lily Tomlin. Of all these comedians, Tomlin shines as a sort of supernova whose act defies categories and boundaries. Tomlin's first Broadway show, *Appearing Nitely,* written by longtime friend and collaborator Jane Wagner, introduced a fresh notion of what a one-woman show could be, as Tomlin portrayed such diverse characters as a bored housewife, a cocktail pianist, and a male pickup artist operating out of a disco. "I construct a character essence that is as real as I can get it," Tomlin says. "I don't go for laughter, I never play for a joke per se. If the joke gets in the way, I take it out." [32] Her uncanny ability, not just to mime, but seemingly to *become* these disparate eighties types, earned Tomlin a Tony Award.

But it is in their latest theatrical venture, *The Search for Signs of Intelligent Life in the Universe* that Tomlin and writer-collaborator Wagner have created what might almost be called a new art form. Trudy, the Bag Lady who flip-flops back and forth between communicating with other worldly observers and commenting on the most hypocritical hijinks of contemporary America, is no mere victim, but a shrewd cracker-barrel philosopher in the tradition of Josh Billings and Artemus Ward. It is the element of compassion that Wagner/Tomlin bring to their work that is most remarkable and suggests not only a "difference" from male humor but a new possibility and direction for American humor, period. Strictly speaking, there is little violence in this humor (though there is anger at male chauvinism and even at some versions of the new "feminist" man). But

one does learn of violent forces beyond the stage (Reaganom-
ics, etc.) that have caused Trudy to become a Bag Lady and the
other women characters to suffer the delusions that bedevil
them.

Though the thrust of the humor is sharp as a knife, there is
also an underlying compassion, unusual in a time when most
humor is distinguished by savagery and mockery (cf., Kinison
and Murphy). In Agnes Angst, who wants to vomit every morning when she wakes, and looks upon her family like a detached
retina; in Kate, the jaded socialite who claims she is actually
dying of boredom; in Paul, the swinging sperm donor; in Bob,
the holistic capitalist; and, of course, in Trudy, who notes that
humankind first laughed the day we made an ass of ourselves
and suggests a better idea than the survival of the fittest might
be the survival of the wittiest, Wagner has drawn types who
recall the turmoil of our recent social history. Wagner is also
not above taking an occasional potshot at male megalomania.
Commenting on Henry Kissinger's remark that power is the
ultimate aphrodisiac, Edie quips, "The bombing in Vietnam
shows what it takes for *him* to get it up." The occasionally salty
humor licks our wounds, our scars. As Agnes says, "Life is like
that candle flame and we are like Gordon Liddy's hand hovering over it. And it hurts like hell, but the trick is not to mind
it."

Richard Pryor speaks of Tomlin as a "soul mate": "I mean
the characters we do literally take possession of us. You can see
the physical change take place when she's working. It's eerie."
Kevin Kelly of the *Boston Globe* echoes Pryor's feeling: "Awe-
infinitum is pretty close to what you feel when you watch Lily
Tomlin changing flesh and blood and soul as she creates one
character after another [in] a kind of staccato chamber piece
with a haunting coda." As Elizabeth Stone has noted, "Most
comedians work by demoting those presumed to be 'up a peg'
. . . but Tomlin most often works by bringing her characters 'up
a peg' or revealing the humanness of those in whom it had not
been apparent . . . the resulting laughter is inclusive, glad at
the enrichment of the human province." Dave Richards of The
Washington Post has called *Signs* "a chronicle of the human
heart, trying to mend its bruises, and ease its disappointments."

The *New York Times,* Frank Rich proclaims it "the most genu-
inely subversive comedy to be produced in years." Pretty
heady praise, perhaps, though Tomlin and Wagner's shoulders
seem wide and strong enough to stand up under the weight of
such encomia. It seems clear also that their example may suggest ways and means for other younger comedians, such as San-
dra Bernhard, Marjorie Gross, and Paula Poundstone to free
themselves from sexist definitions.

Not all female comics are like Tomlin. As Jane Anderson
says, "Comedy is not nice. It never was and never will be. And
I hope to keep it that way." Carol Siskind echoes that sentiment. A Siskind sample: "If you come home and he's using
your diaphragm for an ashtray, you know it's over." Whoopi
Goldberg likes to think Moms Mabley and Lenny Bruce are
leading her on by saying, "Do it. It's going to piss a lot of
people off." The most unabashed female comic might be Robin
Tyler, whose comedy has been blatantly sexist. "I think the
democratic emblem should be changed from a donkey to a pro-
phylactic. It's perfect. It supports inflation, keeps production
down, helps a bunch of pricks, and gives a false sense of secu-
rity when one is being screwed." To the men in her audience,
she says, "If anyone gets insecure, just do a crotch check. It's
still there." When a heckler asks if she is a lesbian, she barks
back, "Are you the alternative?" So there is as much variation
in subject and delivery among contemporary female comics as
men.

The battle has begun, and the struggle continues. Nancy
Walker has observed of the conventional view: "The humorist
occupies a position of superiority; women are inferior so
women's humor presents not boasters but victims of cultural
expectations, their political humor is usually diverted to gen-
der-specific issues such as female suffrage, and the absurdity
they present is the fundamental absurdity of oppression." The
upshot seems to be, when you come to female comics,
"You've come a long way, baby," but the journey is not yet over.

· · ·

Beside (or following) the ladies, there are a host of other fine
male stand-up comics working as well. There's Robin Williams,

who's been described as "a Jonathan Winters on speed." And Rodney Dangerfield, who makes a living out of getting "no respect at all" and tells a story about breaking up with his psychiatrist: "One day I told him I had suicidal tendencies. He told me, from now on, I had to pay in advance." And satirists, such as Shelley Berman, Nichols and May, Mort Sahl ("I'm for capital punishment. You've got to execute people. How else are they going to learn?"). And Steve Martin is still out there, that wild and crazy guy; and Steve Allen, so consistent, so generous; and young comics like Stephen Wright—one could, and perhaps should, go on and on.

But in many ways what seems a department store of riches is really the same bag. Most American comics employ the techniques of frontier humor to exploit the difference between apparent reality and what Lenny called "the truth truth." As Mel Brooks puts it, "Comedy is a red rubber ball, and if you throw it against a soft, funny wall, it will not come back. But if you throw it against the hard wall of ultimate reality it will bounce back and be very lively." To change metaphors, the best of our stand-up comedians—Lenny, Pryor, Carlin, Tomlin—have played, and continue to play, with a full deck; they show us all the cards so that we will get the full implications of the joke— and see the world behind the punch line.

Our best comics are hip, as Lenny would say, to the physical and emotional violence around them. The bad guys (so they tell us time and time again) are the deniers who claim that everything is "cool." *Oh, yeah?* our comics say, well just try this on for size, smartass. As Tom Lehrer sings in "Bright College Days:"

> Soon we'll be sliding down
> the razor-blade of life . . .

Often, especially with Pryor and Tomlin, we not only see but feel the hurt. But the dynamics of stand-up also encourage a curious aggression, sometimes bordering on outright hostility, with some comics, like Rickles and Kinison, hungry for victims. Yet, in one very important sense, comics *are* pointmen for the truth, directing us to look at what we might prefer to ignore. We laugh, not because what they say is so awful (though it sometimes is), but because it is so true.

ROUND NINE

The Black Humor of the
Red, White, and Blue

*Our guardians ought not to be overmuch given to
laughter. Violent laughter tends to provoke an
equally violent reaction.*   —Plato

*Politics is the best show in America. I love animals
and I love politicians and I like to watch both of 'em
play either back home in their native state or after
they have been sent to a zoo or to Washington.*
                                        —Will Rogers

*Where I was born they always hang a man who can't
take a joke.*   —Mark Twain

Plato might have had a point; but since long before Will Rogers
was twirling his lariat, our politicians have certainly been providing our humorists with an amusing circus, and long after
Twain breathed his last, those who can't take a joke—and particularly politicians who can't take a joke—are being pilloried,
if not hanged.

American politics *is* a tough game, "a profoundly atavistic
sport," according to Hunter Thompson, and, as Bitter Bierce
defined it, nothing more than "a strife of interests masquerad-
ing as a contest of principle." The secret to politics, observed
Artemus Ward, Twain's old mentor is simple—"You scratch my
back, and I'll scratch your back."

But humorists and politicians often make scratchy bedfel-
lows. Twain said acidly, "America has no native American
criminal class—except Congress." Ward looked on with mordant disdain: "At a special Congressional 'lection in my district

the other day I delib'ritly voted for Henry Clay. I admit that
Henry is dead, but inasmuch as we don't seem to have a live
statesman in our national congress, let us by all means have a
first-class corpse." Ward's favorite president, he said, was
George Washington because "he never slopt over." Petroleum
Vesuvius Nasby, another "Phunny Phellow," announced his
availability for office with refreshing honesty:

> 1st I want an office
>
> 2nd I need an office
>
> 3rd An office would suit me; therefore
>
> 4th I should like to have an office.

America's *real politik* sometimes creates its own satire. When
Tammany ward boss George Washington Plunkitt, reflecting on
his own considerable pork barrel accomplishments, proclaimed, "I seen my opportunities and I took 'em," and Ivan
Boesky found a fit precursor. On a more recent occasion, Gerald
Ford, embroiled in a presidential debate over Jimmy Carter,
saw fit to pound his fist on the table and insist that there certainly had been no Russian influence in Eastern Europe during
his tenure in office. Ronald Reagan once said, "If you're right
90 percent of the time, who cares about the other 3 percent."
Reagan's statistical gaffes bring to mind Will Rogers's comment
"It's not what he *doesn't* know that bothers me, it's what he
knows for sure that just aint so."

But *could* we have better men in office? H. L. Mencken, the
Sage of Baltimore, thought not—he reckoned it made no more
sense to try to attract better men for office than to fill bawdy
houses with virgins, because "either the virgins would leap out
of the windows, or they would cease to be virgins." Mencken
called the political scene a Carnival of Buncombe and noted
that, in a democracy, power not only corrupted but seemed to
do so with a ludicrous and chummy venality. As Bill Arp
shrugged, "Government officials always have friends." More
recently, Hunter Thompson compared President Reagan's in-
stalation of his buddy Ed Meese as head honcho of the Justice

Department to "putting Charlie Manson in charge of the gym, at a prison for teen-age girls."

Perhaps corruption is inevitable under any system. "Politics is the apology of plunder," Josh Billings said, "every man has a weak side, and some have two or three." But, as Alexis de Tocqueville shrewdly observed over 150 years ago, American democracy causes every man on the street to feel he has the right not only to express his views but to condemn at will the rascals in Washington. So once again we have a contradiction between appearance and reality, between the claim for the moral superiority of democracy and the betrayal of those ideals in the day-to-day running of the government. Like Bierce, Mencken thought that to claim a providential goodness was farcical:

> Democracy is that system of government under which the people, having 35,717,342 native-born adult whites to choose from, including thousands who are handsome and many who are wise, pick out a Coolidge to be head of the State. It is as if a hungry man, set before a banquet prepared by master cooks and covering a table an acre in area, should turn his back upon the feast and stay his stomach by catching and eating flies.

He offered an absurdist equation: "If x is the population of the United States and y is the degree of imbecility of the average American, then democracy is the theory that x times y is less than y."

Mister Dooley, Finley Peter Dunne's turn-of-the-century Irish-American mouthpiece, also elaborated on this theme, and revised Abe Lincoln's famous phrase, "Th' modhren idee of government is 'Snub th' people, buy th' people, jaw th' people." Dunne was particularly amused by the high-minded hypocrisy and flag-waving inspired by President McKinley's interventionism in the Philippines:

> "I know what I'd do if I was Mack," said Mr. Hennessey. "I'd hist a flag over th' Ph'lippines, an I'd take in th' whole lot iv thim.
> "An yet," said Mr. Dooley, "tis not more than two months since ye larned whether they were islands or canned goods."

Dunne's disdain for our shenanigans in China echoed Twain's call to bring the missionaries home. Says Dooley crisply:

> But the Chinymen have been on earth a long time, an' I don't see how we can push so many iv them off iv it. Annyhow, 'tis a good thing f'r us they ain't Christyans an' haven't larned properly to sight a gun.

Throughout his long career, Dunne mocked American jingoism through Mr. Dooley's country-man's common sense. When confronted by Hennessey to defend his own fireside, Dooley replies, "I don't need to. If I keep on coal enough, me fireside will make it too hot f'r anny wan that invades it." In the face of Hennessey's boast that we're a "gr-reat" people, Mister Dooley shrugs; "We ar-re. We ar-re that. An' the best iv it is, we know we ar-re." Mr. Dooley's own political philosophy is more modest but shrewd: "Trust ivrybody—but cut the cards."

. . .

When it comes to politics, even our cartoonists get in on the act. Thomas Nast pictured Plunkitt and his Tammany cronies as a bunch of buzzards hovering over a hapless Manhattan. In the 1950s and 1960s, Walt Kelly's *Pogo* targeted the absurdities of American political life through a kind of *Animal Farm* parody of some of our more outrageous politicians. Lynx-like Simple J. Malarkey organizing an "anti-bird" crusade to protect the swamp from "immigrant" birds was an obvious take-off on the red-baiting senator from Wisconsin, Joe McCarthy; and Kelly's graphic caricatures included a George Wallace gamecock, a Robert Kennedy wind-up toy, a Lyndon Baines Johnson dopey longhorn steer, and even a piggy Nikita Khrushchev.

Berke Breathed and Gary Trudeau head a list of talented contemporary cartoonists with satirical bite. Breathed's *Bloom County* has traced the peregrinations of the Meadow Party with frazzled, inarticulate Bill the Cat heading the ticket and sweet Opus the Penguin as his Veep; and one of his longest running series deals with an invasion of Antarctica which bore a strong resemblance to our own "intervention" in Grenada. In one

Doonesbury strip, Gary Trudeau's B.D. exclaims to his father, "Sure, Dad, we'll have another war, you'll see! Our country will prosper again." Trudeau portrayed Ronald Reagan as a mindless "Ronnie Headset" and has burlesqued an invisible George Bush replaced by his brother Skippy. Jokes, of course —("Just joking, sir," as George Carlin says), but, once again, we can see the comic gargoyle at work deflating pomp and circumstance.

Political satirist Edward Sorel's sharp pen has taken on violence and hypocrisy in often brutal fashion. In one Vietnam era cartoon, Sorel portrays New York's Cardinal Cooke as a crazed madman swathed in the American flag, his ornate cross dangling like a trinket. The caption reads:

QUESTIONS WITHOUT ANSWERS

Cardinal Cooke visited Vietnam and told American soldiers there: "You are friends of Christ by the fact that you come over here." Question: would the Cardinal have taken a less benevolent attitude had our soldiers been firing at fetuses instead of men?

This is an intellectually demanding cartoon, perhaps because of what one has to know about Cardinal Cooke's strong anti-abortion position and the Catholic church's policy on the "just" war. But Sorel can be simple, too. In another cartoon he designed like a recruiting poster, Sorel portrayed a bullet-headed Spiro Agnew in khaki, swathed in the American flag, pleading:

SUPPORT OUR BOYS IN WASHINGTON
BUY A U.S. GOVERNMENT OFFICIAL.

Tom Wolfe (yes, *that* Tom Wolfe of *Electric Koolaid Acid Test* fame) is also an accomplished caricaturist. In Wolfe's case, it is "style," which not only portrays but betrays a person. One Wolfe drawing shows a California teenager lolling in the parking-lot of a drive-in hamburger joint and packed into a tight t-shirt which proclaims defiantly, "MOTHER WAS WRONG." In another, we see Hugh Hefner scrunched up like a fetus in a gigantic round bed supported by the shrunken heads of former female "conquests." Jay Leno claims that comedy is basically conservative: "The joke is about how things are out of whack." Certainly Wolfe, despite his fascination for fringe groups and fanatic politics, is a conservative. His first (and extremely popular) novel, *Bonfire of the Vanities,* takes as its model Thackeray's *Vanity Fair,* which pilloried English folly. But *Bonfire of the Vanities* is also very American in the violence of its frame story (the "accidental" killing of a black man by two rich whites in a Mercedes on the streets of the Bronx), and is the symbols and reactions of the class struggle (the "donkey" Irish cops, the wasp-waisted WASP women, the brutalization and exploitation of the underclass, etc.), the power-trip of the legal system, and the self-righteousness of the new Wall Street multimillionaires who make something out of nothing to spend it wildly.

Comedians not only use politicians as whipping boys—and they are stepping up the attack. "A "Tonight Show" host can say the previously unsayable," Peter Tauber wrote in a recent article. "He is both allowed and expected to make the Official National Jokes." And Tauber cites examples from Jay Leno. During John Tower's lengthy (and eventually unsuccessful) confirmation hearing for secretary of defense, Leno quipped: "It's alleged that John Tower may have a drinking problem. Well, that's important to know. I'd hate to think World War III started out as a bar fight." On another night, Leno said that Dan Quayle was an insurance policy for George Bush: "Who's gonna take a shot at the guy now? Even Hinckley went, Dan Quayle, Whoa, ho! No way."

There seems almost no limit to the attacks our comic satirists can make. One slightly hoary anecdote hinges on Mayor Daley's alleged vote-stealing during the 1960 election:

> In 1967, Johnson and Humphrey went to Chicago to discuss a matter of importance with Mayor Daley and for security reasons decided to take a rowboat out into Lake Michigan to talk about it there. Some distance from shore, the boat began to leak so much they knew it could only hold one of them, so they held a secret ballot to find out who would stay on board. Mayor Daley won by three votes to two.

To Tom Wolfe, Jimmy Carter was "an unknown down home matronly voiced Sunday-schoolish soft-shelled watery-eyed sponge-backed Millennial lulu." Mark Russell threw in another twist. When Carter traveled to Philadelphia for the Bicentennial, Mark Russell quipped, "Jimmy laid his hand on the Liberty Bell and the crack healed! Hallelujah!" Gerald Ford, after a series of accidents which included his stumbling down the stairs of Air Force One in Salzburg, Austria, became a target for many comedians—most notably *Saturday Night Live's* Chevy Chase. "There are two ways to become an authority on humor," Ford later observed stiffly. "The first way is to become one of the perpetrators. You know them: comedians, satirists, cartoonists, and impersonators. The second way to gain such credentials is to be victims of their merciless talents." Ford tried to take most of it in stride. When Chase did a take-off on him at a Radio and Television Correspondents dinner, which ended by his saying, "I have asked the Secret Service to remove the salad fork embedded in my left hand," Ford then rose, pretending to get tangled up in the tablecloth and spilling his notes from the podium, and then nodded toward his adversary, "Mister Chase, you are a very funny suburb."

Our politicians better know what it is to take a joke because they risk getting laughed right out of town if they can't. Ford was, in some measure, getting some of his own back, and we have had many politicians who could more than hold their own in the joking wars. Lincoln, for instance, had a notoriously droll sense of humor. In one of his famous debates, he observed Douglas's argument was "as thin as the homeopathic soup made by boiling the shadow of a pigeon that had been starved to death." Challenged to a duel, he suggested cow dung as an appropriate weapon. He once wrote to his chief of staff, who many felt was too fond of retreat, "My dear McLellan: If you don't want to use the army I should like to borrow it for a while. Yours respectfully, A. Lincoln." Coming upon some recruits constructing a one-hole privy for the general, he sighed, "Thank God it's a one-holer, for if it were a two-holer, before McLellan could make up his mind which to use, he would beshit himself." Of one self-righteous politician, Lincoln observed, "He reminds me of the man who murdered both his parents, and then pleaded for mercy on the grounds he was an orphan."

But Lincoln was often roundly criticized for taking things too lightly. Editorial cartoonists cruelly lampooned his big ears and hangdog features; and minstrel performers milked easy laughs by references to "Abe-olition." In one of the bitterest anti-Lincoln cartoons, Columbia asks accusingly, "Where are my fifteen thousand sons murdered at Fredericksburg?", while Lincoln is seen looking away and saying, "This reminds me of a little joke . . ." But Lincoln maintained that jokes were a necessity. Like Twain, he saw himself as speaking to the Belly of the masses who would understand. "A hearty laugh relieves me," he said, "and I seem better able to bear my cross." If, as Aristotle observed, melancholy men are of all others the most witty, Lincoln was a case in point. "I laugh because I must not cry," he admitted poignantly. "That is all. That is all."

Wit has nothing to do with goodness, of course. One particularly memorable scalawag was Earl Long, the controversial governor of Louisiana, and a man Adlai Stevenson called "a comedian for subversive purposes." Long was a great stump speaker who used humorous stories to highlight his own populist policies. One particular shaggy-dog story was aimed at a rival politician who wanted to cut aid to education ("aid to spastics who can't even vote," as Long put it) which Long said reminded him of the tightwad at the Pearly Gates who tried to negotiate past St. Peter on the grounds that he had given a nickel for charity on three separate occasions, only to have St. Peter say, "Give the sum-bitch back his fifteen cents and tell him to go to Hell." Even the "goo-goo" prospect of voting machines did not faze Long: "If I have da raight commissioners, I can make dem machines play Home Sweet Home."

In the right hands, cutting epigrams can be a formidable political weapon; and nobody was better at it than Adlai Stevenson. "Someone must fill the gap between platitudes and bayonets," he once said. He described Richard Nixon as "the kind of politician who would cut down a redwood tree, then mount the stump for a speech on conservation." Of the Republican's vaunted symbol, Stevenson observed: "The elephant has a thick skin, a head full of ivory, and as everyone who has seen a circus parade knows, proceeds best by grasping the tail of its predecessor." Sometimes a well-turned dart sticks and can never be pulled out. After Franklin Roosevelt's Secretary of the Interior Harold Ickes invited the public to see Republican candidate Thomas Dewey as "the little man on top of the wedding cake," Dewey remained forever so—and was left standing at the altar.

John Kennedy employed humor to defuse some of the most scathing of the "floating" accusations about his excessive privilege. At the Gridiron Club in Washington (a notorious "roasting" platter), Kennedy read what purported to be a wire from his Daddy: "Dear Jack—Don't buy a single vote more than necessary. I'll be damned if I'm going to pay for a landslide." After appointing his brother Robert as attorney general, he deadpanned "I don't see what's wrong with giving Bobby a little experience before he starts to practice law." (Senator Barry Goldwater, no mean wit himself, observed: "Bobby Kennedy's finally on the right track, I think, about adequate defense. He's in favor of a large standing army—in the South, that is." When Kennedy welcomed Nobel Prize winners from all over the world to a state dinner, he quipped, "This is the most extraordinary collection of talent, of human knowledge, that has ever been gathered together at the White House—with the possible exception of when Thomas Jefferson dined alone."

Perhaps these are just wisecracks (certainly if you don't like Lincoln or Kennedy you might think so), just a way politicians have of amusing the unwashed and deflecting our gaze from real problems. In 1940, Gracie Allen (the dumbest of the dumb Doras, as she was dubbed) stood in as a candidate, flying the flag of the Surprise Party under the slogan, "Down with common sense, vote for Gracie, Governess of the State of Coma." Abbie Hoffman and the Yippies ran a pig for president in 1968, and comedian Pat Paulsen is a perennial candidate who promises to do nothing. Funny business. But politicians have to be careful not to be *too* funny—few Americans, despite their enthusiasm, really want an Abbie Hoffmann, a Pat Paulsen or some other stand-up comedian as president. For all his wit, Stevenson was defeated twice; Ike, on the other hand, made few memorable sallies but served two terms. Senator Tom Corwin once advised Garfield: "Never make people laugh. If you would succeed in life, you must be solemn as an ass. All great monuments are built over solemn asses." But we must hope

Corwin was wrong—that there's a place for wit and humor in the face of the unrelenting miseries that pack the daily papers.

Not all are as shrewdly solemn as Corwin. Many politicians are fond of "roasts," at which they themselves can let their hair down, speak the unspeakable—all in good clean fun of course. At one such roast, Massachusetts Representative Margaret Clapprood (herself a strikingly sexy blonde) questioned how *Playgirl* could vote Michael Dukakis one of the ten sexiest men in America. "Who did they ask?" she wondered aloud, "Brain-dead former cheerleaders? The society for the perpetually frigid? Dukakis' idea of a big evening is to get a sundae at Brigham's and tell them to hold the nuts." But a politician can be roasted just as well on the editorial pages of the local daily newspaper or on the floor of the state house. The *Boston Globe* quoted George Keverian, the Speaker of the Massachusetts Senate, as saying he knew of a way to save the three billion dollars necessary to depress the Central Artery: "Let Mike Dukakis talk to it, and it will slowly depress itself." ("And he could bore the third tunnel, too," added another wag.)

While it may be difficult to imagine a Soviet premier or Japanese prime minister allowing himself to be subjected to this sort of public humiliation, in the American political arena ridicule is *de rigeur.* In his recent campaign, George Bush struggled with the "wimp factor"—until he defused it with a series of macho chest-thumpings uncharacteristic of the prep-school reared and mild-mannered Bush. When politicians fight back, Americans like it. We admired the feistiness of Harry Truman and made a best-selling album out of "The Wit of John Fitzgerald Kennedy." Ronald Reagan's one-liners are an integral part of his popularity. While being rolled into the operating room after the assassination attempt, Reagan said to his doctors, "I hope all of you are Republicans." Asked how the shooting had happened, Reagan shrugged his most endearing, aw-shucks shrug, and said: "I forgot to duck." Such humor, however, is not always providential. Testing a microphone in 1984, Reagan got himself in hot water when he joked, "My fellow Americans, I am pleased to tell you today that I've signed legislation which outlaws Russia forever. The bombing begins in five minutes." At the Gridiron Club recently, President Bush joshed, "Let's face it. If I had been funnier than Ronald Reagan, *I* would have won in 1980, and *he* would be up here trying to laugh off the Bush deficit."

Echoing Vonnegut's fears about humor defusing anger, however, politicians can and often do manage to co-opt even their most savage critics. Political humor can be a double-edged sword. Refusing to leave the field to impersonator Vaughn Meader, John Kennedy parodied himself and his family—with a wink. Editorial cartoonist Herblock portrayed Nixon henchmen Haldemann and Ehrlichman as sly thugs, only to have them request "originals" of Herblock's most scathing caricatures to display in their private offices. But such aplomb, such hubris, Herblock confesses, causes him to shudder. Burke Breathed, too, complains about the "apparent warmth" politicians display toward him. Impersonator David Frye worries aloud, "I hope I'm giving the country relief, but sometimes it's like making fun of cancer."

Some jokes stick in the public craw, whatever politicians' responses. Perhaps the darkest, most bitter jokes followed hard upon the Watergate scandal, which provided a field day for satirists. As Will Rogers once said, "There's no credit in being a comedian when you have the whole government working for you." And Watergate provided satirists and political cartoonists with a field day. Mark Russell admitted to hoping Watergate would never end: "If it does, I'll have to go back to writing my own material. Now I just tear it off the news service wires." Bumper stickers prompted drivers to "Honk if you think he's guilty," and vendors peddled a host of buttons aimed at Nixon's throat: "Behind every Watergate Stands a Milhous" and "Bail to the Chief." Sorel, in one cartoon, portrayed an angry Nixon emerging from a closet to proclaim "CRIMINALS' LIB!" The Watergate escapades inspired, among others, Emile de Antonio's film-satire, *Millhouse: A White Comedy,* and Philip Roth's vicious quasi-novel, *Our Gang.* David Frye parodied Nixon's infamous (but, alas, not definitive) California exit-speech: "Esteemed executioner, honored guests—this is my last press conference. I appreciate this opportunity to make myself perfectly clear. As for this great country of ours, ladies and gentlemen, I HATE America. Try spending twenty-one years in Whittier,

California—try loving America after that." People joked, Arthur Dudden speculates, because this laughter "offered almost the only way out of the well-nigh universal dismay and chagrin at the Watergate scandal."

No doubt. But sometimes even the critics palled. The Watergate book, even for convicted criminals like John Dean and Gordon Liddy, Tom Wolfe observed, became "one of the decade's new glamor industries." Hunter Thompson called Nixon "a foul caricature of himself" and "a man with no inner convictions, with the integrity of a hyena and the style of a poison toad." Tricky Dick, said Harry Truman, was "just a shifty-eyed goddam liar and the public knows it." For all the jokes and the naked insults, in the end it was the Congress (and himself of course) that did Nixon in.

. . .

Political humor is by no means restricted to the politicians themselves. Their deeds offer other obvious targets. Along these lines, there is another genre in which Americans have excelled that deserves special mention: the war comedy. Of course, there has always been war comedy; we can think of *Don Quixote, Good Soldier Schweik, The Tin Drum*, even Homer's *Iliad* has humor in spots, such as Achilles' sulking in his tent and the pop-art grotesquerie of that original *miles gloriosus*, hulking Ajax. Early American filmmakers produced memorable efforts as well. Chaplin made *Shoulder Arms*, and Laurel and Hardy donned uniforms in more than a dozen films. But these are "service comedies" (like the more recent efforts, *Mr. Roberts* and *Private Benjamin*) which satirize the red-tape of military experience rather than question the idiocy and barbarity of war itself. (*Duck Soup*, of course, was a notable exception.) More recently, America has produced a number of especially rich, dark variations of war comedy and brought the genre—both in print and on the screen—to a new height and fresh ferocity. Of the many fine war novels, besides Vonnegut's *Slaughterhouse Five*, there is also Joseph Heller's indelible *Catch-22* and Thomas Pynchon's inimitable *Gravity's Rainbow*.

Catch-22 is a bitter satire, set only tenuously in the Italy of World War II where Heller himself served as a bombardier. In many ways, *Catch-22* suggests Every War, a paranoid state of being in which the combatants no longer have any idea of why they are fighting. Survival is paramount, and all the major decisions take place offstage so that the airmen seem to be puppets pulled by unseen strings. The war in *Catch-22* is but the outcropping of a sick society; and the sickest (and therefore the sanest) character is Milo Minderbinder, that Chico-like hustler who cuts a deal with the Germans to bomb his own base and thereby benefit the "corporation." The catch, *Catch-22*, whereby the insane is expected and insanity therefore discountable, is the watchword for the crazy logic of the modern world. This logic is also hilarious, or would be if it were not so evil. But the illogic of war, Heller suggests, is emblematic of a general madness where there is only farce and death the final cruel joke.

Gravity's Rainbow, Thomas Pynchon's 887-page multileveled novel set in World War II, is an interesting case to note as well. Pynchon has always been interested in the interrelationships between sex, violence, and comedy; and he often works like a stand-up comic. For instance, in one short story, "The Small Rain" (1959), Lardass Levine has to get corpses out of the water after a hurricane: "One corpse they unhooked from a barbed wire fence. It hung there like a foolish balloon, a travesty; until they touched it and it popped, hissed and collapsed." Often, too, in Pynchon's works, sex, *le petit mort* (the little death, as the French call it) functions in the very midst of the great death. In *Gravity's Rainbow*, Pynchon describes a bomber as a "giant white cock in the sky" and Rachel Owlglass making love to her MG auto. Through such images, Pynchon suggests that, in war, *Eros* is perverted by *Thanatos*. In *Gravity's Rainbow*, the animate seems always to succumb to the mechanical, inverting Henri Bergson's comedy formula and making humor an adjunct to nihilism, thus eliminating it as a means of salvation. Pynchon, however, maintains his own strange sense of humor, even sending "Professor" Irwin Corey, a master of comic double-talk, to accept his National Book award for *Gravity's Rainbow*.

In the field of war comedy, our moviemakers have been active, too. Fine film adaptations of Vonnegut's *Slaughterhouse Five* and Heller's *Catch-22* have been made (*Gravity's Rainbow* has so far eluded Hollywood). But the ultimate classics in the field of cinema must be Stanley Kubrick's *Dr. Strangelove —Or How I Learned To Stop Worrying And Love The Bomb* (1964) and Robert Altman's adaptation of "M*A*S*H" (1970). Kubrick was intrigued by a straight suspense thriller, *Red Alert*, written by former R.A.F. navigator Peter George, which posited a nuclear disaster following upon the collapse of certain "failsafe" procedures. But Kubrick found himself unable to film the novel straight because the story kept defining itself as a kind of "nightmare comedy," so he and Buck Henry worked up their own script. Kubrick made the film in England, employing such quintessentially American actors as George C. Scott, Keenan Wynn, and Sterling Hayden and employing that brilliant chameleon Peter Sellers in three roles: as an American president, a British aide-de-camp, and Dr. Strangelove, the ex-Nazi who heads the American nuclear program (echoes of Henry Kissinger and Wernher von Braun). Despite its British roots, Kubrick's film deals with the precarious Soviet-American nuclear brinksmanship as seen from an American perspective.

In *Strangelove*, a veneer of plausibility overlies the most farcical elements. In the opening shot, mountains stick sensuously through the clouds, as we watch Strategic Air Command bombers being refueled. A close-up makes them seem like giant praying mantises copulating—an apt metaphor, perhaps, for the comic battle we are to witness between what Freud called the Life Force and our nuclear Death Wish. Cut to SAC Headquarters where General Jack D. Ripper has called for Wing Attack Plan R. Cut to a SAC bomber commandeered by Major Kong (played by Slim Pickens, the original redneck second banana), who dons his cowboy hat before calling on his "boys" to get ready for toe-to-toe combat with "the Rooskies." Cut to General Buck Turgidson's bedroom, where he is entertaining his secretary and disgusted because the Red Alert threatens to take him away from his lovemaking.

From then on, the film toggles back and forth from the War Room to SAC HQ to Slim Pickens's bomber—as the attack draws ominously closer to its targets. After the well-meaning American president invites the Russian ambassador into the War Room over the outraged protests of his generals, he calls Premier Kissoff, who is drunk at his dacha. (The theme, always, is that of human fallibility.) But the coordinated efforts to stop the bombers are thwarted when Kissoff reveals the existence of a "Doomsday Machine," which is designed to explode and make the earth a desolate wasteland if it so much as senses an attack on Russian soil—and which cannot be disengaged. The Russian ambassador sighs, "We couldn't keep up with the arms race and the peace race—we were afraid of a Doomsday Gap."

After all attempts at recall fail, Slim Pickens jumps into the jammed bomb bay to ride the bomb down like a cowboy riding a steer ("Yahoo!"), and a mushroom cloud slowly fills the screen. Cut to the War Room, where Dr. Strangelove has already begun laying plans for the aftermath—selected supermen will take ten women apiece down a mine shaft to wait things out, etc.—but his right arm keeps giving the Nazi salute, throttling him even as he bites it. At last, in a final bitter paradigm, he struggles out of his wheelchair to shout, "Mein Fuhrer, I can walk!" Kubrick cuts again to the clouds (echoing the beginning), while we hear that World War II British standard sung so valiantly by Vera Lynn, "We'll meet again . . . don't know where, don't know when . . . we'll meet again some su-u-unny day."

Strangelove is scathingly funny—without slapstick. It is the inappropriate apposition that draws our attention and suggests the humor and the horror. Signs outside SAC HQ proclaim PEACE IS OUR PROFESSION—as a battalion of Americans attacks the base. While the battle rages, General Ripper offers a rambling monologue on fluoridation as a Communist conspiracy to contaminate "our vital bodily fluids." While General Turgidson and the Russian ambassador roll around on the floor, the president scolds them, "Gentlemen, you can't fight in here —this is the War Room!" The SAC survival kit contains morphine, weapons, a Russian phrase book—and nylons and condoms. Colonel Bat Guano refuses to blow up a Coke machine to get change for Lieutenant Mandrake to call the White House ("That's private property, you deviated prevert!"). Yet, throughout this casual heaping up of one absurdity after another, everyone remains serious—and the film, too, beneath its ironies, is serious. We laugh despite the horror—and our terror. Certainly, as a scathing indictment of the profession of war and the good old boys who can't see the forest for the trees, *Strangelove* points a finger at those politicians and bureaucrats who have created a Catch-22 system they can no longer fully control. Now basking in the soothing prospect of "glasnost," we no longer hear agonized debates over "missile gaps" and "space gaps." But, with a Star Wars deployment still in the works, we know a Doomsday Machine is no archaic nightmare and that, despite the "limited" test-ban treaty and glowing promises to ban chemical warfare, America and Russia retain nuclear arsenals capable of destroying the world. So *Strangelove* remains an oddly contemporary film—and probably always will —because it depicts a nuclear world. How will it all end—with a whimper, a bang, or both? We await the mushroom cloud—or could *Strangelove* have a sequel?

. . .

That other war comedy of distinction, Robert Altman's "M*A*S*H," a black comedy about field hospital "operations" during the Korean War opens with a helicopter lifting off, body-bags tied to its pontoons. A gentle song plays over, but the lyrics are skewed, eerie, nihilistic:

> Suicide is painless
> it brings on too many changes . . .
> I can take it or leave it if I please
> and you can do the same thing . . .
> The game of life is hard to play
> you're going to lose it anyway.

Surely, a far cry from the positivist message of Norman Vincent Peale and other "saviors" of the American fifties.

We swing down to the base where officers and enlisted men are talking through and over and past each other. A radio broadcast announces that MacArthur is leaving Korea, Eisenhower is doing, *well*, something—we can't quite make it out. (Chaplin and Keaton would have approved; words hardly matter because nobody listens—all is gibberish.) The first fight we see is between Americans (the "enemy" throughout remains invisible); and in the confusion Hawkeye steals a jeep to get to his post at the Mobile Army Surgical Hospital—where his first move is to try to pick up a cute nurse. Soon we are in the operating room, a butcher shop with blood and guts all over, where Hawkeye is sawing away while a nurse scratches his nose. Afterward, "Chest-cutter" Trapper John, snapping bubblegum, appears at Hawkeye's tent in a parka and produces a jar of olives for the obligatory martinis.

But what appears to be callous actions on the part of the surgeons, Altman suggests, are necessary survival tactics. Hawkeye and Trapper's job is rescue and succor. But there is simply too much to keep up with as the unseen, yet very real, war keeps manufacturing casualties faster than they can cope. So they joke—and play jokes—to retain their sanity. Like Huck, they rarely laugh—their world also is too grim for that. But they do revel, as does Altman, in baiting such "Great Pretenders" as Frank, the Puritanical hypocrite who vindictively accuses one young recruit of having "killed" a man through delay, and "Hotlips" Houlihan, the prissy perhaps-blonde who is his fellow-scold and erstwhile succor. In one of their most imaginative pranks, Hawkeye and Trapper wire Frank's bedroom to broadcast his and Hotlips's steamy lovemaking to the whole camp.

Often, too, the pranks have good intentions. When Painless, the well-hung dentist, suddenly can't "get it up" and announces he wants to commit suicide, they all laugh—no Good Samaritans here. But Painless is serious. So Hawkeye prepares a "host supper" and gives him a "black capsule" to send him on his way, and his buddies bring him gifts as he lies in his coffin: a bottle of Scotch, *Playboy*, etc. The black capsule, however, is really a placebo, and Hawkeye convinces a lovely nurse to "sacrifice" herself to "raise" Painless from the dead. Success! Painless is "up" in the morning. Throughout, the intercom announces a nightly fare of such patriotic movies as World War II's *When Willy Comes Marching Home*; but the movies, with

their "heroes' welcomes" and "incredible feats of bravery,"
seem anachronistic and naive amid the chaos. Altman's *Grand
Guignol* humor constantly reminds us of the bloody mess that
war really is. "M*A*S*H" seems the real thing because, as in
Strangelove, nothing improbable happens despite the absurdity. The real bloodshed may be happening offscreen, but underlying the jokes is a lot of actual death; and Altman never
allows us to forget that the real culprits are those running the
war.

"M*A*S*H" has a gritty, albeit batty, integrity to it. The images
Altman offers (of the riotous surgeons and the bloody O.R. with
its twitching bodies; of Hawkeye and Trapper blithely hitting
golfballs off bomb-cratered hills; of the vicious "combat" of an
interdivisional football game complete with ringers) cohere
into a vision of a world gone mad. "I have nothing to say,"
Altman said recently, "I just have something to show. Truth
exposes itself." The humor of "M*A*S*H" is savage, deflating,
sexist, even occasionally sophomoric; but it also seems truer to
anything we have had in "war" films before or since. Pauline
Kael has called it, "the best American war comedy since sound
came in, and the sanest American movie of recent years." Certainly, in its bloody integrity, it stands to remain a black humor
classic.

But is there not something also disturbing about what these
films indicate about the level of cynicism American artists are
offering as paradigms of the contemporary political scene? With
Strangelove and "M*A*S*H," the violent comedy of the Marx
Brothers and W.C. Fields seems to have evolved into something perhaps best described as a comedy of violence. But *can*
you have a comedy of violence? S. J. Perelman thought not.
After seeing "M*A*S*H," Perelman was shaken. "Reality has
overcome the comic writer," he said. "For the first time I was
struck by something that was actually beyond satire. Not war
itself, but the horror of people being blown to bits and then
patched together again. It is called black, but it is not humor.
Certainly, these films suggest a world so hopelessly and over-
whelmingly violent one feels almost guilty to be laughing."
One must agree—which is, of course, no comfort. Farce, as
Bermel points out, laughs at the foolishness of men and women

and at their bad luck, but surely there must be a limit to the extent we wish to be reminded of our foolishness or bad luck.

These films have helped spawn a new generation of war films, and a new, even more disturbing, genre. What we get, in the war films of the eighties, is something quite different, the quasi-documentary. Oliver Stone's *Platoon* and Kubrick's *Full Metal Jacket* (and a host of clones) seem designed to rectify the gloss and hype of John Wayne's *Green Berets* and such "hero" films as *Bridge Over the River Kwai* and *Bridge Too Far;* but they stray far from the searing black comedy of *Strangelove* and "M*A*S*H." Here the *modus operandi* seems to be to make war as realistic—and as ugly—as possible, and if there is much sarcasm and cynicism, there is little humor. In many ways, the "patriotic gore" of these films ironically encourages riotous applause, as when Rambo blows away a North Vietnamese platoon. The American audience very often tends to see these films as "kick-ass" exercises, much like a karate film, and the merits of such films are debated on the basis of how imaginatively sadistic the killings are or how realistic the intestines look. In a sense, they are—throwbacks to the world of such horror films as *The Texas Chainsaw Massacre.* Lincoln himself observed tartly of war stories: "Military glory—that attractive rainbow that rises in a shower of blood, that serpent's eye that *charms* to destroy." Even with their Marine Corps Advisers, there does seem a practical limit to how far these quasi-documentaries can go, and they may have already gone all the way. It will be interesting to see the direction good film directors will take in dealing with fresh absurdities; certainly there's enough gobbledygook around for a saturnalian feast.

But even to mention such films, alongside *Strangelove* and "M*A*S*H," is to remind ourselves of how far we *have* come from the world of Laurel and Hardy. Like Vonnegut, we might look back with longing at the strange sweetness and innocence of their time where most of the destruction was private, the primary hazards domestic. Our world is stranger, and darker by far. Now our leaders can have bombs dropped anywhere in the world—and occasionally they do, as Reagan did in Libya to spank Khadafi. *Funny is* is not always as *funny does.* "I am worried about the current meanings of the word funny," James

Thurber observed over fifty years ago. "It now means ominous, as when one speaks of a funny sound in the motor; disturbing, as when one says that a friend is acting funny; and frightening, as when a wife tells the police that it is funny, but her husband hasn't been home for two days and nights." Or we might add, in a rueful update, "funny" as when the world prepares to annihilate itself.

· · ·

American political humor, it seems, is an endless serial that keeps playing itself back over and over. For our humorists, the American political scene remains a rich, and seemingly bottomless, compost heap. But the spectacle and the stench infuriates as it amuses. Sometimes one feels present at (or even within) the Theater of the Absurd. What is one to say, for instance, when one hears White House spokesman and erstwhile stand-up comic Marlin Fitzwater opine that he has forsaken *Doonesbury* because Trudeau is glorifying drugs? But, Marlin, Marlin, we *need* more opiates. Hunter Thompson calls ours "The Time of the White Trash."

One thing is clear: if our composite urge to ridicule and to level is a legacy and a right of democracy, the products are often disturbing and grim. In one Civil War story making the rounds, a white man asks an old black man, "The men of the northern and southern states are killing one another on your account, why don't you join in and fight yourself?" The black man replies, "Have you ever seen two dogs fighting over a bone? Well, did you ever see the bone fight?" Another story set during the era of The Great Society has Lyndon Johnson in the South Bronx to announce his all-out War on Poverty, only to have one little man in the back pipe up, "I just want to say one thing— we surrender."

For as the crackling of thorns under a pot, *Ecclesiastes* tells us, so is the laughter of the fool. But if American politics is the boiling pot, that crackling we hear might be the laughter of the very politicians who are fueling (or fooling) the pot. Thompson refers to today's politicians as "a generation of swine," and cites Coleridge's Ancient Mariner, "A thousand thousand slimy

things lived on, and so did I," as an apt description of the
motives and the methods of Washington. The picture he paints
is bleak:

> It is difficult for the ordinary voter to come to grips with the
> notion that a truly *evil* man, a truthless monster with the brains
> of a king rat and the soul of a cockroach, is about to be sworn in
> as president of the United States for the next four years. . . . And
> he will bring his *gang* in with him, a mean network of lawyers
> and salesmen and pimps who will loot the national treasury,
> warp the laws, mock the rules and stay awake 22 hours a day
> looking for at least one reason to declare war, officially, on some
> hapless tribe in the Sahara or heathen fanatic like the Ayatollah
> Khomeini.

And yet (always [sometimes?] *and yet*) things may not be as
bleak as Thompson and the other cynics insist. As Lukes and
Galnoor suggest in the introduction to their anthology *No
Laughing Matter*, political joking may be a healthy form of
coping because "[e]ven when the situation is bad, and the jokes
become destructive and vicious, they still represent a collective
intimacy, a sign that people belong, that they care, and conse-
quently that they entertain hope." Hope, a comforting notion.
Certainly, the thrust of the caricatures, cartoons, jokes, and satirical blasts of our American humorists is to argue against the
perversion of democratic ideals and the uses of violence. Perhaps, they also seem to hope, readers and listeners will get the
point and become more aware of present dangers and act on it.
That is the hope—the *only* hope.

ROUND TEN

The End of the Dream
or the Dream of the End
—or Something Like That

*There's no violence out here, and no blood. Nobody
gets killed here, so you don't have to worry. There's
no violence in public.*
      —Joseph Heller, *We Bombed in New Haven*

*Violence demonstrates the "real" nature of man, his
fundamental disorderliness and will to destruction,
his hatred of constraints, his resentment of ideas and
ideals and all other artificial constructions. Hence the
artist who deals honestly with violence becomes a
kind of nose-rubber or mirror-holder, someone rub-
bing the spectator's nose in the disagreeable, and
holding up a mirror in which he can contemplate the
essential filthiness, nastiness, and beastliness of mankind, or at least of unregenerate bourgeois mankind.*
      —John Fraser, *Violence in the Arts*

Before (perhaps blessedly) concluding, it might be interesting
to consider the state of the comic art of the comic state within
this world of "unregenerate bourgeois mankind." And when
one speaks of unregenerate bourgeois mankind, one's mind
wanders to television, our most popular medium, which I have
so far (*note bene*, George) studiously avoided mentioning, and
of which Groucho Marx's old buddy Goodman Ace observed
tartly, "Perhaps we call it a medium because nothing's well
done."

So into the breach at once I must dive. After all, the average
American, or so we're told, spends some twenty or so hours a

week in front of this "lava lamp with sound," as "Saturday Night Live" writer Michael O'Donoghue calls it. "A child's mind must inevitably rot looking at the dreary procession of nonsense night after night," Groucho himself complained years ago, "and I think the next ten years will produce a population composed entirely of goons. When I was a kid, we used to read." Even Newton Minow, mogul that he was, confessed that he found television "a vast wasteland." Hunter Thompson calls it "some kind of cruel and shallow money trench through the heart of the journalism industry, a long plastic hallway where thieves and pimps run free and good men die like dogs, for no good reason."

But perhaps we should not be so hasty with the tar brush. Certainly, there has been good television comedy—from the Sid Caesar and Milton Berle shows of the early fifties and Jackie Gleason's "Honeymooners" (with that other great slapstick performer Art Carney and Audrey Meadows of the wonderful deadpan); fine comics like Carol Burnett, Steve Allen, Dick Van Dyke, Mary Tyler Moore; and break-through programs like "All in the Family," "The Bill Cosby Show," and, of course, "Laugh-In" and "Saturday Night Live." The late night talk-show hosts—Jack Paar, Johnny Carson, David Letterman—are, and have been, primarily comics as well; and they gear their shows for laughs and have introduced much of America to wonderful comic monologists like Alexander King, Oscar Levant, Jonathan Winters, Mort Sahl, and Robin Williams.

But, blow for blow, it must be said, the product is not up to the standards of print or cinema—and how can it be? It is difficult, if not nigh unto impossible, to come up with quality comedy week after week, and the whimsical nature of Nielsen ratings only adds to the problem. Since television goes directly into the home, that most sacred of all American institutions, censorship is also a sensitive issue. So it seems (to paraphrase Lincoln) the goal, often, is to please as many of the people as much of the time in the most inoffensive manner possible.

We can see how this laundering of language and imagery works when we look at that immensely popular TV "spin-off" of "M*A*S*H," which managed not only to sanitize the operating room (all shots from the waist up), but to reduce the horrors of war to clever one-liners and atrocious puns—e.g., Hawkeye smirking, "If I touch that gun I'll just trigger an argument." We can see this principle at work also in Norman Lear's comedies, particularly in "All in the Family" which, despite its "liberal" viewpoint, makes Archie out to be a loveable bigot. And we can see it in "The Bill Cosby Show," with its own Harvard psychologist-consultant to maintain a "positive" portrait of blacks and its commitment to working everything out neatly in a half hour. Noncontroversial comedy is what television demands, and what it gets.

So what's the gripe, you might ask? Aren't such shows valuable, particularly after a hard day? Yes, of course, and I often find them so. But they should not be confused with the genuine article. Comedy is a tough task-master, one that demands its message be based on reality—on what Lenny called "things as they are." As I hope to have shown, the greatest comic writers and performers—the Twains and the Chaplins—take us past the giggle stage to something more. Their art is grounded not in sentimentality, but in truth; and it is a truth that enables us to see clearly and laugh at ourselves as well. Only through such truth do we think on the day *after* the laughter stops.

Maybe the one thing television does not want the public to do *is* to think. In its giant maw, television has, like Moby Dick, swallowed and regurgitated many of its brightest and most resourceful comedians—people like Lenny and Jackie Mason, even Lily Tomlin. But the situation is perhaps not all that dreadful—or that permanent. Today, with less restrictive network censorship standards ("Saturday Night Live" could not have aired in the fifties or even the sixties) and the proliferation of cable stations, fresher and more incisive comedy may also get a viewing. There is even talk of establishing two twenty-four hour comedy channels in 1990. America the beautiful! Certainly, television and its vast influence is not going to go away; we can only hope—and demand—that it get better.

A closer look at "Saturday Night Live" (which first aired in 1975) might help illustrate some of the forces driving for more incisive comedy and the equally strong forces at work to restrain or defeat it. First of all, "Saturday Night Live"like "The Sid Caesar Show" of the fifties, *was* live, which not only made it seem that we were right there in the screaming audience, but allowed for a topicality which could, and often did, include the latest, right up to the minute political absurdity. Live meant *now*, and the risk attracted us.

But where did it come from—what did it intend? Tony Hendra sees "Saturday Night Live"as a direct outcropping of "baby boomer" humor, with roots in such magazines as *MAD* and *The National Lampoon* (of which "Saturday Night Live" writer Michael O'Donoghue was once an editor); the underground comics of R. Crumb; and such improvisational troupes as Chicago's Second City, which fed in "Bully Boys" John Belushi, Dan Ackroyd, and Bill Murray, as well as Gilda Radner and John Candy. In their recent book, *Saturday Night Live: A Backstage History*, authors Jeff Weingrad and Doug Hill concluded: "The tenets of the show's political philosophy were that inspiration, accident, and passion were of greater value than discipline, habit, and control. "Saturday Night Live" was the first program of its kind to commit itself consciously to the subconscious, to emulate as much as it could the spirit of artistic abandon embodied and endorsed by the gods of twentieth-century hip. Baudelaire, Blake, D. H. Lawrence, William Burroughs, Henry Miller, Jack Kerouac, Lenny Bruce, Ken Kesey, the Beatles, and Hunter Thompson were as much the fathers of "Saturday Night Live"as Kovacs, Carson, Benny, and Berle." They cite the writers and producers as having taken as their guiding light Burroughs's maxim: "Nothing is true; everything is permitted." Just as Burroughs's own "naked lunch" was that icy, drug-frozen moment when he really *saw* what was on the end of his fork, and the thumpers of "Saturday Night Live" held out many forks. "Our comedy reflects a violent desperate time," says Michael O'Donoghue. "Humor is a release of tension, and you react to what is happening around you. The world is ready to nuke itself out—Dick Van Dyke and Donna Reed just don't cut it any more."

The performers, in fact, considered themselves comedy commandoes on a mission of truth behind enemy lines. The signals were obvious. As Hendra puts it, "Once the switch was thrown, the audience recognized everything they saw—the 'fuck-you' tilt of the head, that certain edge and edginess." O'Donoghue dubbed it Cut-and-Slash humor, and the premise was: You Can Never Go Too Far. *Too Far* was where they all wanted to go. In that atmosphere, they created routines that were truly weird, even "sick." O'Donoghue worked up one gruesome bit on possible jams: Nose Hair, Mangled Baby Ducks, Monkey Pus, Painful Rectal itch. Eddie Murphy's sly "Mister Robinson" was a wicked, ghetto version of Public Broadcasting's laidback Mister Rogers. Richard Pryor appeared one night during his paranoid druggy days and played out a macabre word association duet with Chevy Chase, that built toward edgy venom:

Chase:		Pryor:	
	white		black
	bean		pod
	Negro		whitie
	tarbaby		what'd you say?
	tarbaby		ofay
	colored		peckerwood
	burrhead		cracker
	spearchucker		white trash
	jungle bunny		honky
	spade		honky honky
	nigger		dead honky

One night, the *Dr. Strangelove* screenwriter and "Saturday Night Live" regular Buck Henry called for the violent overthrow of the American government. Another night, Belushi introduced The All Star Dead Band, with lead vocalists Janis Joplin and Jim Morrison, Brian Jones on rhythm guitar, Duane Allman on slide guitar, and Jimi Hendrix on lead guitar. "Okay," yelled Belushi, "a one-two-three-four." And then the silence of the grave. O'Donoghue set another sketch in a Grand Guignol White House where the Reagan family hacked Jane Fonda to pieces and ate her.

"If this is a joke—I don't get it," comic David Brenner is said to want as his epitaph; and certainly many folks do not *get* the humor of "Saturday Night Live," and do not *want* to get it. "This new candor," complained TV-critic Harriet Van Horn, "has made the boob-tube the lewd tube on Saturday night. Let us cry enough to the vulgarity which spits in our faces." Hendra theorized on another reason for viewer resentment: "Clowns do not comment on wars; clowns make you laugh. Clowns who did comment on wars were stepping out of their floppy shoes and baggy pants, were becoming indistinguishable from station owners." But some objections have come from unexpected quarters. Gary Trudeau, speaking at Colby College in 1981, attacked what he called "this screw-you humor which adroitly mocks society's victims by convincing them that they are no-bodies, that to be so un-hip as to be disadvantaged, to be igno-rant, to be physically infirm, or black, or even female is to invite contempt. What worries me about Slash and Burn Humor is that it reflects a sort of callousness so prevalent in the survival ethic." Steve Allen, while admiring of Belushi's gifts as a phys-ical comic, saw also "an ugliness of spirit, a self-centeredness" and "an almost barbaric social irresponsibility." Even George Carlin is not quite sure: "The show made me laugh but it didn't take on a lot of issues. It *seemed* daring, and there were things that were sort of irreverent, but mostly they didn't present any alternate ideas, they just tore down—which is a form of comedy I can live with but don't love."

So, alongside its legions of admirers, the wildness and irrev-erence of "Saturday Night Live" has caused indignation, dis-gust, and dyspepsia. But though this controversy is extreme, it certainly is not unique in television-land. The Smothers Broth-ers' infamous battles with the networks and the "sock-it-to-me" humor of "Laugh-In" caused head-shaking and concern as well. There will always be those whose idea of humor runs more along the safe lines of "Gilligan's Island, Hogan's Heroes, Pet-ticoat Junction," and "The Beverly Hillbillies." "I don't under-stand what "Mary Hartman" is all about," complained Lucille Ball (whose own "I Love Lucy" was another "white" comedy), "—a kid being electrocuted is supposed to be comedy?" Ball disapproves of Archie Bunker. "I object to the show's bringing certain words—the racial epithets—back into our vocabulary. I think any kind of racial put-down is wrong." But, we might ask, have these racial epithets disappeared in the streets? Is kindly situation comedy enough?

One thing we should note: So many of these controversial shows depended on parody ("Mary Hartman" of soap operas, "Saturday Night Live" of everything), and parody is one of the most subversive and most vicious forms of humor. Parody in-sults people and their beliefs. We can understand why funda-mentalists were upset (and many were) by "Saturday Night Live" take-offs on Oral Roberts-type preachers. Parody may be hip, but in the un-hip it unleashes rage.

. . .

What has been happening at the movies—besides rising prices? After the depression, the American cinema seemed to suffer a case of the comic-blahs. Perhaps World War II did it. At any rate, Hollywood designed their comedies—the "road" films of Hope and Crosby, the screwball comedies of Grant and Hepburn, the Jerry Lewis farces, the Doris Day confections, the Beach Party Bingo-dingos—as escapist amusement. Fine and dandy, perhaps, as far as that went, but it didn't go very far. There were, of course, some notable exceptions; the work of Billy Wilder and Preston Sturges come readily to mind. But for the most part, in the sentimental comedies Hollywood produced, reconciliation (Everything's going to be all right!) was the sole intent, so it went down like cotton candy, and now most seem like nothing more than pieces of fluff.

Are there good comedy films still being made? Even as perspicacious and usually generous a critic as Pauline Kael has her doubts. After viewing the Belushi-Ackroyd vehicle *Blues Brothers,* she shrugged that it was just "car chases and bullshit." Modern comedies lack "elfskin," she argues, "that glow that comics emit when they're giving of their best and when everything comes together right."

Perhaps what goes around, comes around—with a twist. Under laxer censorship, the most obvious change in contemporary comedy has been the emergence of the "gross-out" movie—with ex-"Saturday Night Live" comics such as Belushi, Murphy, Murray, and Ackroyd leading the charge. *Animal House,* featuring Belushi as Bluto the bloated sophomore who savages anything and anyone who gets in his way from stuffy deans and prissy housemothers to coddled coeds and preppy nerds, is perhaps the ultimate gross-out movie. In his "id-ness," his need to satisfy his simple desires, Belushi is not of the same school as Harold Lloyd's inept but benevolent freshman; and certainly in such scenes as when Belushi imitates a zit by squirting mashed potatoes through his swollen cheeks, comedy has rarely been uglier. Sure, it is funny; but we are not touched, as we are by Chaplin's Little Tramp or the cheerful valor of Laurel and Hardy. Instead we are invited to laugh at the "gross-out," the excess, as Sennett invited us to do in his films. So perhaps we've come full circle. When Belushi-Bluto screams, "Nothing is over till we say it's over," young people hoot and holler; and it seems quite clear they are applauding the "giving the bird" to all authority. *Animal House* is a kind of postscript to the violence of the sixties, a reminder that things are never quite going to be the same; the little white house with the nice, white picket fence just doesn't cut the mustard anymore.

Fortunately, "gross-out" movies are not the only kind of comedy films being made. The underrated Frank Oz film, *Little Shop of Horrors*, for instance, a clever spoof of horror movies, features a hilarious performance by Steve Martin as a nitrous-gas-guzzling, plier-plying dentist, which brings back the shades of W. C. Fields. Mel Brooks and Woody Allen also have worked outside of the gross-out formula, and often quite brilliantly. Brooks films are almost all parodies (*Blazing Saddles* of the Western, *Young Frankenstein* of the horror film, *The Producers* of the Broadway musical) in which Brooks operates as a third-rate ham but demonstrates a first-rate originality. In Brooks's films, the clunky "home movie" quality is part of the joke; and he welcomes us to groan along with him at a particularly dumb pun or hackneyed piece of action. Woody Allen, perhaps the most intelligent comic going, has raised the wise-crack to a distinctive level not heard since Groucho. But, like Lenny, he has used his hip, Jewish outsider status to poke fun at the milk-and-cookies life-style of America's heartland. More recently, however, Allen seems to be drifting away from the hilarious slapstick of his earlier films like *Bananas* and *Everything You Wanted To Know About Sex * But Were Afraid To Ask* (in which a community is attacked by a giant breast and sperm cells dressed as astronauts prepare for possible exit and entry) to a Manhattan-based comedy of manners. The irony now, of course, is how "in" Woody Allen is.

Punch Line (no relation to this book), a recent and interesting dark comedy, explores the ruthless dynamics of stand-up comedy. We have had movies on comics before (Dustin Hoffman's *Lenny,* for instance), but nothing quite like this. *Punch Line* deals with the pain at the heart of the comic impulse. Tom Hanks plays a young man forced into medical school by his physician father, who becomes a Lenny-style comedian on the side. Hanks slays them in the aisles—until his father comes to scowl at his act; then he bombs and his father walks out. Hanks's sensitive performance suggests the rough edges (and dark birthplace) of comedy, as he goes for the jugular himself and urges his New Jersey housewife friend to "go for it" by telling the truth-truth about her "funny life."

Punch Line's scenes have a gritty integrity—the sordid coffee shop where Fields buys jokes like a junkie copping bags of heroin; the has-been comic who announces "the love of my life, the lady named comedy"; Hanks's advice to a bumbling, fat history teacher who gets heckled, "Attack, Jerry, attack"; the burnt-out waitress who shrugs off her brief fling with Hanks as "a lotta laughs." Whole chunks of the movie feel right, right down to the cutthroat backstage atmosphere where comics jockey to win a spot on a late-night talk-show—that lurid beacon in the West which promises release from the $15/night hellholes. Hanks is an attack comic with heart ("God's enemy to cartoons," as he puts it), and Sally Fields is quite good, too, as the spunky Hausfrau—if never quite believable as a stand-up comic. The film, unfortunately, ends "soft," with Fields winning the joke-off but ceding to Hanks and going home with her hubby. As Lenny would say, it didn't take it to its real end, man, it finked out. But most of it is quite good indeed.

.   .   .

American stand-up comedy certainly is not dead—its practitioners and surgeons are out there still working, still suturing and unsuturing wounds, and fresh comics are still coming forth out of gaga land to wing it for us. On the radio, monologists like Bob and Ray and Garrison Keillor are still spinning their goofy magic; and in the newspapers, strippers like Trudeau and Breathed (now in a hopefully brief hiatus) get top billing on the comic pages. On stage, we can still catch new works of black comedy by such playwrights as David Mamet, Edward Albee, and Jules Feiffer (both in his mordant cartoons and in stage comedies like *Little Murders*.) Our literary comedians, too, have been *busy, busy, busy,* as Vonnegut would say—Vonnegut himself of course, and Heller, and a host of others like Terry Southern, John Barth, Thomas Berger, Fran Liebowitz, and Nora Ephron—the list goes on almost *ad infinitum.*

One interesting young novelist, for instance, is Jay Cantor whose recent, intriguing novel, *Krazy Kat,*[8] updates that love-struck feline's adventures in the modern world. But Cantor's resurrected Krazy is a far different cat, having become a kind of victimized Patty Hearst-type outlaw, involved in COMISA-LAD (Comic Strip Artists Liberation Army—Division One) under an Ignatz Mouse caught up in his own power trip. "The gangster is the modern American hero," Ignatz tells Krazy, "because he is willing to confront the truth that all success is based on violence." Krazy, for her part, is not a total success as a convert. She can't even manage to swear correctly, spouting instead, "Lick mothers . . . bull-lappers . . . cock-shetters." But Ignatz-Cantor has the last word: "It was the modern era that produced both the comic strip and the atom bomb, so I think it's you comic strip artists who have the knowledge that we desperately need to deal wisely with this new danger." The novel would have value if it did no more than return readers to the surrealistic and violent and oddly romantic imaginings of Herriman's original Krazy Kat strips, still available in many editions.

Yes, American humor is alive, and still kicking. But what does it all *mean*—how far *have* we come or have we come anywhere at all? Some critics worry that our comedy has become too nihilistic. In *The Rise and Fall of American Humor,* for instance, Jesse Bier rehearses of the American humorist's corrosive love-hate relationship with his culture and describes American comedy as "voracious, deflationary, skeptical, cynical, pessimistic, blasphemous, and black." It is certainly all of that, but it is not *only* that. Humor is not death, "the fellow in the bright nightgown," as W. C. Fields called him; humor is life, clawing and scratching perhaps, but still *life.* Gerald Mast, thinking of films (though his thoughts might be applied to all comedy) speculates: "One of the values of a purely destructive form such as comedy, then, is simply its assertion that it is human, that we are human, and that to reveal the paradoxes, ironies, and ambiguities of existence is the art of being human. (Also) in shaking us out of our assumptions comedy reminds us not to inflict pain on those who do not share those assumptions. The comic films are full of pain."

Certainly blacks in this country have suffered pain, and two of our finest black writers have indicated a shrewd awareness of the complex function of our humor. In his introduction to *The Book of Negro Laughter*, Langston Hughes said, "Humor is laughing at what you haven't got, what you wish in your secret heart were not funny but it is and you must laugh. Humor is your own unconscious therapy." In his brilliant essay "Change the joke and Slip the Yoke," Ralph Ellison touches on one of the deepest themes of American humor, the mask. "America is a land of masking jokers," says Ellison. "We wear the mask for purposes of aggression as well as for defense." But the motives behind the mask, Ellison argues, are as numerous as the ambiguities the mask conceals, and "give Americans an ironic awareness of the joke that always lies between the discontinuity of social tradition and that sense of the past which clings to the mind." (Once again, the discrepancy between the what-should-be and the what-is.) "The mask is a strategy common to our culture," Ellison notes; and it is clear that he is not just talking about black Sambo imitations but of the masks all Americans wear. And how much the notion of the mask seems to answer—not only Twain's betrayal of Jim, but Lardner's poker-face, Pryor's jiving, even Kinison's screaming. Could there come a day when we take the masks off? Would it be allowed? Could we *bear* it?

Other observers see some healthy signs. Karen Feldscher points to a notable change, from the humor of Sut Lovingood to that of Woody Allen. "A century later," she writes, "the joke isn't on somebody *else* anymore; it's on *us*. This shift in what we consider comical can be traced directly to changes in the American psyche, influenced by changes in the American way of life." Feldscher may have something; her theory has obvious application to the humor of Pynchon and Heller, and also to that of Lily Tomlin, Rodney Dangerfield, Steve Martin, not to mention such odd developments as Cantor's *Krazy Kat*. Humor, too, as Earl Rovit reminds us, does have a purging effect: "Ultimately, the comic spirit draws its strength from the realm of possibilities, rather than limitations. Its most profound and healthy appeal is to that creative and destructive explosion

of energies which offers men a renewed promise of themselves
and a recognition of the realistic options that are open to them
in their lives." Performance artist Eric Bogosian says he understands "the power of the spoken word especially when uttered
in the face of the fragility of people's beliefs. I make them laugh
at violence and prejudice, then feel embarrassed for the laughter." In this view then, humor, like an antibody, destroys in
order to heal.

Well, what is it? Should we applaud—or throw tomatoes?

. . .

The best of all humor, particularly the best of American humor
tells the truth—and we also, often, resist that truth. If the ancient Greek kings didn't like the message, they killed the mes-
senger. Can we not be more honest, more brave than that?
Often, things don't work, we don't get what we paid for, our
elected officials chisel us, those we love let us down—and
there *is* violence out there, massive violence, and death, silent
and thunderous; and *that* is what we need our humorists to
point out so that we may laugh—and then think.

To recap for a moment might be helpful. Mark Twain, as we
saw, started his own career by relying on the raucous, broad
humor of the Far West, relying on hoaxes and broad jests, but
the wildness of such fledgling efforts as *The Snodgrass Letters*
tended to minimize any real satirical thrust. It was only in his
mature works, particularly *Huckleberry Finn*, that Twain effec-
tively questioned the violent underpinnings of his society.
Twain's own methodology, too, we saw, changed over his long
career, as he came to rely less on practical jokes, tall-tales, and
burlesque and developed a more broadly-based humor of character. He came to understand that certain brands of humor, such
as practical joking, were rather crude substitutes for violence
itself. But this insight did not provide Twain with any clear-cut
solution to the problem of violence. We were left with a picture
of the aging Twain struggling with the darkness of his own
vision of a violent world in which the human animal hobbles
about, crippled by his own terrible instincts. Ambrose Bierce,
on the other hand, believed that only ruthless force could rem-
pedy the lawlessness of the frontier. Thus he attacked, heaping

invective on the vile "human critter" and asserting his eternal damnation. But in refusing to don the "genial mask," "Bitter Bierce" allowed the general public to dismiss his "bottled bile" as satirical overkill; and in many ways his work seems but another version of the very violence he railed against.

If Twain and Bierce wielded the sword of ridicule, Ring Lardner, we saw, preferred the rubber banana. By distancing himself so clearly from his own disturbed comic creations, Lardner also allowed his audience to distance *themselves* from the subjects of his satire. Lardner the writer, in effect, became his own "self-controlled" gentleman, seldom abandoning his poker face to condemn outright the avarice and the violence he saw around him. But there is a difficulty in such a sophisticated and clever technique. The reader must be smart enough to get the point; and the morally obtuse reader can get off the hook. If Bierce fell victim to his rage, Lardner seems a victim of his comic mask. Kurt Vonnegut is a hard man to pigeonhole. Like the early Twain, he can be outrageous; like Bierce, he can be venomous, especially toward those he judges most responsible for our sorry state; and his obvious concern for common decency suggests Ring Lardner. But Vonnegut's voice has become more strident as he has taken the problem of violence, both public and individual, as the subject of his dark humor; and in putting violence up to the light so we will be more properly appalled, Vonnegut seems to have handled best the dilemma of the humorist as social critic.

In the world of film, we noted how the silent clowns, particularly Keaton and Chaplin, employed slapstick techniques to get laughs and often took the violence of the outside world as the subject for their best comedies. Laurel and Hardy, the Marx Brothers, and W. C. Fields went on from there to create comic metaphors of destruction through ridicule, parody, and insult; and current filmmakers have even managed to devise a slashing black humor out of war. And we have also seen how our stand-up comedians earn their keep by "killing" an audience; and how the dynamics of stand-up comedy infects and affects even our politicians. (Perhaps losing politicians should take up stand-up comedy; they certainly have the training to kill an audience.)

But what have we really learned? Certainly, particulars are more fun, generalizations more difficult; and on the battlefield of humor, there is so much smoke and so many snipers, one generalizes at one's peril. Dick Shawn is reputed to have said, "A critic is someone who comes in after the battle and dispatches the wounded." I hope I have done more than dispatch the wounded—or caused additional wounds through theoretical overkill. I would be the first to concede that, if there is a school for scoundrels, there is no "school" of American humorists—their aims and accomplishments have varied widely. But, on the whole, we can note that these artists have produced an original and variegated comic mosaic of immense vitality, admittedly often corrosive and dark, but liberating and refreshing as well. But if the ridiculous is a species of the ugly, as that old stand-up comic Aristotle once said, we can see that little imp (that gargoyle) everywhere in American humor. If for a moment we might lump these humorists together (like a hive of bees perhaps), certain conclusions suggest themselves:

1. These artists view violence as problematic for Americans.

2. They have evidenced a particular fondness for violent comic methodology—ironically, even when attacking aggression.

3. They have come increasingly to question the effectiveness of humor as antidote to aggression.

4. Their recognition of the violent and unregenerate nature of the "common man," that so-called pillar of American democracy, has caused a certain despair.

So we might understand from this that comic relief from the prevailing violence does not, unfortunately, last very long. We laugh; but as with the proverbial Chinese lunch, we are soon hungry again. Perhaps that should come as no surprise. "Man alone," said Nietsche, "suffers so excruciatingly in the world that he was compelled to invent laughter." Is *that* the punch line? Ian Frazer, in a recent *New Yorker* article, offers a view of our entire, history as one extended and violent punch line:

> This finally is the punch line of our two hundred years on the Great Plains: we trap out the beaver, subtract the Mandan, infect the Blackfeet and the Hidatsa and the Assiniboin, overdose the Arikara; call the land a desert and hurry across it to get to Cali-

fornia and Oregon; suck up the buffalo, bones and all, kill off nations of elk and wolves and cranes and prairie chickens and prairie dogs; dig up the gold and rebury it in vaults someplace else; ruin the Sioux and Cheyenne and Arapaho and Crow and Kiowa and Comanche; kill Crazy Horse, harvest wave after wave of immigrants' dreams and send the wised-up dreamers on their way; plow the topsoil until it blows to the ocean; ship out the wheat, ship out the cattle; dig up the earth itself and burn it in power plants and send the power down the line; dismiss the small farmers, empty little towns; drill the oil and natural gas and pipe it away; dry up the rivers and the springs, deep-drill for irrigation water as the aquifer retreats. And in return we condense unimaginable amounts of treasure into weapons buried beneath the land that so much treasure came from—weapons for which our best hope might be that we will someday take them apart and throw them away, and for which our next best hope certainly is that they remain humming away under the prairie, absorbing fear and maintenance, unused, forever.

There is little humor in Frazier's catalog certainly isn't funny, and maybe the message is that certain punch lines simply just are not, and cannot be, funny.

But the vexing, and still unanswered, question seems to be: If man is a foolish and violent hombre (and *that*, after all, is the subject of so much American humor), then when will he stop being so? Deadness comes over one in the face of so much repetitive violence in the jokes. (Did you hear the one about the butcher who backed into the meat grinder and got a little *behind* in his orders?) However the ingredients in the Great American Joke may vary, the punch line is often depressingly similar—the sly jab in the ribs, the quick poke to the nose, the swift boot in the ass. Just as we find weary men in our homicide bureaus and morgues counting bodies and numbly chalking up revised figures, many of our American humorists—angry but increasingly stoic witnesses—end up tired and cynical. We are forced by such findings, then, to reconsider our earlier working formula. If

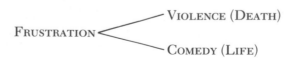

FRUSTRATION < VIOLENCE (DEATH) / COMEDY (LIFE)

then, in America, very often

FRUSTRATION ⟶ COMEDY ⟶ MORE FRUSTRATION ⟶ PESSIMISM

For American humorists, it seems, humor is an escape rather than a true balm. If every country gets the kind of humor it deserves, then the wild and wooly thrust of American humor is a sign of vigorous health. But its violent nature also suggests there is a kind of lingering cancer within the body politic as well. The violent, crude jokes often seem as much a symptom as a diagnosis; and, often, our "phunny phellows" seem to be suffering from the very disease they are doctoring. If Baudelaire is right in suggesting joy as a unity and laughter as a sign of a certain turmoil in the soul, perhaps we must simply accept the fractured response our humorists offer rather than expect any real vision of wholeness. At base, at heart, American humor, like much humor, is not a humor of joy.

What gives one pause is the backdrop of violence and terror that looms behind the humor—an atmosphere so dark and irrational as to make the jokes wear thin. "Mirth is the Mail of Anguish," penned that wise woman Emily Dickinson, "In which it Cautious Arm / Lest anybody see the blood / And 'you're hurt' exclaim!" How often does it seem that the American humorist, having set out daringly and lightly as an amused observer of the American spectacle of violence and corruption, ends up mouthing sardonic fables in a bed of gloom. Violence, the inspiration of much American humor, outlives it. When the jokes grow cold, the guns—unfortunately—are still hot.

But that should not perhaps be the last word. Our humorists have given us not only a "new" deal but a great deal. In their limning of the harsh, barely submerged realities of American life, they have operated as honest craftsmen, telling the story behind the story, so to speak. Despite their portraits of folly, the dream of peace—*their* dream of peace, *our* dream of peace —still hovers about the ragged edges of the comic nightmare. "Humor," as Kierkegaard said, "is the last stage of existential awareness before faith." I should also add—but, ah, I hear a voice from the wings, "Say goodnight, Gracie." *Goodnight, Gracie, and goodnight, Mrs. Calabash, wherever you are ... keep warm.*

THE WRAP

Notes and Sources

I have tried to arrange the notes for convenience, offering an annotated list of the most significant general reference works and anthologies at the beginning and citing particular sources in short form chapter by chapter. Because of varying editions I have, in Twain and Vonnegut, referred to chapters rather than pages in those books where chapters are short. I have also resorted to cluster citations when occasions seemed to warrant. I have not cited sources for jokes or quips that reside within the general circulation where I myself encountered them. My working rule was to make the apparatus succinct so as to keep the book from being bottom-heavy. I owe a great deal to many and hope I have been fair. I trust the reader enjoys the book more than the notes, as I did.

GENERAL REFERENCE WORKS

Bier, Jesse. *The Rise and Fall of American Humor*. Holt, 1968. A contentious but well-argued study which ends by attacking the nihilism of contemporary comedy.

Blair, Walter, and Hamlin Hill. *America's Humor: From Poor Richard to Doonesbury*. Oxford University Press, 1978. The best comprehensive study to date.

Blair, Walter. *Native American Humor*. Chandler, 1960. An excellent introduction to early American humor.

Boskin, Joseph. *Humor and Social Change in Twentieth-Century America*. Boston Public Library, 1979. An incisive study of the social effects of humor.

Cohen, Sarah Blacher, ed. *Comic Relief: Humor in Contemporary American Literature*. Illinois University Press, 1978. Good essays on Faulkner, ethnic humorists, black comedy, and Jewish humor.

Corrigan, Robert W. *Comedy: Meaning and Form*. Chandler, 1965. Excellent source book of comic theory. Cf., W. H. Auden, "Notes on the Comic," 61–72; George Santayana, "The Comic Mask and Carnival," 73–80; Eric Bentley, "Farce," 279–303; Charles Baudelaire, "On the Essence of Laughter," 448–65; George Meredith, "An Essay on Comedy," 466–70.

Dudden, Arthur, ed. *American Humor*. Oxford University Press, 1987. A collection of recent essays with a political slant.

Dudden, Arthur. *The Assault of Laughter*. Yosseloff, 1962. A fine book on our political humorists.

Gale, Steven H., ed. *Encyclopedia of American Humorists*. Garland, 1987. Good bibliographical essays.

Harris, Charles. *Contemporary American Novelists of the Absurd*. Yale University Press, 1971. An excellent study of Joseph Heller, John Barth, and other black humorists.

Hauck, Richard. *A Cheerful Nihilism*. Indiana University Press, 1971). See 77–132, 167–200 for a lively discussion of humor in William Faulkner and Herman Melville.

McGhee, Paul E., and Jeffrey Goldstein, eds. *Handbook of Humor Research*. 2 vols. Springer-Verlag, 1983.

Mintz, Lawrence E. *Humor in America: A Research Guide to Genres and Topics*. Greenwood, 1988. Indispensable and long overdue. See especially Joseph Boskin and Joseph Dorinson, "Ethnic Humor: Subversion and Survival," 163–94. Also Stephen Whitfield, "Political Humor," 195–211.

Rourke, Constance. *American Humor*. Harcourt, Brace and World, 1931. An important early study.

Rubin, Louis. *The Comic Imagination in America*. Rutgers University Press, 1971. An extremely useful collection of essays. See especially Walter Sullivan on Flannery O'Connor and Walker Percy, 339–48; Robert D. Jacobs on Faulkner's humor, 305–18.

Thorp, Willard. *American Humor*. University of Minnesota Press, 1964.

Veron, Enid. *Humor in America*. Harcourt Brace, 1976. An attractive anthology with incisive critical essays.

Walker, Nancy, and Zita Dresner. *Redressing the Balance: American Women's Literary Humor from Colonial Times to the 1980's*. University Press of Mississippi, 1988. An attempt to broaden the canon.

White, E. B., and Katherine S. White, eds. *A Subtreasury of American Humor*. Random House, 1941. A collection of pieces mainly from the "counter-tradition."

Zeidman, Irving. *The American Burlesque Show*. Hawthorn, 1967. Fun.

THE PRELIM

PRIMARY SOURCES

Boskin, Joseph and Joseph Dorinson. "Racial and Ethnic Humor," in Mintz, *Humor in America*, 163–94.

———— "Ethnic Humor and Survival," in Dudden, *American Humor*, 98–117.

Freud, Sigmund. *Jokes and Their Relation to the Unconscious*. The Hogarth Press, 1960.

Koestler, Arthur. *The Act of Creation*. Dell, 1967. See especially 27–97 for analysis of the humor "process" where Koestler argues that laughter is a powerful tool of aggression.

McNamara, Brooks. *American Popular Entertainments: A Collection of Jokes, Monologues and Comedy Routines*. Performing Arts Journal Press, 1983.

May, Rollo. *Power and Innocence*. Norton, 1972.

Morison, Samuel Eliot. *Admiral of the Ocean Sea, A Life of Christopher Columbus*. Houghton-Mifflin, 1942.

———— *Builders of the Bay Colony*. Houghton-Mifflin, 1958.

Pohl, Frederick. *Amerigo Vespucci: Pilot Major*. Octagon, 1966.

Walker, Nancy. *A Very Serious Thing: Women's Humor and American Culture*. Minnesota, 1988. Thoughtful and angry.

Wilde, Larry. *The Complete Book of Ethnic Humor*. Pinnacle, 1978. The best collection of ethnic jokes.

NOTES

p. xi   For Columbus and the Indies, see Morison, *Admiral of the Ocean Sea*, 381, ff.

p. xii   Emerson *English Traits* (1856), q. Pohl, *Amerigo Vespucci*, vi.

p. xiii   For Morton material and Bradford quotes, see Morison, *Builders of the Bay Colony*, 14–18.

p. xv   Leslie Fiedler, *O Brave New World* (Dell, 1968), 380.

p. xvi   Twain on ridicule, *Mark Twain's Notebook*, ed. A. B. Paine (Harper, 1935), 198. Artemus Ward, q. David Sloane, *Mark Twain as a Literary Comedian* (Louisiana State University Press, 1979), 54.

p. xix   These particular jokes are taken from Wilde, *The Complete Book of Ethnic Humor;* there are, of course, infinite others. See also McNamara, *American Popular Entertainments*. See especially "How Adam and Eve Turned White. A Darkey's Sermon to His Congregation," 35, ff. Also, "The Black Breach of a Promise Case," 105, ff. (Judge: "Did ye swear dem all?" Police: "Yes, dey's all bin swearin' for de last half-hour, some ob dem berry badly.")

p. xx   Sick-humor-loving readers are invited to consult Patrick D. Morrow, "Those Sick Challenger Jokes" Vol. 20, 4 (*Journal of Popular Culture*): 179.

p. xx   On women's humor, see especially Walker, *A Very Serious Thing: Women's Humor and American Culture*. On Faulkner, see *Faulkner and Humor*, eds. Doreen Fowler and Ann Abadie (University of Mississippi Press, 1986).

p. xxii   Gregory, *The Nature of Laughter*, q. Koestler, *The Act of Creation*, 51–52. For an overview on the "scary" elements of children's humor, see Janice Alberghene, "Humor in Children's Literature." In *Journal of Children in Contemporary Society* (1989): 223–45.

p. xxii   Freud, *Jokes and Their Relation to the Unconscious*, 102, ff. May, *Power and Innocence*, 171. Burrows and Brooks, q. Boskin, "Racial and Ethnic Humor," 168, 171.

p. xxiii   Walpole, letter to the Countess of Upper Ossory, q. *Bartlett's Familiar Quotations*. Baudelaire, "On the Essence of Laughter," in *Comedy: Meaning and Form*, ed. Corrigan, 448–65.

ROUND ONE.
THE VIOLENCE OF AMERICAN HUMOR

PRIMARY SOURCES

Brack, O. M. Jr. *Essays Presented to John C. Gerber*. Arete, 1977.

Clark, William, and W. Craig Turner, eds. *Critical Essays on American Humor*. Hall, 1984.

Cohen, Hennig and William B. Dillingham, eds. *Humor of the Old Southwest*. Houghton-Mifflin, 1964.

Gardner, Elaine. "Sut Lovingood: Backwoods Existentialist." *Southern Studies* (Summer 1983): 177–89.
Harris, George Washington. *Sut Lovingood's Yarns.* Edited by M. Thomas Inge. College and University Press, 1966.
Hofstadter, Richard. *American Violence.* Knopf, 1970.
Inge, M. Thomas. *The Frontier Humorists.* Archon, 1975.
Nicolson, Harold. *The English Sense of Humor.* Funk & Wagnalls, 1968.

NOTES

p. 1   Japanese joke attributed to Fukurokuju, eighteenth-century Japanese humorist, q. R. H. Blyth in *Oriental Humor* (Hokuseido Press, 1959), 510.

p. 2   Hofstadter, *American Violence,* 8.

p. 3   Twain, q. Blair and Hill, *America's Humor,* 20. Meredith, "An Essay on Comedy," q. Corrigan, *Comedy: Meaning and Form,* 469. Lord Chesterfield, q. Nicolson, *The English Sense of Humor,* 44. Muggeridge, q. Dudden, *The Assault of Laughter,* 21.

p. 4   Morley, *ibid,* Dudden, 21. Auden, "Huck and Oliver," *The Listener,* (1 October 1953), 450–51.

p. 4   Pritchett, "The Cruelty of American Humor," *New Statesman and Nation,* 22, (August 2, 1941), 113.

p. 5   Bentzon and Charpentier, q. James C. Austin, *American Humor in France* (Iowa State University Press, 1978), 70–71. 37. Boyesen, in Dudden, 370. Cox, *Why We Laugh* (Harper, 1876), q. Clark and Turner, *Critical Essays,* 42. Billings, q. Blair and Hill, *America's Humor,* 41.

p. 5   Blair and Hill, 12. Irving, *Ibid,* 11–12. Jarvis, *Ibid,* 110. On the subject of the palatability of early American humor, cf., Blair and Hill's comment: "If we're to laugh at the (early) stories, we have to be amused as our forebears evidently were by drunkenness, recklessness, racism, male chauvinism, violence, sheer cruelty." *Ibid,* introduction.

p. 6   Rubin, *The Comic Imagination in America,* 12. Leacock, *Humor and Humanity* (Knopf, 1933), 218. Breton, "Mark Twain: an Appreciation," *Twentieth Century Views of Mark Twain* (Prentice-Hall, 1963), 30. Reagan, q. Mark Green, *Reagan's Reign of Error* (Pantheon, 1987), 33.

p. 7   West, "Some Notes on Violence," *Contact 1,* no.3 (1932). Brown, q. Hofstadter, *American Violence,* 35. For more on the American he-man tradition, see Rupert Wilkinson, *American Tough: The Tough Guy Tradition and American Character* (Perennial, 1986).

p. 9   For much of the statistical information, I am indebted to Hofstadter's *American Violence*.

p. 9   Davis, *Homicide in American Fiction* (Cornell University Press, 1957), viii.

p. 10   Hofstadter, 8.

p. 10   Hooper, "Simon Plays the Snatch Game," in Cohen and Dillingham, *Humor of the Old Southwest*, 207.

p. 10   "Parson John Bullen's Lizards," *Sut Lovingood Yarns*, 51–59.

p. 12   Wilson, "Poisoned," *New Yorker* (7 May 1959), 150–55.

p. 14   For more on what Twain owed to his precursors and what he redefined, see Kenneth Lynn, *Mark Twain and Southwestern Humor* (Little, Brown, 1959).

ROUND TWO.
THE PAINTED FIRE OF MARK TWAIN.

PRIMARY SOURCES

Anderson, Frederick, ed. *Mark Twain: The Critical Heritage*. Barnes and Noble, 1971.

Auden, W. H. "Huck and Oliver," *Listener* (October 1, 1953): 540.

Benson, Ivan. *Mark Twain's Western Years*. Russell, 1966.

Blair, Walter. *Mark Twain and Huck Finn*. University of California Press, 1962.

——— *The Literary Apprenticeship of Mark Twain*. Russell, 1966.

Brooks, Van Wyck. *The Ordeal of Mark Twain*. Doubleday, 1920. Revised, 1947.

Budd, Louis J. *Our Mark Twain: The Making of His Public Personality*. University of Pennsylvania Press, 1983.

Cardwell, Guy. *Twins of Genius*. Michigan State University Press, 1953.

Cox, James. *The Fate of Humor*. Princeton University Press, 1966.

Covici, Pascal. *Mark Twain's Humor*. Southern Methodist Press, 1962.

DeVoto, Bernard. *Mark Twain's America*. Riverside, 1932.

Ellison, Ralph. *Shadow and Act*. Signet, 1966. "Twentieth Century Fiction and the Black Mask of Humanity," 42–60.

Emerson, Everett. *The Authentic Mark Twain: A Literary Biography*. University of Pennsylvania Press, 1984.

Fatout, Paul. *Mark Twain in Virginia City*. Indiana University Press, 1964.

Geismar, Maxwell. *Mark Twain: An American Prophet*. McGraw-Hill, 1970.

Holbrook, Hal. *Mark Twain Tonight*. Ives Washburn, 1959.

Hill, Hamlin. *Mark Twain: God's Fool*. Harper, 1973.

Howells, William Dean. *My Mark Twain*. Edited by Marilyn Austin Baldwin. Louisiana State University Press, 1967.

Kaplan, Justin. *Mr. Clemens and Mark Twain*. Simon and Schuster, 1966.

Lauber, John. *The Making of Mark Twain*. Heritage, 1985.

Lorch, Fred W. *The Trouble Begins at Eight: Mark Twain's Lecture Tours*. Iowa State University Press.

Lynn, Kenneth. *Mark Twain and Southwestern Humor*. Little, Brown, 1959.

——— ed. *The Comic Tradition in America: An Anthology of American Humor*. Norton, 1968.

——— *Visions of America*. Greenwood, 1972.

Meltzer, Milton. *Mark Twain Himself*. Bonanza Books, 1960.

Paine, Albert Bigelow. *Mark Twain, a Biography*. 3 vols. Harper, 1912.

Pettit, Arthur G. *Mark Twain and the South*. The University of Kentucky Press, 1974.

Pritchett, V. S. "Huckleberry Finn and the Cruelty of American Humor." *New Statesman*, 22 (August 2, 1941).

Read, Opie. *Mark Twain and I*. Reilly and Lee, 1940.

Sloane, David E. *Mark Twain as a Literary Comedian*. Louisiana State University Press, 1979.

Smith, Henry Nash. *Mark Twain: The Development of a Writer*. Belknap, 1962.

——— ed. *Mark Twain: A Collection of Critical Essays*. Prentice-Hall, 1963.

Tanner, Tony. *The Reign of Wonder: Naivete and Reality in American Literature*. Cambridge University Press, 1965.

Taylor, Cooley. *Mark Twain's Margins on Thackeray's Swift*. Gotham, 1939.

Tuckey, Frederick. *Mark Twain and Little Satan: The Writing of "The Mysterious Stranger."* Greenwood, 1963.

Twain, Mark. *The Writings of Mark Twain*. 37 vols. Harper and Brothers, 1922–1925. A "definitive" edition is in process at the Universities of California and Iowa. Several volumes, including *The Mark Twain Papers*, have emerged so far.

—— *The Adventures of Thomas Jefferson Snodgrass*. Edited by Charles Honce. Pascal Covici, Inc., 1968.

—— *The Autobiography of Mark Twain*. Edited by Charles Neider. Harper, 1959.

—— *Clemens of the* Call. Edited by Edgar M. Branch. University of California Press, 1969.

—— *Complete Essays of Mark Twain*. Edited by Charles Neider. Doubleday, 1963.

—— *Complete Humorous Sketches and Tales of Mark Twain*. Edited by Charles Neider. Hanover, 1961.

—— *Editorial Wild Oats*. 1905. Reprinted by Books for Libraries, 1971.

—— *The Forgotten Writings of Mark Twain*. Edited by Henry Duskis. Citadel, 1963.

—— *Letters from the Earth*. Edited by Bernard DeVoto. Harper, 1962.

—— *Life As I Find It*. Edited by Charles Neider. Hanover, 1961.

—— *Mark Twain and the Three R'S*. Edited by Maxwell Geismar. Viking, 1967.

—— *Mark Twain in Eruption*. Edited by Bernard DeVoto. Harper, 1940.

—— *Mark Twain's Letters to Mary*. Edited by Lewis Leary. Columbia University Press, 1963.

—— *Mark Twain's Notebook*. Edited by Albert Bifelow Paine: Harpers, 1935.

—— *A Pen Warmed-up in Hell*. Edited by Frederick Anderson. Harper, 1972.

—— *Plymouth Rock and the Pilgrims: and other Salutary Platform Opinions*. Edited by Charles Neider. Harper, 1985.

—— *The Portable Mark Twain*. Edited by Bernard DeVoto, Harper, 1962.

—— *Satires and Burlesques*. Edited by Franklin R. Rogers. University of California Press, 1967.

—— *Selected Mark Twain-Howells Letters*. Edited by Frederick Anderson et al., Belknap, 1967.

—— *The War Prayer*. Harper, 1970.

Wiggins, Robert A. *Mark Twain: Jackleg Novelist*. University of Washington Press, 1964.

NOTES

p. 18 *Autobiography*, 99. John Marshall Clemens seems best remembered for his stern sense of duty and occasional flashes of violence. See Pettit, *Mark Twain and the South*, 13–20.

p. 20 "First Literary Venture," *Editorial Wild Oats*, 5–6.

p. 20 "Journalism," *ibid*, 14–29.

p. 20 "How I edited," in *Editorial Wild Oats*, 68, ff. "Nicodemus Dodge," in *A Tramp Abroad* (1880), I, ch. xxxiii.

p. 21 *Adventures of Thomas Jefferson Snodgrass*, 224, ff.

p. 22 "On murder, " reprinted from *Virginia City Enterprise* in *San Francisco Golden Era*, November 22, 1863. "Empire City massacre," reprinted in *San Francisco Bulletin*, October 31, 1863.

p. 23 "Rebuke," *Bulletin*, reprinted in *Sacramento Daily Union*, November 2, 1863. Twain on hoax, in *The Galaxy*, (June 1870), 858. "Mummy," *Enterprise*, October 4, 1862, reprinted in *Bulletin*, October 15, 1862.

p. 24 Benson, *Mark Twain's Western Years*, 67. "Aurelia," reprinted in *Complete Humorous Sketches and Tales*.

p. 24 Meriden letter, January 30, 1864.

p. 25 Doten, *Nevada Magazine* (October 1899), q. Benson, 90. "Scandal," q. Fatout, *Mark Twain in Virginia City*, 196.

p. 26 "Absquatulated," *ibid.*, p. 211. McEwen, San Francisco *Examiner*, 1893. "How I Escaped," *Fatout*, 212.

p. 27 "Letter to bandits," *Enterprise*, November 11, 1866. De Quille, q. Fatout 151. "No practical joke," *ibid*, 204. "Good-bye to felons," *Bulletin*, December 14, 1866.

p. 27 Twain on practical joking, *Autobiography*, 48, 50.

p. 28 "Their equipment," *ibid.*, 103. "Amazonian," *Essays*, 171. On Twain's use of the hoax, see *Mark Twain's Humor*, where Covici argues that Twain often hoaxes his readers as well; for example, Covici sees the ending of *Huckleberry Finn* as a hoax on any reader who has identified with Tom.

p. 29 "Mayhem," July 21, 1864. "Accomodating," August 31, 1864. "On planting Democrats," September 25, 1864. All reprinted in *Clemens of the Call*.

p. 30 "The Ching devil," *Life As I Find It*, 78. "On the police court," *Autobiography*, q. Branch, 254–55. "Advice to little girls," *Humorous Sketches*, 47.

p. 31 "Answers to Correspondents," *ibid.*, 48.

p. 35 Paul Bowles, *The Sheltering Sky* (New Directions, 1949), 13–14.

p. 35   "No Californian," *Roughing It*, chap. 54.

p. 36   "On violence" and Slade, chap. 10.

p. 36   "Slough hat," chap. 42.

p. 37   "Trial by jury" and Captain Ned, chap. 49.

p. 38   Arkansaw, chap. 31. Unrevised "Arkansaw," *Roughing It* (University of California Press, 539.

p. 39   On practical jokes, revisiting Washoe, and the moral of the story, chap. 79.

p. 42   "*Huckleberry Finn* and the Cruelty of American Humor," 113. For an exhaustive study of the struggles of composition, see Blair, *Mark Twain and Huck Finn*.

p. 43   "Come in, Huck, chap. 10.

p. 44   Ambush of Buck, chap. 17.

p. 44   Sherburn, chap. 21 and 22. Bricksville, chap. 21.

p. 46   Ellison, *Shadow and Act*, 43.

p. 48   Opie Read, *Mark Twain and I*, 17.

p. 50   *Connecticut Yankee*, chap. 1.

p. 50   Morgan le Fay, chap. 16. Hank's priorities, chap. 9. "In a new country," chap. 33.

p. 51   "Boss," chap. 8.

p. 51   "King," chap. 34.

p. 52   "The Machinery of Self-Preservation," *Twentieth Century Views*, 129.

p. 54   June, 1872. *Twain-Howells Letters*, 9 .

p. 55   "Liars," *Life As I Find It*, 334.

p. 55   "The Conquest of the Phillipines," *Mark Twain and the Three R's*. "Talons," *Life As I Find It*, 335. "Lynching," *Essays*, 679. "White man," *Three R's*, 67.

p. 56   Aborigines, *ibid*, 72.

p. 57   "Wandering Photograph," *Complete Sketches*, 115.

p. 58   *Twain-Howells Letters*, 334.

p. 59   Anderson, *Mark Twain: The Critical Heritage*, 336. Mencken, "The Burden of Humor," *Smart Set* (February 1913): 331.

p. 60   Twain on Swift, q. Taylor, *Mark Twain's Margins of Thackeray's Swift*, 55. Twain on Harte, *Autobiography*, 296. Twain to Read, *Mark Twain and I*, 17.

ROUND THREE.
THE BOTTLED BILE OF
AMBROSE BIERCE

PRIMARY SOURCES

Bierce, Ambrose. *The Collected Works of Ambrose Bierce.* 12 vols. Walter Neale, 1909–1912.

——— *The Shadow on the Dial and Other Essays.* Edited by S. O. Howes. A. M. Robertson, 1909.

——— *The Collected Writings of Ambrose Bierce.* Edited by Clifton Fadiman. Citadel, 1945. A good one-volume "selection." Fadiman advises that Bierce, like poison, should be taken in small doses.

——— *The Sardonic Humor of Ambrose Bierce.* Dover, 1963. A grab-bag without citations.

——— *The Enlarged Devil's Dictionary.* Edited by Ernest Hopkins. Doubleday, 1967. Includes many worthy entries omitted from Bierce's *Works.*

——— *The Ambrose Bierce Satanic Reader.* Edited by Ernest Hopkins. Doubleday, 1968. A compendium of Bierce's "invective journalism."

——— *Letters of Ambrose Bierce.* Edited by Bertha Clark Pope. California Book Club, 1922. Includes Bierce's letters from 1892–1913 and a memoir by George Sterling.

Fatout, Paul. *Ambrose Bierce, the Devil's Lexicographer.* Oklahoma Press, 1951. Good readable biography.

Fuentes, Carlos. *The Old Gringo.* Harper & Row, 1985. An award-winning novel imagining Bierce's life and demise in Mexico.

Grattan, C. Hartley. *Bitter Bierce: A Mystery of American Letters.* Doubleday, 1929. Reprinted by Cooper Square, 1966. A well-written study assessing Bierce's philosophy.

Martin, Jay. "Ambrose Bierce." In Louis Rubin, *The Comic Imagination in America,* 195–205. Rutgers University Press. Good terse article with no citations, however.

Morrill, Sibley. *Ambrose Bierce, F. A. Mitchell-Hedges, and the Crystal Skull.* Cadleon, 1972. A spectacularly outlandish book.

Neale, Walter. *The Life of Ambrose Bierce.* Doubleday, 1929.

O'Connor, Richard. *Ambrose Bierce: A Life.* Little Brown, 1962. The most thorough factual account.

Starrett, Vincent. *Ambrose Bierce.* Kennikat, 1920. A starry-eyed memoir by an admirer.

NOTES

p. 61   Bierce, q. Martin, "Ambrose Bierce," 201.

p. 61   "Cynic" and other Bierce "definitions" taken from *The Enlarged Devil's Dictionary* (alphabetized). For much biographical material, I am indebted to Richard O'Connor.

p. 62   Albert Bierce, q. George Sterling, "The Shadow Maker," *American Mercury* (October 1925), 44. "United States," *WASP*, December 12, 1885.

p. 63   Pope, *Letters*, p. ix.

p. 63   "To say of a man," q. Martin, 198. "On delicate humor," *ibid*, 200.

p. 64   "The wittiest man", *Satanic Reader*, 24. On Howells and James, *ibid.*, 183–84. "Humor is tolerant," Bierce, *Works*, 10, 101.

p. 64   "Chuck him," *Satanic Reader*, 9. "Satire," *Devil's Dictionary*.

p. 66   Bierce on Twain's marriage, q. O'Connor, 77.

p. 67   Bierce on dead babies, q. *Satanic Reader*, 3.

p. 69   O'Connor, 120.

p. 69   "McFarland," *Satanic Reader*, 59. "Anthem," *Sardonic Humor*, 91. On anarchists, *Shadow on the Dial*, 9.

p. 70   On "vox populi," *Satanic Reader*, 59. For "democracy" and "republic," see *Devil's Dictionary*.

p. 70   Fadiman, "Portrait of a Misanthrope," *Collected Writings*, xviii.

p. 72   Bierce dressed in black, Pope, *Letters*, xv. Letter to Helen, O'Connor, 298.

p. 73   Last letter, December 16, 1913, q. O'Connor, 303.

p. 73   Sibley Morrill, *Crystal Skull*, 43. Torres, q. O'Connor, 305.

p. 74   Carlos Fuentes, *The Old Gringo*, 68–76, ff.

p. 76   Agee, November 26, 1937. *Letters to Father Flye* (Braziller, 1962), 96–97. Mencken, *Prejudices*, 6th Series (Knopf, 1927), 293.

p. 76   Neale, *Life*, 97–98.

p. 77   Fadiman, *Collected Writings*, xiii. Vonnegut, "Interview with Robert Scholes," in Klinkowitz, *The Vonnegut Statement*, 99.

p. 77   Bierce on mullahs and dervishes, *Letters*, 123.

ROUND FOUR.
RING LARDNER: SAD SACK IN
THE FUN HOUSE

PRIMARY SOURCES

Anderson, Sherwood. "Four American Impressions: Gertrude Stein, Paul Rosenfeld, Ring Lardner, Sinclair Lewis," *New Republic*, 32 (October 11, 1922), 171–73.

—— "Meeting Ring Lardner," *The New Yorker*, 9 (November 25, 1933), 36–38.

—— *No Swank*. Appel, 1970.

Drennan, Robert E. *The Algonquin Wits*. Citadel, 1975.

Elder, Donald. *Ring Lardner*. Doubleday, 1956.

Fadiman, Clifton. "Ring Lardner and the Triangle of Hate," *Nation* 136 (March 22, 1933): 315–17.

Fitzgerald, F. Scott. "Ring," *New Republic* (October 11, 1933): 254–55.

—— *The Crack-up*. New Directions, 1956.

Geismar, Maxwell. *Ring Lardner and the Portrait of Folly*. Crowell, 1972.

—— "Ring Lardner: Like Something Was Going to Happen," *Writers in Crisis: The American Novel Between Two Wars*. Houghton-Mifflin, 1942.

Lardner, Ring. *Bib Ballads*. P. F. Volland, 1915.

—— *You Know Me Al*. Doran, 1916.

—— *Gullible's Travels*. Bobbs-Merrill, 1917. Reprinted by Scribner's, 1967, with an introduction by Josephine Herbst.

—— *How to Write Short Stories (with Samples)*. Scribner's, 1924.

—— *What of It?* Scribner's, 1926.

—— *The Story of a Wonder Man*. Scribner's, 1927.

—— *Round Up: The Stories of Ring Lardner*. Scribner's, 1929.

—— *The Ring Lardner Reader*. Edited by Maxwell Geismar. Scribner's, 1963.

—— *Some Champions*. Edited by Mathew Bruccoli and Richard Layman. Scribner's, 1976. Twenty-six previously uncollected stories and sketches with a forward by Ring Lardner, Jr.

—— *Ring Around Max: The Correspondence of Max Perkins and Ring Lardner*. Northern Illinois University Press, 1973.

Lardner, Ring, Jr. *My Family Remembered*. Harper and Row, 1976.

Masson, Thomas. "Ring Lardner," *Our American Humorists*. Moffat, 1922.

Patrick, Walton. *Ring Lardner*. Twayne, 1963.

Schwartz, Delmore. "Ring Lardner: Highbrow in Hiding," *Reporter* (August 9, 1956): 52–54; reprinted in *Selected Essays* (Chicago University Press, 1970).

Wilson, Edmund. "Mr. Lardner's American Characters." *Dial* (July 1924): 69–72.

Yardley, Jonathan. *Ring*. Random House, 1977. The most thorough biography.

Yates, Norris. *The American Humorist: Conscience of the Twentieth Century*. Iowa University Press, 1964. Perceptive essays which deal with the humorist as social critic.

NOTES

p. 78 "Us three youngest," from "What I ought to have Learnt in High School," *American Magazine* (November 1923): 10. On school and gas-office, q. Masson, *Our American Humorists*, 206–7.

p. 79 Herbst, *Gullible's Travels*, v-vi. Tittle, *Century* (25 July, 1926): 313: Anderson, *No Swank*, 1–2.

p. 80 Fitzgerald, "Ring," *The Crack-up*, 40.

p. 81 "Commencement," q. Geismar, *Ring Lardner and the Portrait of Folly*, 13. "The C or not the C," *ibid.*, 19. *Bib Ballads*, n.p.

p. 82 "The Other Side," *What of It?*, 3.

p. 82 "All the music," *ibid.*, 9. "Blue Laws of Scotland," 33–34. "Old saw," 27. "Bullfight," 12–13.

p. 83 "Fitzgerald," *ibid.*, 14. "My parents," 225.

p. 84 "Young Immigrunts," *ibid.*, 232, 254, 255. "Soon my father," 238–239.

p. 84 "Legal wife," *ibid.*, 259–260. "But at 35," 267.

p. 85 Play citations, *What of It?*, 42, 45, 52.

p. 86 Lardner, *The Story of a Wonder Man*, v. Lardner remained self-deprecating about the "writing game" throughout his career. "Personally I never feel comfortable at my desk unless they's a dozen large rats parked at my ft. These inst. will give you an idear of how different tempermunts effects diffrent writers but, as I say, each writer has to choose for theyself what tempermunt to have, and I might advise you to try writing in a public garage, whereas you might do your best work setting in a eel trap." Cf., "Inside Facts on the Writing Game," Masson, *Our American Humorists*, 198.

p. 86 *Wonder Man*, 117, 24, 29, 71, 102.

p. 87 Fitzgerald, *The Crack-up*, 38.

p. 88   "I promised the wife," *Gullible's Travels*, 45.

p. 88   "We aint swelled," *ibid.*, 46–47. "Mrs. Potter," 82. "Lord,"
85.

p. 89   "Scenery," "Cairo," and "work," *ibid.*, 51–53.

p. 90   Gullible's "jokes," *ibid.*, 49, 59, 65.

p. 90   Herbst, introduction to *Gullible's Travels*, xi. Geismar, *Portrait of Folly*. Yates, *American Humorist*, 181.

p. 91   Herbst, *op cit.*, xii.

p. 92   "Champion," *Round Up*, 109, 110, 11.

p. 92   "That wop," 112. "Just a kid," 125.

p. 94   Sherman, *The Main Stream* (Scribner's, 1927), 171.

p. 95   Miss Lyons, *Round Up*, 72. Mr. Drake, *ibid.*, 57–58.

p. 97   "Haircut," *Round Up*, 23–34.

p. 98   Fadiman, "Ring Lardner and the Triangle of Hate," *Nation* (March 22, 1933), 315.

p. 98   Yates, *American Humorist*, 193. Schwartz, *Selected Essays*, 224.

p. 99   Woolf, quoted by John Lardner, introduction to *You Know Me Al*, 6.

p. 100   Anderson, "Four American Impressions," 171.

ROUND FIVE.
KURT VONNEGUT, JR.:
HUMORIST IN THE COMBAT ZONE

PRIMARY SOURCES

Elliott, Robert C. *The Power of Satire*. Princeton University Press, 1960.

Goldsmith, David. *Kurt Vonnegut: Fantasy of Fire and Ice*. Bowling Green, 1972.

Klinkowitz, Jerome and John Somers, eds. *The Vonnegut Statement*. Delacorte, 1973.

Reed, Peter J. *Writers for the 70's: Kurt Vonnegut, Jr.* Warner, 1974.

Scholes, Robert. "Cat's Cradle and Mother Night," in *The Fabulators*. Oxford University Press, 1967.

Vonnegut, Kurt, Jr. *Player Piano*. Houghton-Mifflin, 1952. Reprinted, Avon, 1969.

———— *The Sirens of Titan*. Copyright 1959. Reprinted Dell, 1966.

———— *Mother Night*. Fawcett, 1961.

———— *Cat's Cradle*. Dell, 1963.

———— *God Bless You, Mister Rosewater*. Holt, 1965.

———— *Slaughterhouse Five or the Children's Crusade: A Duty-dance with Death*. Delacorte, 1969.
———— *Breakfast of Champions*. Delacorte, 1973.
———— *Welcome to the Monkey House*. Dell, 1973.
———— *Wampeters, Foma, and Granfaloons.* Delacorte, 1975.
———— *Slapstick*. Delta, 1976.
———— *Jailbird*. Delacorte, 1979.
———— *Deadeye Dick*. Delacorte, 1982.
———— *Palm Sunday*. Delacorte, 1984.
———— *Galapagos*. Delacorte, 1985.
———— *Bluebeard*. Delacorte, 1987.

NOTES

p. 101   On satirists, see Elliott, "The Satirist and Society," *Modern Satire*, 148–51.

p. 102   "Jokesters," *Palm Sunday*, 183.

p. 103   In the early novels, for the reader's convenience, I have cited chapters. "A step backward," *Player Piano*, chap. 32.

p. 103   Finnerty "on the edge," *ibid*, chap. 9. "canary," chap. 25.

p. 105   Unk, *Sirens of Titan*, chap. 9. On Indianapolis, epilogue.

p. 106   Vonnegut on *Connecticut Yankee*, *Palm Sunday*, 171.

p. 106   Black Fuhrer, *Mother Night*, chap. 17.

p. 107   Campbell on hate, *ibid*., chap. 43. "Hangwomen," chap. 20. Heinz, chap. 21.

p. 108   Campbell, *ibid*., chap. 21.

p. 108   Newt, *Cat's Cradle*, chap. 81. Bokonon, chap. 18.

p. 109   Minton, *ibid*, chap. 114. Hauck, *A Cheerful Nihilism*, 244.

p. 110   Bokonon, *Cat's Cradle*, chap. 127.

p. 111   Mary O'Hare, *Slaughterhouse Five*, chap. 1. "ripping sound" and description of Billy, chap. 2. "war a comical thing," chap. 4. Weary, chap. 2.

p. 111   "The box-car," chap. 3.

p. 112   Trout on Gospels, chap. 5. Trout's robot, chap. 8. British, chap. 5. Vonnegut on Dresden, *Palm Sunday*, 301–2.

p. 113   Harold, *Happy Birthday, Wanda June*, 142, 168.

p. 113   Woodly, *ibid*, 189, 194. "I have no culture," *Breakfast of Champions*, chap. 1.

p. 114   "The Big Space Fuck," *Palm Sunday*, 226. Dwayne, *op. cit*, chap. 4.

p. 114   "Impolite," *ibid*., chap. 1. "Nazis," chap. 15. Vonnegut on culture, letter to the author, 30 March, 1987.

p. 115 "Requiem: The Hocus Pocus Laundromat," *New American Review* (December 1986): 31–35.

p. 116 Eliza, *Slapstick*, chap. 22.

p. 116 Nixon on Sermon on the Mount, *Jailbird*, 15. Ruth on evil, 23. Mary on crap, 158. Starbuck on planet, 238. (Note page citations because later novels have longer chapters.)

p. 117 "My boys," *Deadeye Dick*, 60; "Deadeye/Rudy," 69; "victim's husband," 87.

p. 118 Trout on dead woman, *Galapagos*, 244; on big brains, 147; on nuclear weapons, 82–83. Vonnegut on Bob and Ray, *Palm Sunday*, 142.

p. 118 Rabo on genocide, *Bluebeard*, 3; on merchandising death, 67; on pitying writers, 176.

p. 119 Rabo on the bombardier, *ibid.*, 293; on the Japanese, 286. Vonnegut on gallows humor, *Wampeters, Foma, and Granfaloons*, 256.

p. 120 Vonnegut on jokes, *ibid.*, 258; on the belly laugh, 118. "Biafra," *Wampeters*, 145–46. "Vonnegut as black humorist," see Hauck, *A Cheerful Nihilism*.

p. 120 "Hesse," *Wampeters*, 108. Schickel, in Klinkowitz, *The Vonnegut Statement*, 108. On Republicans, "In a Manner That Must Shame God Himself," *Wampeters*, 198. Graham Greene, *The Comedians* (Viking, 1966), 135.

p. 122 "Address," *Wampeters*, 161; "visitor," *ibid.*, 168.

p. 122 *Ibid.*, 185.

p. 124 "Wonderful jokes," *Wampeters*, 285. "The bugler," *Palm Sunday*, 84. "Noble jokes," *ibid.*, 327.

ROUND SIX.
CELLULOID PUN(CH)STERS:
THE SILENT CLOWNS

PRIMARY SOURCES

Agee, James. "Comedy's Greatest Era," in Veron, *Humor in America*, 281–97.

Bermel, Albert. *Farce*. Simon and Schuster, 1982.

Chaplin, Charles. *My Autobiography*. Penguin, 1966. Arrogant, trite, and tedious. No doubt indispensable.

Dardis, Tom. *Keaton: The Man Who Wouldn't Lie Down*. Scribner's 1979. A readable biography.

Keaton, Buster with Charles Samuels. *My Wonderful World of Slapstick*. Doubleday, 1960. Fascinating on early life.

Kerr, Walter. *The Silent Clowns*. Knopf, 1975. A lovely study of the mechanics and art of the early films.

McCaffrey, Donald W. *Four Great Comedians: Chaplin, Lloyd, Keaton, Langdon*. Barnes, 1968.

Mast, Gerald. *The Comic Mind: Comedy and the Movies*. Chicago University Press, 1979. The finest book on film comedy.

Pratt, George. *Spellbound in Darkness:* History of the Silent Film. New York Graphic Society, 1966.

Robinson, David. *Chaplin: His Life and Art*. McGraw-Hill, 1985. The best biography.

Sennett, Mack. *King of Comedy*. Doubleday, 1954.

Sobel, Raoul and David Francis. *Chaplin: Genesis of a Clown*. Quartet Books, 1977.

Speaight, George. *Punch and Judy*. Studio Vista, 1970.

Toll, Robert C. *The Minstrel Show in Nineteenth-Century America*. Oxford University Press, 1974. Tyler, Parker. *Chaplin: The Last of the Clowns*. Horizon, 1972.

Yallop, David. *The Day the Laughter Stopped*. St. Martin's, 1976. Definitive account of Arbuckle's trial and demise.

NOTES

p. 125   Agee, "Comedy's Greatest Era," reprinted in Veron, *Humor in America,* 281, ff.

p. 125   Sennett, q. by Dreiser, *Photoplay* No.3, August 1928.

p. 126   Bermel, *Farce,* 21.

p. 127   On Grimaldi, Speaight, *Punch and Judy,* 129.

p. 127   For a provocative discussion of the racist roots of minstrel-show humor, see Toll, *Blacking Up,* 11, ff.

p. 129   Sennett, *King of Comedy,* 32, ff.

p. 130   Bentley, q. Bermel, *Farce,* 164.

p. 132   Broun, q. Robinson, *Chaplin,* 178.

p. 133   Chaplin's preference for automats, Constance Collier, *Harlequinade* (1928), q. Robinson, 190. Chaplin on being mobbed, to Thomas Burke, q. Robinson, 455–56.

p. 134   Fields, q. William Everson, *The Art of W. C. Fields* (Bobbs-Merrill, 1967), 157. "A good player," Samuel McKechnie, *Popular Entertainments Throughout the Ages* (Low, Marston, 1931), 68.

p. 134   On his Elizabethan style of humor, Sobel and Francis, *Chaplin: Genesis of a Clown,* 42.

p. 135   On casting a dog, Robinson, 230. Fiske, *Harpers Weekly*, (6 May 1916).

p. 136   On tragedy, q. Robinson 334–335.

p. 137   On the rich, *American Magazine*, n.d., Robinson, 203.

p. 138   Chaplin on comedy and luxury, *Autobiography*, q. Robinson, 412, 431.

p. 139   On patriotism, q. Robinson, 437. On dialogue, *ibid.*, 465. Mast, *Comic Mind*, 301.

p. 140   Cocteau, *My Voyage Round the World*, q. Robinson, 481. On the Nazi horrors, q. Robinson, 485.

p. 141   "More than machinery," speech from *The Great Dictator*.

p. 142   Chaplin on how he'd have testified, press conference 11 April 1947, q. Robinson, 547. Chaplin on violence, q. *ibid.*, 538.

p. 142   Marceau, q. John McCabe, *Laurel and Hardy* (Bonanza Books), 7. For much Keaton material, I am indebted to Keaton, *My Wonderful World of Slapstick* and Dardis, *Keaton: The Man Who Wouldn't Lie Down.*

p. 148   See *My Wonderful World*, 34, ff. for additional hair-raising descriptions of the Keaton act.

p. 149   Bermel, *Farce*, 56.

p. 149   Kerr, *The Silent Clowns*, 120, ff.

p. 149   Lorca farce, q. Dardis, *Keaton*, 281–84. Keaton quotes from *My Wonderful World.*

ROUND SEVEN.
THE SOUND AND THE FURY:
THE TALKING CLOWNS

PRIMARY SOURCES

Adamson, Joe. *Groucho, Harpo, Chico (and Sometimes Zeppo).* Simon and Schuster, 1973.

Allen, Steve. *More Funny People.* Stein and Day, 1982.

Durgnat, Ronald. *The Crazy Mirror: Hollywood Comedy and the American Image.* Dell, 1972. Perceptive and readable.

Everson, William K. *The Films of Laurel and Hardy.* Citadel, 1967.

———— *The Art of W. C. Fields.* Bobbs-Merrill, 1967.

Fields, W. C. *W. C. Fields by Himself: His Intended Biography*, ed. Ronald Fields. One hopes not.

———— *Drat: Being the encapsulated view of W. C. Fields in his own words*, ed. Richard Anobile. Signet, 1969. Slightly better.

Green, Stanley. *The Great Clowns of Broadway*. Oxford, 1984. Cf., 67–82 on Fields's stage routines.

McCabe, John. *Mr. Laurel and Mr. Hardy*. Signet, 1968.

——— *Laurel and Hardy*. Bonanza, 1983. Excellent study with marvelous stills.

Marx, Groucho with Richard Anobile. *The Marx Bros. Scrapbook*. Crown, 1973. Raunchy Groucho at the end.

——— *The Groucho Letters: Letters from and to Groucho*. Simon and Schuster, 1967.

——— *Memoirs of a Mangy Lover*. Woodhill, 1978.

Marx, Maxine. *Growing Up with Chico*. Limelight, 1986.

Monti, Carlotta, with Cy Rice. *W. C. Fields and Me*. Prentice-Hall, 1971. Chatty and frightening account by a longtime former Fields's mistress.

Skeetvedt, Randy. *Laurel and Hardy*. Moonstone, 1987.

Sklar, Robert. *Movie-made America: A Cultural History of American Movies*. Random House, 1975. Fascinating and literate.

NOTES

p. 151   q. Adamson, *Groucho, Chico, Harpo (and Sometimes Zeppo)*, 37. Sklar, *Movie-made America*, 104.

p. 152   Hardy, "the dumbest kind of guy," q. Allen, *More Funny People*, 178. Marceau, q. McCabe, *Laurel and Hardy* (Bonanza Books), 7.

p. 154   Durgnat, *The Crazy Mirror*, 102.

p. 158   Allen, *More Funny People*, 182.

p. 159   Sons of the Desert, q. McCabe, *Laurel and Hardy*, 399.

p. 163   Hill, "The Future of American Humor: Through a Glass Darkly," in Clark and Turner, *Critical Essays on American Humor*, 221.

p. 164   Fields on pain and humor, q. Blair and Hill, *America's Humor*, 511.

p. 165   See Anobile, *The Marx Bros Scrapbook* for accounts of the Marx Brothers' zany early life.

p. 165   Ronald Durgnat, "New Humor," *Crazy Mirror*, 20–21.

p. 166   Chaplin, q. Blair and Hill, *America's Humor*, 450. Artaud, q. Adamson, 161.

p. 168   Groucho on Chico, Adamson, 20.

p. 169   Durgnat, *The Crazy Mirror*, 37.

ROUND EIGHT.
THE COMICS. Or Sick, Sick, Sick (sic)

PRIMARY SOURCES

Allen, Steve. *Funny People*. Stein and Day, 1981.

—— *More Funny People*. Stein and Day, 1982.

Berger, Phil. *The Last Laugh: The World of the Stand-up Comics*. Ballantine Books, 1975. A terrific read.

Borns, Betsy. *Comic Lives: Inside the World of American Stand-Up Comedy*. Simon and Schuster, 1987. Incisive interviews with contemporary comics.

Bruce, Kitty. *The (Almost) Unpublished Lenny Bruce*. Running Press, 1984.

Bruce, Lenny. *How to Talk Dirty and Influence People*. Playboy, 1972. Bruce's autobiography. Much better than the run-of-the-mill celebrity bio.

—— *The Essential Lenny Bruce*, ed. John Cohen. Ballantine, 1967. The best collected material.

—— *Thank You, Masked Man* (Fantasy 7019).

—— *Live at the Curran Theatre* (Murray Hill 5-2952).

—— *I am Not a Nut, Elect Me* (Fantasy 7007).

—— *The Sick Humor of Lenny Bruce* (Fantasy 7003).

—— *Lenny Bruce—American* (Fantasy 7011).

Carlin George. *Playing With Your Head*. Home Box Office, 1987.

—— *Sometimes a Little Brain Damage Can Help*. Running Press, 1984.

Collier, Denise and Kathleen Beckett. *Spare Ribs: Women in the Humor Biz*. St. Martin's, 1980.

Dorinson, Joseph and Joseph Boskin. "Racial and Ethnic Humor." In *Humor in America*, ed. Lawrence Mintz, 163–94. Greenwood, 1988.

Foxx, Redd and Norma Miller. *Encyclopedia of Black Humor*. Ward Ritchie, 1977.

Friedman, Bruce Jay. *Black Humor*. Bantam Books, 1965.

Goldman, Albert. *Ladies and Gentlemen, Lenny Bruce*. Ballantine, 1974. The most thorough biography.

Goldstein, Jeffrey. *The Psychology of Humor*. Academic Press, 1972.

Goldthwaite, Bobcat. *An Evening with Bob Goldthwaite: Share the Warmth*. Home Box Office Special, February, 1988.

Gregory, Dick. *Nigger*. Pocket Books, 1964.

—— *The Two Sides of Dick Gregory*. (Vee-Jay LP 4005).

Haskins, Jim. *Richard Pryor: A Man and His Madness*. Beaufort Books, 1984.

Hendra, Tony. *Going Too Far*. Doubleday, 1987.

Kaufman, Gloria and Mary Kay Blakely, eds. *Pulling Our Own Strings: Feminist Humor and Satire*. Indiana University Press, 1980.

Kinison, Sam. *Stranger in Town*. HB 0047, 1987.

Kofsky, Frank. *Lenny Bruce: The Comedian as Social Critic and Secular Moralist*. Monarch, 1974.

Koziski, Stephanie, "The Standup Comedian as Anthropologist," *Journal of Popular Culture* (Fall 1984): 57–76.

Martin, Linda and Kerry Seagrave. *Women in Comedy*. Citadel, 1986. An excellent source book.

Midler, Bette. *A View from a Broad*. Simon and Schuster, 1980.

Pryor, Richard. *Richard Pryor Live*. Vestron, 1979.

—— *Richard Pryor Live on the Sunset Strip*. Vestron, 1984.

Rivers, Joan. *The Life and Times of Heidi Abramovitz*. Dell, 1984.

Smith, Ronald Lande. *The Stars of Stand-up comedy: A Biographical Encyclopedia*. Garland, 1986. A wealth of fascinating material, including jokes and routines.

Stillman, Deanne and Anne Beatts, eds. *Titters: The First Collection of Humor by Women*. Collier, 1976. Not the first, but interesting.

Wagner, Jane. *The Search for Signs of Intelligent Life in the Universe*. Harper and Row, 1986.

Wilde, Larry. *How the Great Comedy Writers Create Laughter*. Nelson-Hall, 1976.

—— *The Great Comedians*. Citadel, 1973.

NOTES

p. 170   Roth himself admits to having been influenced as a writer by a certain sit-down comic named Franz Kafka.

p. 171   Bolster, q. Borns, *Comic Lives*, 148.

p. 171   Borns, 248. Schlatter, "Laugh In," interview printed in Fitchburg, Mass. *Sentinel* (17 September 1987): 8. also quoting Skelton.

p. 171   Carlin, et al., q. Borns, 28, ff.

p. 172   Borns on comics as cerebral strippers, *Comic Lives*, 14. Stephanie Koziski sees this process as a valuable catharsis: "Many stand-up comedians jar their audience's sensibilities by making individuals experience a shock of recognition. This occurs as deeply-held popular opinions people hold about themselves—even the hidden underpinnings of their culture—are brought to an audience's level of conscious awareness. The stand-up comedian can elevate his audience to a new cultural focus." Cf., "The Standup Comedian as Anthropologist," 57. Seinfeld on Bruce, *Comic Lives*, 168.

p. 172 "My Permit?" *Bruce, How to Talk Dirty and Influence People*, 87. Bruce on satire, 8. Smith. *Stars of Stand-up Comedy*, 37.

p. 174 "Prison Break" is assembled from several books and records (cf., *The Essential Lenny Bruce*, 179–83.) Because of his improvisation, no Bruce routine was ever definitive.

p. 174 Keepnews, q. Kofsky, *Lenny Bruce*, 109. On truth, *Essential Lenny*, 235. On niggers, *ibid.*, 15.

p. 177 On the South, *Essential Lenny*, 19. Castro, *ibid.*, 96.

p. 179 Feiffer, q. Hendra, *Going Too Far*, 84.

p. 180 The "what should be," *Talk Dirty*, 235. On women, *Essential Lenny*, 167. Chicken story, *ibid.*, 195–196.

p. 180 On Las Vegas, *Talk Dirty*, 228. On Honey, *ibid.*, 117. On the Legion of Decency, breasts and capital punishment, *Talk Dirty*, 91–92.

p. 181 On killing Christ, *Talk Dirty*, 197. Pilot story, *Essential Lenny*, 187.

p. 182 On truth, *ibid.*, 112. On Zsa Zsa, q. Kofsky, 25. On cruel comics, *Talk Dirty*, 125.

p. 183 "Kiss my bruce," and where's the toilet, *Talk Dirty* 192–99.

p. 184 On war, *Essential Lenny*, 288. Tynan, Foreword to *Talk Dirty*, vi. Paar, liner notes of *Live at the Curran Theatre*. Hentoff, *op. cit.*, 143; Gelb, 45. Pryor, q. Smith, *Stars*, 163. "It's all over Lenny," *ibid.*, 34.

p. 185 Slave routines, q. Dorinson and Boskin, "Racial and Ethnic Humor," 174–75.

p. 186 Gregory, *Nigger*, 133–35.

p. 186 Restaurant story, *ibid.*, 144. Cambridge, q. Smith, *Stars*, 47. Murphy, *ibid.*, 154.

p. 188 Kael on Pryor, *Taking It All In* (Holt, 1986), 323. "The black ghost of Lenny" and Pryor on Lenny, q. Smith, 163.

p. 188 Pryor, q. Smith, *Stars*, 164.

p. 192 Carlin on blacks, q. Hendra, 161.

p. 192 Carlin on Ali, q. Smith, *Stars*, 51. Carlin's "hostility scoreboard," q. Koziski, 68.

p. 194 Rivers, q. Smith, 171.

p. 195 McCormick, q. Smith, 170. Rickles on style, *ibid.*, 168.

p. 195   Goldthwaite, *Sharing the Warmth*. Charboneau, Nick's Comedy Stop (Boston) 9/11/87. Sullivan, *Boston Globe* (8 August 1988). Kinison, *Stranger in Town*.

p. 196   Ludovici, *The Secret of Laughter* (Constable, 1932), q. Goldstein, *Psychology of Humor*, vi.

p. 197   "Edith Ann," Tomlin, *And That's the Truth* (Polydor PD 5023).

p. 198   "Resume," *The Portable Dorothy Parker* (Penguin, 1973), 99.

p. 198   Martin and Seagrave, *Women in Comedy*, 20. Radner, q. ibid., 56. For good accounts of the history and difficulties of women's comedy, see also Collier and Beckett, eds., *Spare Ribs: Women in the Humor Biz*.

p. 199   Diller, Rivers, Radner, Schuster, in Collier and Beckett, *Spare Ribs*, 3–4, 7, 137, 166. See *Titters* for more of Stillman's argument.

p. 200   Tomlin, q. Martin and Seagrave, 372.

p. 201   Stone, *Psychology Today* (July 1977). Pryor, q. *Women in Comedy*, 375.

p. 202   Comedy routines from *Women in Comedy*. Walker, *A Very Serious Thing*, 12.

p. 203   Brooks, q. Smith, 166.

ROUND NINE.
THE BLACK HUMOR OF THE RED, WHITE, AND BLUE

PRIMARY SOURCES

Berger, Arthur Asa. *The Comic-Stripped American*. Walker, 1973.

Block, Herbert. *Herblock Through the Looking Glass*. Norton, 1984.

Boller, Paul. *Presidential Anecdotes*. Oxford University Press, 1981.

Breathed, Berke. *Penguin Dreams and Stranger Things*. Washington Post, 1985.

Dudden, Arthur, ed. *American Humor*. Oxford University Press, 1987.

——— *The Assault of Laughter*. Yosseloff, 1962.

Dunne, Finley Peter. *Mister Dooley on Ivrything and Ivrybody*. Selected by Robert Hutchinson. Dover, 1963.

——— *Mister Dooley in Peace and War*. Small-Maynard, 1898.

Ford, Gerald. *Humor and the Presidency*. Arbor Hill, 1987.

Frye, David. *I Am the President*. (Elektra EKS 75006).

Feiffer, Jules. *The Great Comic Book Heroes*. Dial, 1965.

—— *Jules Feiffer's America from Eisenhower to Reagan*. Knopf, 1982.

Galnoor, Itzhak and Stephen Lukes, eds. *No Laughing Matter: A Collection of Political Jokes*. Routledge and Kegan Paul, 1985.

Goldstein, Jeffrey. *The Psychology of Humor*. Academic Press, 1972.

Green, Mark and Gail MacCall. *Reagan's Reign of Error*. Pantheon, 1987.

Harris, Leon. *The Fine Art of Political Wit*. Bell, 1964.

Heller, Joseph. *Catch-22*. Simon and Schuster, 1961.

Kael, Pauline. *Deeper into the Movies*. Atlantic, 1973.

—— *Taking It All In*. Holt, 1986.

Lewin, Leonard, ed. *A Treasury of American Political Humor*. Dial, 1964.

Lincoln, Abraham, *Wisdom and Wit*, ed. Louise Bachelder. Peter Pauper, 1965.

Mahony, Patrick, ed. *Barbed Wit and Malicious Humor*. Institute for the Study of Man, 1983.

Meader, Vaughn. *The First Family*. (Cad 3060 25060).

Mencken, H. L. *A Carnival of Buncombe*. Johns Hopkins, 1956.

Pynchon, Thomas. *Gravity's Rainbow*. Viking, 1973.

Roth, Philip. *Our Gang (Starring Tricky Dicky and His Friends)*. Random, 1971.

Schutz, Charles E. *Political Humor: From Aristophanes to Sam Erwin*. Associated University Presses, 1977.

Sorel, Edward. *Superpen: the Cartoons and Caricatures of Edward Sorel*. Edited and designed by Lidia Ferrara. Random House, 1978.

Tauber, Peter, "Jay Leno: Not Just a Funny Face." *New York Times Magazine*, (26 February, 1989) 32. ff.

Thompson, Hunter. *Generation of Swine. Gonzo Papers Vol. 2: Tales of Shame and Degradation in the '80s*. Vintage, 1988.

Whitfield, Stephen J. "Political Humor." In Lawrence E. Mintz, *Humor in America*, 195–212. Greenwood, 1988.

—— "Richard Nixon as a Comic Figure." *American Quarterly* 37 (Spring 1985): 114–132.

Wolfe, Tom. *In Our Time*. Farrar, Strauss, 1982.

—— *Bonfire of the Vanities*. Farrar, Strauss, 1987.

NOTES

p. 204   Rogers, q. Dudden, *American Humor*, 59–60. Plato, q. Elmer Blistein, *Comedy in Action* (Duke, 1964), xiii. Thompson, *Generation of Swine*, 260, Bierce, *Devil's Dictionary*.

p. 204   Ward on politics, q. Dudden, *The Assault of Laughter*, 27. Ward on voting, q. Sloane, *Mark Twain as a Literary Comedian*, cf. 47. Nasby, q. Dudden, *op. cit.*, 285. Reagan, q. Green, *Reagan's Reign of Error*, 12.

p. 205   Rogers, q. *ibid*, 9. Mencken, on better politicians, q. Dudden, *Assault of Laughter*, 63. Arp, *ibid*, 288. Thompson on Meese, *Generation of Swine*, 300. Billings, q., *op. cit.*, 296.

p. 206   Mencken on democracy, *The Assault of Laughter*, 361–362. Mencken, "x times y," q. Louis Rubin, "If Mencken Were Only Alive," in Rubin, *The Comic Imagination*, 273. Mr. Dooley on government, on the Philippines, on "Chinymen," Dunne, *Mr. Dooley on Ivrything*, 53, 14, 233.

p. 207   "We are gr-reat," Dunne, *Mr. Dooley on War*, 8.

p. 208   Trudeau, q. Blair and Hill, 514. America's Humor Sorel, on Cooke and Agnew, *Superpen*, n.p.

p. 209   Wolfe, *In Our Time*, 93, 73. Leno, q. Peter Tauber, "Jay Leno: Not Just a Funny Face." 32.

p. 209   Daley story, q. Galnoor and Lukes, *No Laughing Matter*, 86. Wolfe on Carter, *In Our Time*, 22. (See also Jeremy Rifkin and Ted Howard, eds., *Redneck Power: The Wit and Wisdom of Billy Carter* (Bantam, 1977). Russell, q. Blair and Hill, 43.

p. 210   Ford, *Humor and the Presidency*, 15. Lincoln anecdotes, q. Harris, *The Fine Art of Political Wit*, 99–104. "He reminds me," Lincoln, *Wisdom and Wit*, 50.

p. 211   Lincoln "cartoon," *op. cit.*, 14. Lincoln, 'I laugh because," Boller, *Presidential Anecdotes*, 123.

p. 211   Long, q. Harris, 231–32. Stevenson, *ibid.*, 238–41.

p. 212   Kennedy, q. Harris, 258, ff. Goldwater, *ibid.*, 262–63.

p. 213   Ike was reported to have made one amusing sally: When John Foster Dulles showed him where Washington was said to have flung a silver dollar across the Potomac, Ike said, "A dollar went a lot further in those days." q. Mahony, *Barbed Wit*, 148. Corwin, q. Schutz, *Political Humor*, 24.

p. 213   For more Reagan one-liners, see Boller, 354–56. Reagan at mike (8/11/84), Green, *Reagan's Reign*, 59.

p. 215   Breathed, q. Dudden, 14. Frye, q. Smith, *Stars of Stand-up Comedy*, 89–90. For Nixon material, see Whitfield, "Richard Nixon as a Comic Figure," 14–32. Dudden on Watergate, *American Humor*, 69. Wolfe, *In Our Time*, 16.

p. 221 Kael, *Deeper into the Movies* (Atlantic, 1973), 95.

p. 221 Perelman (*Cue*, 11 November 1974).

p. 222 Lincoln, *Wit and Wisdom*, 68.

p. 223 Thurber, "The Future, If Any, of Comedy," *Harpers*, (July 1961): 223.

p. 223 Civil War story and Great Society stories, q. Galnoor and Lukes, *No Laughing Matter*, 148, 128. Thompson, *Generation of Swine*, 281.

p. 224 *No Laughing Matter*, xi.

ROUND TEN.
THE END OF THE DREAM OR THE
DREAM OF THE END—OR SOMETHING LIKE THAT

PRIMARY SOURCES

Bacon, James. *How Sweet It Is: The Jackie Gleason Story*. St. Martin's, 1985.

Begosian, Eric. *Drinking in America*. Vintage, 1987.

Cantor, Jay. *Krazy Kat*. Knopf, 1987.

Cohen, Sarah Blacher, ed. *Comic Relief: Humor in Contemporary American Literature*. Illinois University Press, 1978.

Dickinson, Emily. *Final Harvest*. Edited by Thomas H. Johnson. Little, Brown, 1961.

Ellison, Ralph. "Change the Joke and Slip the Yoke," *Shadow and Act*, 61–73. Signet, 1966.

Ephron, Nora. *Crazy Salad*. Bantam, 1978.

Feldscher, Karen. "Laughing Matters." *Northeastern University Alumni Magazine* (April 1989): 22–27.

Fraser, John. *Violence in the Arts*. Cambridge University Press, 1974.

Heller, Joseph. *We Bombed in New Haven*. Scapegoat Productions, 1967.

Hendra, Tony. *Going Too Far*. Doubleday, 1987.

Hill, Doug and Jeff Weingrad. *Saturday Night: A Backstage History of Saturday Night Live*. William Morrow, 1986.

Hughes, Langston. *The Book of Negro Humor*, Dodd-Mead, 1966.

Keillor, Garrison. *Happy To Be Here*. Atheneum, 1982.

——— *Lake Wobegon Days*. Viking, 1985.

Lebowitz, Fran. *Metropolitan Life*. Fawcett, 1978.

Lehrer, Tom. *That Was the Year That Was*. Reprise (RS-6179).

Mast, Gerald. *The Comic Mind: Comedy and the Movies.* Chicago University Press, 1979.

McCrahan, Donna. *The Second City: A Backstage History of Comedy's Hottest Troupe.* Putnam, 1987.

Morreall, John. *The Philosophy of Laughter and Humor.* State University of New York Press, 1987.

Whicher, George. *This Was a Poet.* Ann Arbor, 1957. See 170–88, on Dickinson's humor.

Woodward, Bob. *Wired: The Short Life and Fast Times of John Belushi.* Simon and Schuster, 1984.

NOTES

p. 226   Groucho to Goodman Ace, "Touching on Television," *Groucho Letters.* Thompson, *Generation of Swine,* 43.

p. 228   Hill and Weingrad, *Saturday Night Live,* 119.

p. 228   O'Donoghue, q. *Newsweek,* 25 April 1983. Hendra, *Going Too Far,* 3.

p. 229   Pryor and Chase routine, Hill and Weingrad, 118. Van Horne, q. *ibid.,* 188.

p. 229   Hendra, *Going Too Far,* 161. Trudeau, q. Hill and Weingrad, 183–84. Allen, *More Funny People,* 46. Carlin, *ibid.,* 51.

p. 230   Ball, q. Blair and Hill, *America's Humor,* 527.

p. 231   Kael, "Elfskin." *Deeper into the Movies* (Atlantic Monthly, 1973), 59–62.

p. 234   Cantor, *Krazy Kat,* 48, ff.

p. 234   Bier, *Rise and Fall,* 5. Mast, *Comic Mind,* 324. Hughes, *Negro Humor,* vii.

p. 235   Ellison, *Shadow and Act,* 68–70. Feldscher, "Laughing Matter," 22.

p. 236   Rovit, "College Humor and the Modern Audience," in *Comic Relief,* Cohen, ed., 247. Begosian, *Drinking in America,* 15.

p. 238   Nietsche, q. Goldstein, *The Psychology of Humor,* 20. Frazer, "Reporter at Large." *New Yorker* (6 March. 1989): 66–67.

p. 240   Dickinson, No. 165, *Final Harvest,* 17. As a student, Dickinson, that saddest and wisest of American poets, co-edited a humor magazine called *Forest Leaves* at Amherst Academy. (Whicher, *This Was a Poet,* 175.)

p. 240   Kierkegaard, q. Morreall, 37.

INDEX

ABOUT THE AUTHOR

Bill Keough is a Boston Irish native, which he feels may account for both his interest in humor and violence.

Though Keough has earned a B.A. from Harvard, an M.A. and M.F.A. from the University of Iowa, and a Ph.D. from U/Mass-Amherst, he claims to have been truly educated (and flaggelated) at St. Theresa's Grammar School in West Roxbury and Boston College High School. In these pages, he hopes he has not embarrassed anyone besides himself and is grateful, along with all those who have had to deal with him, that the book (many years in the making as they say in Hollywood) finally is to see the light of day.

On the plus side, he scuba dives, cross-country skis, jogs, and all that healthy stuff; but he also drinks and smokes too much, and is really fortunate in being blessed with two fine children and many loyal friends who scold him toward sanity. He describes himself, as a tragically happy man, that is, when he is not writing too many metaphors.